Fallen Women

The prostitute in literature and life, in fantasy and reality: these are the two basic themes of Martin Seymour-Smith's new book. To trace the prostitute's antecedents, the author has gone back to the earliest records. He follows the story from the Paris of Villon to the London of Nashe, Jonson and Shakespeare, from the Byzantium of Justinian and Theodora to the world of Boswell, *Fanny Hill*, and the anonymous Victorian 'Walter', and from there down to the present day.

In the past and into modern literature an absurd sentimentality is often found contrasted with sensitive realism, but in a prostitute–client relationship is the man necessarily more exploiter than exploited, or vice versa? To what extent, in any case, is the prostitute a manifestation of the male need for fantasy – an erotic need not always satisfied in 'normal' situations. In posing these questions, the author distinguishes myth from reality and puts in a strong plea for a socially more realistic, less hypocritical attitude.

THE NATURAL HISTORY OF SOCIETY
EDITOR: ALEX COMFORT

MARTIN SEYMOUR-SMITH

Fallen Women

A sceptical enquiry into the treatment of prostitutes,
their clients and their pimps,
in literature

NELSON

THOMAS NELSON AND SONS LTD

36 Park Street London W1
P.O. Box 2187 Accra
P.O. Box 336 Apapa Lagos
P.O. Box 25012 Nairobi
P.O. Box 21149 Dar es Salaam
77 Coffee Street San Fernando Trinidad

THOMAS NELSON (AUSTRALIA) LTD
597 Little Collins Street Melbourne 3000

THOMAS NELSON AND SONS (SOUTH AFRICA) (PROPRIETARY) LTD
51 Commissioner Street Johannesburg

THOMAS NELSON AND SONS (CANADA) LTD
81 Curlew Drive Don Mills Ontario

First published 1969
Copyright © 1969 by Martin Seymour-Smith

17 138030 4

Printed in Great Britain by Western Printing Services Ltd Bristol

DEDICATION

To

Giles Gordon
and
Harold Brooks

ACKNOWLEDGEMENTS

I AM grateful to many people for help in the writing of this book (my gratitude to the two friends mentioned in the dedication goes beyond its scope): to the general editor of the series, Alex Comfort, for invaluable and constructive suggestions; to James Mitchell, for his encouragement, forbearance and generosity as a publisher; to Peter Ford, for helping me to put it into shape; to my daughters, for help with photocopying and for advice about *Fanny Hill* and *My Secret Life*; to my parents, for help with books and useful discussions; to the London Library and its staff (as always); to the staff of the East Sussex County Library, especially Miss Butler, at Bexhill-on-Sea; to my friend C. H. Sisson, for allowing me to make extensive use of his superb versions of Catullus; and to my wife, for much typing, re-typing and criticism, and for her general support (of a wholly moral nature).

Bexhill-on-Sea   M.S–S.
March 1969

And the Creature run from the cur: there thou might'st behold the great image of Authoritie, a Dogg's obey'd in office: Thou, Rascall Beadle, hold thy bloody hand: why dost thou lash that whore? Strip thine owne backe, thou hotly lusts to use her in that kind, for which thou whip'st her. The userer hangs the Cozener. Thorough tatter'd cloathes great Vices do appeare: Robes, and Furr'd gownes hide all. Plate sinnes with Gold, and the strong Lance of Justice, hurtlesse breakes: Arme it in ragges, a Pigmies straw do's pierce it. None do's offend, none, I say none, I'le able them; take that of me my Friend, who have the power to seale th'accusers lips. Get thee glasse-eyes, and like a scurvy Politician, seeme to see the things thou dost not. Now, now, now, now. Pull off my Bootes: harder, harder, so.

King Lear, IV, v

PROSTITUTE. A necessary evil. A protection for our daughters and sisters, as long as we have bachelors. Should be harried without pity. It is impossible to go out with one's wife owing to the presence of these women on the boulevards. Are always poor girls seduced by wealthy bourgeois.

Flaubert, *Dictionary of*
Accepted Ideas, translated
by Jacques Barzun

INTRODUCTION

SINCE this is a study of the prostitute in literature – the literary notion of literature here being extended to include anything written – it is first necessary to establish a working definition of the term 'prostitute'. A concise dictionary definition reflects the general opinion: 'woman given over to indiscriminate sexual intercourse for hire', but is not comprehensive enough; the word also refers, of course, to men who hire themselves out to women for money (gigolos), to men who will perform homosexual acts for money, and presumably to animals who exchange immoral sex-services for food, warmth and affection.* Fernando Henriques' definition, in the preface to his three-volume *Prostitution and Society*,† is essentially an extension of this:

Prostitution consists of any sexual acts, including those which do not actually involve copulation, habitually performed by individuals with other individuals of their own or the opposite sex, for a consideration which is non-sexual. In addition, sexual acts habitually performed for gain by single individuals, or by individuals with animals

* A difficult problem for society, with which I shall not be dealing here, is how to punish, harry and ostracize such animal prostitutes. Too many British pets are thus tainted.

† Fernando Henriques, *Prostitution and Society* (3 volumes): *The Pretence of Love, The Immoral Tradition* and *Modern Sexuality*, MacGibbon and Kee, London, 1962–8.

or objects, which produce in the spectator some form of gratification,
can be considered acts of prostitution. Emotional involvement may or
may not be present.

This, solemnly though it may read, is perhaps as near as one
can get to a comprehensive definition, although the ambiguity
of 'habitually' has been criticized. Again, the non-sexuality of the
'consideration' – usually financial – for which the sexual acts are
performed must surely be regarded as only apparent. Henriques
is right, however, to avoid the deliberate, and originally Pauline
error of confusing prostitution with fucking in general.* Nevertheless, his definition can be slightly improved upon. Acts of
prostitution are overtly sexual, whereas the rewards for them,
while they may be sexual, are not overtly so – except where the
exclusively sexual services of a pimp, ponce or (most accurately)
cunt-pensioner, could be established as the chief 'consideration'
for which a woman prostitutes herself.

Throughout this book the term 'prostitution' will be interpreted as broadly as possible, without undue straining after a
'correct' definition. An Income Tax Inspector (is he a member
of 'the oldest profession'?) might be susceptible of definitions
ranging from 'A vicious man who gains sexual gratification
from stealing his fellow-citizens' money so that it may be utilized
by the government of the day in order to maintain its power and
for other immoral purposes' to 'An honourable, imaginative
official who collects justified taxes for the universal benefit of all
mankind'. The first definition would be dismissed as prejudiced
or worse; and even Lord Salisbury would demur at the second.
Neither, of course, is true, although each might in particular
instances have some merit. But society has agreed, in the case of
prostitutes, always to apply definitions of the first type. I prefer
however, to keep at least as open a mind about the profession of
prostitution as society officially does about that of tax-collecting.

The word 'prostitute' itself derives straightforwardly and
unexceptionally from the Latin verb *'prostituere'* meaning 'to
expose publically, offer for sale'; but 'whore', which – although
sometimes taken to mean, as distinct from 'prostitute', 'woman

* See pp. 45–51.

who will fuck for nothing because she likes it; free fornicator'
(as by soldiers) – is its synonym, seems to exhibit in its etymology
some of the same kind of ambivalence as society has shown towards the subject of prostitution. It appears to derive immediately
from a group of Old English, Old Dutch and other words
meaning 'base'; but the conjectural Indo-European root *qar-*
appears in the Latin *carus*, 'dear', and the Old Irish *cara*, 'friend'
and *caraim*, 'I love'. . . .

There is no such equivocation about the derivation of 'harlot',
which before the fifteenth century meant, variously, 'vagabond',
'rascal', 'male servant' and even merely 'fellow': this, as conveniently pejorative, was taken over. The fourteenth-century
'strumpet' is of unknown origin. *Strommel*, meaning 'hair' –
hence *strum*, 'wig' – from which by association with pubic hair
it could derive, seems unknown before the early sixteenth century.
Strum, in its meaning of 'fuck', is much later and puns on 'strumpet', *strum* (wig) and perhaps vaguely on the rhythmical movement contained in the verb 'to strum'. 'Tart', now mostly
pejorative except perhaps in Australia, used to be wholly affectionate, and originally derives from the notion of 'sweetness' in
women.

A Dutch criminologist, W. A. Bonger, impelled either by
a sense of fairness towards a much abused profession or (more
likely) by an extreme sense of morality, proposed that an act of
prostitution is 'intrinsically equal to that of a man or woman who
contracts a marriage for economical [*sic*] reasons'. But the definition that may be inferred from this statement, however just,
is too wide for any practical purpose. First, it allows no significance to the element of sexual indiscriminateness that characterizes prostitution. Secondly, there are countless sexual or
quasi-sexual acts that are 'intrinsically equal' to acts of prostitution: using sex in commercial advertising, or as emotional black-
mail, or to gain fame and money as an author or playwright, or
to sell 'fearlessly clean' newspapers, or to organize 'clean up'
campaigns, involving interference with the private lives of other
people, in order to gain vicarious sexual pleasure. . . .

Prostitution has frequently and foolishly been described as

'the oldest profession', and has attracted a huge literature. This
book is a critique of some – I hope some of the more interesting
and revealing – of that literature. It embodies no preconceived
theory about prostitution in any age, although it attempts to
analyse the motives or attitudes inherent in the literature about
it, and may in this way cast some light upon its nature.

The members of any profession invariably have fewer characteristics in common than otherwise, which makes generalization
a hazardous business. Perhaps it is a feeling of righteousness that
has given some writers on prostitution a special confidence. Not
yet being under instruction from the Roman Catholic Church,
the Bob Jones University, Mr David Holbrook or any similar
fountain of unimpeachable moral authority, I cannot share this
confidence. We know so little about the sexual behaviour of
other people, especially in detail, that it is particularly unsafe to
draw general conclusions. We know even less about their sexual
feelings. There is no agreement among people as to what sexual
happiness is. In any case, the only criterion by which such questions may be answered is happiness-in-general, a concept of
dubious value, for we certainly do not know what universal
happiness might be.

However, the hitherto perpetual quest for it, both theoretical
and practical, has largely involved – no one will deny it – the
matter of sexual relationships between human beings. It can hardly
be frivolous, then, to examine the response of society to the fact
of prostitution, for in the attitudes to this necessarily reside
most, if not all, of its attitudes to sex as a whole.

My account could not be other than selective, and the arrange-
ment is chronological – with exceptions the reasons for which
will be obvious. I have concentrated (I hope appropriately in a
series called *The Natural History of Society*) upon the distinction
between prostitutes as natural history – that is to say, as each one
of them was or is or could have been in particular – and prostitutes
as male fantasy-figures of various types, or as the subject of
male generalizations. Whatever conclusions we may like to draw
from the evidence of our senses, we must first – presumably – try
to get the evidence of our senses as right as we can. My book

suggests that St Paul was not concerned to do this, but that Zola
(for all his personal confusions) was; and that Procopius and
others may have had mixed motives. It is not a book, therefore,
for transcendentalists – at least, only for those who feel obliged to
postpone the process of transcendentalization until the point at
which all the available evidence is 'in'. This is an important
distinction.

Chapter One

1

ALTHOUGH it is not the first allusion to prostitution in literature, one of the earliest and most famous stories about an act of pseudo-prostitution (it does not involve a habitual prostitute) is told in Genesis 38. Judah married his eldest son, Er, to Tamar. When Er was slain by the Lord for some unnamed wickedness, Judah told Onan, his second son:

Go in unto thy brother's wife, and marry her, and raise up seed to thy brother. And Onan knew that the seed should not be his; and it came to pass, when he went in unto his brother's wife, that he spilled it on the ground, lest that he should give seed to his brother. And the thing which he did displeased the Lord: wherefore he slew him also. Then said Judah to Tamar his daughter in law, Remain a widow at thy father's house, till Shelah my son be grown: for he said, Lest peradventure he die also, as his brethren did. And Tamar went and dwelt in her father's house.

And in process of time the daughter of Shuah Judah's wife died; and Judah was comforted, and went up unto his sheepshearers to Timnath, he and his friend Hirah the Adullamite. And it was told Tamar, saying, Behold thy father in law goeth up to Timnath to shear his sheep. And she put her widow's garments off from her, and covered her with a vail, and wrapped herself, and sat in an open place, which is by the way to Timnath; for she saw that Shelah was grown, and she was not given unto him to wife. When Judah saw her, he thought her to be an harlot; because she had covered her face. And he turned unto her by the way, and said, Go to, I pray thee, let me come in unto thee; (for he knew not that she was his daughter in law). And she said, What wilt thou give me, that thou mayest come in unto me? And he said, I will send thee a kid from the flock. And she said, Wilt thou give me a pledge, till thou send it? And he said, What pledge shall I give thee? And she said, Thy signet, and thy bracelets, and thy staff that is in thine hand. And he gave it her, and came in unto her, and she conceived by him. And she arose, and went away, and laid by her vail from her, and put on the garments of her widowhood. And Judah sent the kid by the hand of his friend the Adullamite, to receive his pledge from the woman's hand: but he found her not. Then he asked the men of that place, saying, Where is the harlot, that was openly by the way side? And they said, There was no harlot in this place. And he returned to Judah, and said, I cannot find her; and also the men of the place said, that there was no harlot in this place. And Judah said, Let her take it to her, lest we be ashamed: behold, I sent this kid, and thou hast not found her.

And it came to pass about three months after, that it was told Judah, saying, Tamar thy daughter in law hath played the harlot; and also, behold, she is with child by whoredom. And Judah said, Bring her forth, and let her be burnt. When she was brought forth, she sent to her father in law, saying, By the man, whose these are, am I with child: and she said, Discern, I pray thee, whose are these, the signet, and bracelets, and staff. And Judah acknowledged them, and said, She hath been more righteous than I; because that I gave her not to Shelah my son. And he knew her again no more. And it came to pass in the time of her travail, that, behold, twins [Pharez and Zarah] were in her womb.

Onan was a rebel against his society in two ways. First, he refused to accept the custom (it was not peculiar to the Israelites, and still exists in various forms among some peoples, such as the Tallensi of Northern Ghana) of the levirate, which required that if a married man died without a son, his eldest brother should marry the widow in order to ensure his posterity and to preserve his patrimony ('raise up seed' to him). Secondly, he expressed this refusal by a further offence against custom: at the point of orgasm, he withdrew his penis and came on the ground – that is he performed what is now euphemistically referred to as *coitus interruptus*. Thus, the term 'onanism', for masturbation, is a misnomer, coined in the early eighteenth century – a misnomer which *Webster's* but not the *Oxford Dictionary* recognizes. The eager suggestion that Onan, in order to add fuel to the fire of the campaigners against 'self-abuse' of nearly 3,000 years thence, masturbated rather than withdrew and came on the ground is hardly worth considering. The real crime, for which he was slain by the Lord, was to evade what was then regarded as his duty, as this passage from Deuteronomy 25 makes clear:

If brethren dwell together, and one of them die, and have no child, the wife of the dead shall not marry without unto a stranger: her husband's brother shall go in unto her, and take her to him to wife, and perform the duty of an husband's brother unto her. And it shall be, that the firstborn which she beareth shall succeed in the name of his brother which is dead, that his name be not put out of Israel.

If the Levitical law that considered unions between brother and sister-in-law incestuous was really an unsuccessful attempt to abolish the often inconvenient levirate marriage, then the legendary protest of Onan has a special significance.

At all events, when Judah refused to abide by the custom, Tamar cleverly tricked him into making her pregnant by posing as a prostitute. Harold Krich and Aron Greenwald comment on this passage in their annotated anthology *The Prostitute in Literature*.* While they incidentally imply both that levirate marriage was peculiar to the Hebrews, and that the term onanism is unexceptionable, they also suggest that here

... we have immediately the theme which explains why a woman may choose the path of prostitution for other than economic reasons. . . . When Judah forgets his promise, Tamar seduces him while disguised as a harlot. Here is the classic revenge motive of the prostitute.

Feeling that an injustice has been done her, she revenges herself against society through assuming the trade of a prostitute. But, like many contemporary prostitutes, Tamar's revenge is even more diabolical. In addition to degrading herself, Tamar succeeds in degrading

* Harold Krich and Aron Greenwald, *The Prostitute in Literature*, Ballantine Books, New York, 1960.

Judah, the object of her revenge, and exposing his hypocrisy. It is re-markable that in this earliest reference to prostitution in the Judaeo-Christian world, the ethical standards revealed are in some way [*sic*] higher than those of our own times. In our society, the motives of the prostitute are not taken into consideration at all when she is sentenced to imprisonment, but in biblical times, in the year 1700 B.C., Judah had the unmatched courage to proclaim, 'She hath been more righteous than I,' and to declare, therefore, that she should not be punished for her transgression.

Krich and Greenwald, it should be noted, consider the modern female prostitute to be a singularly maladjusted, suffering per-sonality, 'almost always completely frigid with her clients', and primarily motivated by 'a deep feeling of anger . . . against the parents'.* This view may sometimes be justifiable, although 'almost always' is an unwarranted phrase; but Krich and Green-wald's attempt to find support for it in an Old Testament story is clearly inappropriate – in the way that attempts to superimpose modern psychoanalytical interpretations upon historical or legen-dary material usually are.

First, Tamar acted not against her own father but against her father-in-law. Secondly, even if she was prompted by motives of revenge, this is only incidental: her primary motive was to ensure that the family of Judah should 'raise up seed unto' her dead husband. Judah, afraid that his third son might suffer the fate of his brothers, had tried to deny her this right, and was punished by being tricked into providing it himself. Nor does Tamar either 'degrade' Judah or 'expose his hypocrisy'. Judah makes no attempt to disguise that he has been with a harlot: he makes every effort to find her so that he may discharge his debt to her, openly telling the Adullamite and 'the men of that place' what he has done. None of this suggests that he felt de-graded or that his behaviour over his encounter with the harlot was anything but straightforward and entirely unhypocritical – or, indeed, that anyone would have expected him to feel ashamed. The point is not that Tamar was driven into prostitution by motives of revenge, but that she gained her right by imitating a

* See H. Greenwald, *The Call Girl*, Ballantine Books, New York, 1958.

prostitute on a single occasion. It is wrong to draw any but historical conclusions from this story, which tells us nothing about the motives for prostitution either in the second millennium B.C. or in the twentieth century.

However, it does tell us something about what, from other sources, we already know: the nature of prostitution in Israel. This is important, because the attitude of the twentieth century to prostitution has, with ample justification, appeared to some commentators to have more in common with Jewish than with Greek experience.

From Leviticus 19:29, 'Do not prostitute thy daughter, nor cause her to be a whore; lest the land fall to whoredom, and the land become full of wickedness', we may infer both that prostitution existed and that the legislators disapproved of it. In fact it flourished, as is evident from the frequency with which harlots and even brothels (e.g. Joshua 2:1, 2:6, 2:7) are mentioned, but Leviticus 21:9 suggests that there was a penalty for it only when the daughter of a priest profaned herself 'by playing the whore': 'she shall be burnt with fire'. This suggests that the lawgivers were most concerned to stamp out prostitution amongst their priests. However, Krich and Greenwald assert that 'Prostitution, forbidden to women of the faith, is relegated to the "foreign" woman whose use by the male is not interdicted'; this is slightly misleading. The story of Tamar shows that harlots kept their faces covered (a custom of which she made neat use), but not that they were necessarily always foreign.

However, many of them were – and were no doubt encouraged as preservers of family life. Proverbs speaks twice (2:16, 6:24) of the evils of 'strange' women.

But the Samarian 'dogs' who licked up dead King Ahab's blood, and washed his armour (Kings 22:38), were sacred prostitutes. For what is called 'sacred' prostitution, male and female, existed side by side with 'lay' prostitution. So far as the Israelites are concerned, discussion of the subject is made confusing by chronological and other difficulties; all that is clear is that the Jewish law consistently fought against it as a practice both offensive and alien to Yahweh, and that it was finally wiped out by

King Josiah, who 'broke down the houses of the sodomites, that
were by the house of the Lord, where the women wore hangings
for the grove' (2 Kings 23:7). The practice, which was common
among the Semites in general and particularly among the Canaan-
ites, appears to have been regarded by Yahwism as only one more
aspect of the Jewish tendency to apostasy. Hosea, in a tirade
typical of so many in the Old Testament, said,

> I will not punish your daughters when they commit whoredom . . .
> for themselves are separated with whores, and they sacrifice with har-
> lots: therefore the people that doth not understand shall fall. Though
> thou, Israel, play the harlot. . . . The Lord liveth. . . . For Israel slideth
> back as a backsliding heifer. . . .

It is true that whoredom became a frequent metaphor for back-
sliding; but this may originally have been as much because the
practice of sacred prostitution was regarded as non-Jewish as
because of any innate 'puritanism'. As important an aspect of
the development of the Jewish moral code as its strictness is its
function of settling its adherents off from their neighbours, and
thus of creating a sense of national identity.

2

But sacred, or Temple prostitution – though prostitution is not
an appropriate term – long antedates the emergence of the Israelites as a separate people. There is little agreement as to its real
nature or origins. Richard Lewinsohn's view is that it arose
simply because males needed 'a free area' in which they could
'satisfy their sexual desires without incurring subsequent obligations'.* 'The fact that prostitutes acted as servants of the gods
and that contemporary reports call them "holy",' he writes,

* Richard Lewinsohn, *A History of Sexual Customs*, translated by Alexander Mayce,
Longmans, Green, London, 1958.

'does not alter the realistic nature of their business', which is 'the sexual act . . . without either a long prologue or an epilogue'.

These are, however, generalizations: facile modern projections onto a complex ancient situation. For if by the Jewish second millennium there existed a distinction between Temple and another kind of prostitution, then undoubtedly the two practices had co-existed before that. Which leads to the question, was Temple prostitution actually prostitution – in any sense of the term that is meaningful today – at all? Harry Benjamin and R. E. L. Masters, in their *Prostitution and Morality*,* one of the best of all the many books on the subject, quote Maryse Choisy as saying that 'Between a sacred courtesan and a call girl there is the same difference as between a priestess who offers holy wine and a bartender'. This remark is valueless, since it evinces a merely rhetorical disapproval of call girls and bartenders, and a subjective preference for temple women and priestesses. B. Z. Goldberg's point that 'it is the motive that determines whether a sexual union is prostitutional or not' deserves more serious consideration. It is not a question of deciding whether extra-sexual motives are superior to sexual ones, but which were paramount in this case.

Prostitution as we now know it in the West may not exist merely because there is a demand for it; but certainly it is viable only for that reason. If sacred prostitution did not, at any rate originally – and before it began to merge with the lay kind – exist by virtue of a demand for extra-marital sexual union, but for other reasons, then it is something quite distinct from it and should not be called prostitution. The view that 'religious' motives necessarily conceal only sexual ones, as exemplified in Lewinsohn, may or may not be cynical; certainly it is crude and unhistorical, and does not even make an attempt to outline any Freudian – or other – machinery by which this might be so.

Fernando Henriques in his *Prostitution and Society* speaks of 'prostitution' as being 'an essential part of the worship of the gods', and of the resultant union of 'religion and sexuality'; and

---

* Julian Press, New York, 1964; Souvenir Press, London 1965; paperback edition entitled *The Prostitute in Society*, Mayflower, London, 1966.

J. G. Frazer, in *The Golden Bough*, even while asserting that the custom which obliged women in various parts of the ancient world to 'submit themselves' to strangers before marriage was not regarded as 'an orgy of lust, but as a solemn religious duty performed in the service of that great Mother Goddess of Western Asia whose name varied, while her type remained constant', speaks of their 'prostituting' themselves. But, while we have no grounds upon which we may condemn the economic (or other) motives of 'lay' prostitution, can we usefully or truthfully define religious sexuality as synonymous with it – especially if the two practices co-existed?

The situation seems a confused one at this distance of time, with genuine religious sexuality changing into something different at different rates, at different times, and in different ways, and with genuine tarts always taking advantage of the opportunities offered; but the two practices were originally distinct from each other. It is not a question of quality, but of the difference between two kinds of act.

It may be that important clues to the origins of religious prostitution will be found in the most recent anthropological theories of the nature of marriage, such as that put forward by Claude Lévi-Strauss. Marriage in primitive societies is seen as being, essentially, a means of communication between groups of men. It seems that even today many men who have recourse to prostitutes are really trying to communicate with other men.

3

Krich and Greenwald, although consistently humane in their attitude, are always anxious to point out that prostitutes feel ashamed of their profession to the extent of frequently denying that they follow it. To illustrate their point, they quote a story about Setna and Tbubui from Flinders Petrie's translation of the Doulaq Papyrus (*c.* 1400 B.C.).

Setna, a Pharaoh's son about whom there are many legends, saw a beautiful woman, dressed in gold and attended by fifty-two servants, outside the temple of Ptah. He immediately wanted her, and sent his page to speak to her maidservant, who told him that her mistress was Tbubui, daughter of the prophet of Bastit, and that she was now going to the temple to pray to Ptah. Setna then gives his page certain instructions. The narrative continues:

When the young man had returned to the place where Tbubui was, he addressed the maidservant, and spake with her, but she exclaimed against his words, as though it were an insult to speak them. Tbubui said to the young man, 'Cease to speak to that wretched girl; come and speak to me.' The young man approached the place where Tbubui was; he said to her, ' I will give thee ten pieces of gold if thou wilt pass an hour with Setna-Khamois, the son of Pharaoh Usimares. If there is necessity to have recourse to violence, he will do so, and will take thee to a hidden place where no one in the world will find thee.' Tbubui said, 'Go, say to Setna, "I am a hierodule, I am no mean person; if thou dost desire to have thy pleasure of me, thou shalt come to Bubastis into my house. All will be ready there, and thou shalt have thy pleasure of me, and no one in the world shall know it, and I shall not have acted like a woman of the streets." ' When the page had returned to Setna, he repeated to him all the words that she had said without exception, and he said, 'Lo, I am satsified.' But all who were with Setna began to curse.*

Setna went to Tbubui's house, and

. . . she came down, she took the hand of Setna, and she said to him, 'By my life! the journey to the house of the priest of Bastit, lady of Ankhutaui, at which thou art arrived, is very pleasant to me. Come up with me.' Setna went up by the stairway of the house with Tbubui. . . . Tbubui said to him, 'Will it please thee to rest thyself?' He said to her, 'That is not what I wish to do.' . . . 'Let us accomplish that for which we have come here,' Setna said. She said to him, 'Thou shalt arrive at thy house, that where thou art. But for me, I am a hierodule, I am no mean person. If thou desirest to have thy pleasure of me, thou shalt

* Quoted in Krich and Greenwald, op. cit.

make me a contract of sustenance, and a contract of money on all the things and all the goods that are thine.' He said to her, 'Let the scribe of the school be brought.' He was brought immediately and Setna caused to be made in favor of Tbubui a contract for maintenance, and he made her in writing a dowry of all things, all the goods that were his. An hour passed, one came to say this to Setna, 'Thy children are below.' He said, 'Let them be brought up.' Tbubui arose; she put on a robe of fine linen and Setna beheld all her limbs through it, and his desire increased yet more than before. Setna said to Tbubui, 'Let us accomplish now that for which I came.' She said to him, 'Thou shalt arrive at thy house, that where thou art. But for me, I am a hierodule; I am no mean person. If thou desirest to have thy pleasure of me, thou wilt cause thy children to subscribe to my writing that they may not seek a quarrel with my children on the subject of thy possessions.' Setna had his children fetched and made them subscribe to the writing. Setna said to Tbubui, 'Let me now accomplish that for which I came.' She said to him, 'Thou shalt arrive at thy house, that where thou art. But for me, I am a hierodule; I am no mean person. If thou dost desire to have thy pleasure of me, thou shalt cause thy children to be slain, so that they may not seek a quarrel with my children on account of thy possessions.' Setna said, 'Let the crime be committed on them of which the desire has entered thy heart.' She caused the children of Setna to be slain before him, she had them thrown out below the window, to the dogs and cats, and they ate their flesh, and he heard them while he was drinking with Tbubui. Setna said to Tbubui, 'Let us accomplish that for which we have come here, for all that thou hast said before me has been done for thee.' She said to him, 'Come into this chamber.' Setna entered the chamber; he lay down on a bed of ivory and ebony, in order that his love might be rewarded, and Tbubui lay down by the side of Setna. He stretched out his hand to touch her; she opened her mouth widely and uttered a loud cry.

When Setna came to himself he was in a place of a furnace without any clothing on his back. After an hour Setna perceived a very big man standing on a platform, with quite a number of attendants beneath his feet, for he had the semblance of a Pharaoh. Setna was about to raise himself but he could not arise for shame, for he had no clothing on his back. . . .

Whether all prostitutes suffer from a sense of shame or not, this story gives the notion no support. Krich and Greenwald suggest

that Tbubui was 'a successful business woman', in whom 'we
can discern the prototype of the Greek *hetaira* . . . and the latter-
day mistress'; they compare her reiterated statement, 'I am a
hierodule, I am no mean person', with the modern call-girl's
indignant 'He acted as if I was a street girl!' when she is reporting
the offer of a low fee. But this is entirely to miss the point.

However obscure the exact meaning of this ancient and
frightening story may now be, clearly one of its chief themes is
to illustrate the fact that not even a Pharaoh's son can with im-
punity make the error of treating a hierodule as a 'mean person',
such as a prostitute, or of threatening her with violence. Setna's
crime was that he tried to use a sacred woman as his whore.
There is no evidence that Tbubui had gained her wealth from, as
Krich and Greenwald assert, 'selling her body' (she was a prophet's
daughter). When she repeatedly warns Setna of her position she
means exactly what she says; she is not 'driving a hard bargain', or,
indeed, any bargain at all. Had she been what Setna treated her as,
an expensive whore, her maidservant would not have 'exclaimed
against his [page's] words, as though it were an insult to speak
them'. The story indicates, in fact, the difference between a
particular hierodule and a prostitute – a distinction Krich and
Greenwald choose to ignore, perhaps because of their eagerness
to assume that all promiscuity is essentially prostitutional. They
are fortunate to have been spared the fate of Setna, who made
the same error. The difference between a whore's protesting that
she is not a whore and a girl who is not a whore saying so is not
a very subtle one. . . .

The best-known account of religious 'prostitution' in the
ancient world, however, and one which is quoted in virtually
every history and anthology of prostitution, is Herodotus'
account of the cult of Mylitta in Babylon, which Krich and Greenwald date as '*c.* 300 B.C.'. Herodotus, in fact, died not later than
425 B.C. Doubtless the practices he described had existed in more
or less the same form for a very long time before he recorded
them:

There is one custom among these people which is wholly shameful:
every woman who is a native of the country must once in her life go

and sit in the temple of Aphrodite and there give herself to a strange man. Many of the rich women, who are too proud to mix with the rest, drive to the temple in covered carriages with a whole host of servants following behind, and there wait; most, however, sit in the precinct of the temple with a band of plaited string round their heads – and a great crowd they are, what with some sitting there, others arriving, others going away – and through them all gangways are marked off running in every direction for the men to pass along and make their choice. Once a woman has taken her seat she is not allowed to go home until a man has thrown a silver coin into her lap and taken her outside to lie with her. As he throws the coin, the man has to say, 'In the name of the goddess Mylitta' – that being the Assyrian name for Aphrodite. The value of the coin is of no consequence; once thrown it becomes sacred, and the law forbids that it should ever be refused. The woman has no privilege of choice – she must go with the first man who throws her the money. When she has lain with him, her duty to the goddess is discharged and she may go home, after which it will be impossible to seduce her by any offer, however large. Tall, handsome women soon manage to get home again, but the ugly ones stay a long time before they can fulfil the condition which the law demands, some of them, indeed, as much as three or four years.*

It is not possible to relate this custom to what we now understand by prostitution. The women appear to have had no choice in the matter, and no doubt at least the 'tall handsome' ones accepted it as a matter of course; but in any case it has always been usual for some of those who participate in accepted customs to kick against the pricks. Once again Krich and Greenwald miss the point in their comment on the passage. They write:

One of the most common myths about prostitution is that in other periods or in other places, somewhere it was practised without shame. . . . Yet Herodotus in writing about [the cult of Mylitta] says 'The Babylonians have one most shameful custom,' so that Herodotus did not consider Temple Prostitution anything but shameful. However, it is possible that Herodotus . . . looked upon this institution as shameful, while the Babylonians accepted it. . . . However, Herodotus states, 'Many of the wealthier sort drive a covered carriage to the precinct,'

* Translations of Heroditus are from *The Histories*, translated by Aubrey de Selincourt, Penguin Books, Harmondsworth, 1954.

i.e. in order not to be seen. . . . The act is designed to prevent women from acting out the prostitution fantasies which may have been as prevalent then as they are today.

Herodotus, although born at Halicarnassus in Ionia, knew Athens, where real prostitution flourished, well. The Babylonian custom seems shameful to him, I suggest, precisely because it is primarily religious. As he writes, the value of the silver coin thrown by a man into the lap of the waiting woman 'is of no consequence; once thrown it becomes sacred . . .'. And almost immediately before the passage describing this custom, Herodotus has a note on real prostitution in Babylonia. He has been describing their marriage customs, which he calls 'ingenious': the rich men buy the pretty girls at auctions, while the 'humbler folk, who had no use for good looks in a wife, were actually paid to take the ugly ones . . .'. He goes on:

This admirable practice has now fallen into disuse and they have of late years hit upon another scheme, namely the prostitution of all girls of the lower classes to provide some relief from the poverty which followed upon the conquest [by Cyrus] with its attendant hardship and general ruin.

Thus, Herodotus clearly distinguishes between real (though enforced) prostitution, which he does not call 'shameful' – indeed, he seems to feel that it is as 'admirable' as the practice whose place it took – and the rites of Mylitta.

Krich and Greenwald's speculations, that shame and, presumably, guilt, caused some of the women to drive to the precinct in covered carriages, and that the purpose of the custom was to prevent women from enacting 'prostitution fantasies', can only be described as grotesque. Travelling in a covered carriage would not in any way have spared the woman the alleged shame of sitting in the precinct itself! No doubt the rich habitually travelled in closed carriages. If shame had been felt then it would have been evident, and Herodotus would have mentioned this in support of his own view of the custom. Krich and Greenwald's second speculation is hardly worthy of discussion. Why should this custom 'inoculate' a woman against prostitution at all, or prevent 'prostitution fantasies'? It is as likely to encourage prostitution. But Krich and Greenwald's main fault is that they view the varying sexual attitudes of antiquity as if they were equivalent to what they regard as those of twentieth-century America. There are few aspects of these ancient attitudes that we can confidently describe; but they were certainly most unlike our own.

Chapter Two

1

PROSTITUTION in Greece is well, if not always precisely enough for our liking, documented. Full accounts of its organization may be found in most histories of the subject. The Athenian statesman and poet, Solon, was appointed 'archon and reconciler' in about 594 B.C., to found a constitution more acceptable to the majority of people in Athens. One of his acts is said to have been to put prostitution on a legal basis. The apparently long-lived dramatist Philemon of Syracuse (c. 360–c. 263 B.C.), a naturalized Athenian and poet of the New Comedy, which provided the Greeks and Romans of three and four centuries later with so much inspiration, praised Solon for his action:

The place [i.e. the brothel] was unquestionably necessary . . . in a city where the impetuous young could no longer restrain themselves from yielding to the most potent of nature's injunctions [homosexuality]. . . . Thou didst avert great mischief . . . by installing women in certain houses.

This much later view of Solon's act, however, which is anti-homosexual in tone, gives no certain clue as to Solon's motives, or to contemporary attitudes to his legislation.

Henriques speaks of Solon's being 'far-sighted' in his handling
of 'the problem'. But was it then regarded as a social problem?
Not, certainly, in anything like the same way as it is today, for
then there were no strictly moral overtones.

What is interesting, however, is that Solon's chief virtues are
usually regarded as having been his reasonableness and his wisdom.
Although he did not found a democracy, he undoubtedly helped
to initiate a democratic spirit. The Victorian scholar of the Greek
city-state, the Rev. W. Warde Fowler, mentions that Solon
tried to educate the people in 'morality and self-respect, to curb
luxury . . . to direct them on the road towards intellectual as well
as political liberty'. There is no reason to doubt this; but neither
is there reason to doubt that his legalization of prostitution, which
Warde Fowler did not mention, was in the same spirit. Adultery,
although occasionally practised because the deceptions involved
were exciting, was frowned upon by the Greek authorities both
then and for long afterwards. One of Solon's motives in creating
state brothels, which he stocked with foreign whores, could have
been to discourage adultery; thus supplementing government
finances at the same time. In the absence of detailed evidence it is
impossible to go further than this.

The position of 'respectable' women in Athens was, from a
modern point of view, a depressed one. This is one of the reasons
why the position of prostitutes – non-respectable women – had
become, by 150 years or so after Solon, an elevated one. The wives
and daughters of the Homeric age were never subjected or
secluded in the way their descendants were, even though they
may be over-romantically portrayed in the *Odyssey*. But by the
beginning of the fifth century all they had, in Athens, was their
status – which was worth nothing to them in terms of personal
liberty. For all the subtle and delicate treatment of noble women
in the Greek literature of the classical age – although this does, as
has many times been noted, eschew the theme of young love
except in the case of Haemon and Antigone in Sophocles' *Antigone* – the Greeks showed little sign of appreciation of such noble
women in their daily lives. Athens may have developed into a
democracy, but it was essentially a democracy for free men,

rather than for their wives or daughters, who had little say in the nature of their own lives, let alone anyone else's. However, women were by no means forgotten.

Classical Greek society was, it hardly needs to be said, bisexual, with a spiritual bias towards homosexuality; but emphasis upon this sometimes tends to diminish the extent to which certain women were valued, both for their femininity and their beauty. It is true that the Greek ideal seems to have been the total elimination of love from marriage; but this was not necessarily the result of a fundamentally homosexual attitude. Women may have played no official part in public life, but classical Greek literature never ignores them. Plato was dissatisfied with their absence from state affairs; and even Aristotle's assumption of masculine superiority, which suited the prevailing temper, is more idiosyncratic than symptomatic of a generally homosexual situation. Rather than regarding it as 'degenerate' or 'unnatural', one might think of Greek homosexuality as a highly intellectualized, aesthetically self-conscious, development of a kind of situation that now exists among the males of an anonymous Melanesian community as reported by the anthropologist William Davenport.* The males here (but not the females) enjoy homosexual relationships, which usually include buggery, before marriage, with no trace of 'civilized' 'shame'. Admittedly, the Greek pattern was different – a youth would be sexually, emotionally and intellectually loved by an older man; then, after an interval of some twenty years in which he married and reared children, he would in his turn seek out a youth – but the absence of 'shame' in this connection is similar. At any rate, the Greeks certainly created for themselves the social opportunity to enjoy full relationships with women as well as men – but in the sphere of prostitution rather than of marriage. Prostitution was both extremely highly organized and universally accepted.

There were three classes of prostitutes: the aristocrats of the profession, the *hetairai* (the word, which means 'companion', was used by Sappho to mean 'intimate female companion'); the dancers and flute-players who entertained men in more ways

* Paper in *Sex and Behaviour*, ed. F. A. Beach, John Wiley, New York, 1965.

than one, the *auletrides*; the street-walkers and brothel prostitutes, the *dicteriades* or *pornai*. Concubines, being slaves, can hardly be classed as prostitutes: what choices they had, if any, is not known.

If literature did not represent the situation truthfully, then we do not know what the situation was, for virtually the whole of our evidence comes from literature. But since such disapproval or hostility as is on record is directed against individual prostitutes, on account of their personal behaviour, rather than against the practice of prostitution, we may assume that no one regarded it as a 'moral' problem.

Sexual passion was usually represented in classical Greece as either a recreation or a disease. It might be homosexual or directed towards prostitutes. It was never 'holy'. It is discussed without moral reservations. According to Plato, Sophocles, who being a poet was (admittedly) probably typical only in a rather special sense, called lust 'a savage and fierce master', and was glad, although he had had relationships with *hetairai*, that he had escaped from it in old age. But this means no more than that it was regarded as tiresome; it does not imply that it was thought of as a 'sin'. Homosexual relationships between men, which Socrates idealized (Plato was not quite consistent on the matter), might certainly have represented themselves as a convenient and noble escape from the misfortunes of heterosexual love. However, although women were subjugated in the marriage relation, the Greeks do not seem to have blamed women exclusively for the 'tiresomeness' of sex: they admired them in their role as prostitutes, most particularly, of course, as *hetairai*. Thus Socrates' friend, the bisexual Alcibiades, whose career, as it is recorded by Plutarch, appears shameless by official modern standards, treated his wife Hipparete as a dowry-fetching chattel, but had himself painted with the courtesan Nemea in his arms. Only 'such of the Athenians as were more advanced in years' were displeased.

Contemporary evidence for the high regard in which *hetairai* were held is abundant. Xenophon's Socrates attributed his knowledge of higher love to what he had learned from the *hetaira* Diotima; he told another, Theodota, to employ procurers if she wanted to improve business.

Once the Christians gained power, however, they destroyed as much of this kind of material as possible; fortunately an Egyptian of the third century A.D. called Athenaeus incorporated many scraps of such information in a dull, invaluable collection called *The Deipnosophists*. Titbits from this, quotations from otherwise lost works describing the power of the *hetairai* over almost every one of the great men of the classical age, are often given in histories of prostitution. They titilated the palates of readers of recent generations because of their 'naughtiness', but now read tediously. But they demonstrate beyond doubt that the *hetairai* were regarded as in many ways the intellectual equals of men: they studied or lived with such philosophers as Plato, Aristotle and Epicurus, and their witty sayings were anthologized. All this can be ascertained by reference to the Loeb translation of Athenaeus* or, if its seven volumes of parallel translation are too formidable, then in C. D. Yonge's earlier translation in Bohn's Classics.†

However, while it is one thing for the historians of prostitution to quote from the authentic fragments contained in Athenaeus' erratic disguised encyclopedia-cum-anthology, it is quite another to quote from such writers as Alciphron and Lucian. In the first volume of his *Prostitution and Society*, in the chapter called 'Classical Greece', Henriques quotes three times apiece from each; Krich and Greenwald anthologize a passage from Lucian's *Dialogues of the Courtesans*; 'Lujo Bassermann' (Herman Otto Ludwig Schreiber), in the English translation, *The Oldest Profession*, of his *Das Alteste Gewerbe: eine Kultwigeschichte* (1965),‡ quotes from a famous letter' by 'a certain Megara', which is, he states, 'included in the collection made by Alciphron'.

One of the most celebrated and expensive of the Greek *hetairai* of the period after the Persian Wars was Phryne, mistress of the sculptor Praxiteles, who was charged with impiety at the height of her career. The story is in Athenaeus and in Plutarch. Either the orator defending her, Hypereides, or she herself gained her acquittal by baring her breasts to the judges. Henriques claims

* Heinemann, London, 1927–30.† Bell, London, 1854.
‡ Translated James Cleugh, Barker, London, 1967.

that another *hetaira*, Bacchis, 'is said to have written to
Hypereides', and quotes part of the letter. He also quotes from
the letter by 'Megara'; and, to illustrate his assertion that prostitutes were 'not above fleecing . . . affluent lovers', says that
'Philumena writes to her lover, Criton, in this style: "Why do
you trouble yourself with long letters? I want fifty gold pieces,
but no letters . . .".'

These quotations are misleading, as is Professor Henriques'
remark in the third volume of his study to the effect that 'The
sentiment expressed by Alciphron in the first of his *Letters from
Courtesans* . . . is not to be found in the Christian era': Alciphron,
although his exact dates are unknown, was certainly of 'the
Christian era', even if his sentiments were un-Christian. His most
quoted letter is probably the one describing a party attended by
a number of *hetairai*, from which both Basserman (who coyly
omits some details) and Henriques quote. Here is a bit of it:

What a party we had (why, pray, shouldn't I vex your heart?). . . .
Songs, jests, drinking till cockcrow, perfumes, garlands, sweetmeats.
We reclined under the shade of some laurels. There was only one thing
we lacked – you but nothing else. . . . But the thing that gave us the
greatest pleasure, anyhow, was a serious rivalry that arose between
Thryallis and Myrrhina in the matter of buttocks – as to which could
display the lovelier, softer pair. And first Myrrhina unfastened her
girdle (her shift was silk), and began to shake her loins (visible through
her shift), which quivered like junkets, the while she cocked her eye
back at the wagglings of her buttocks. And so gently, as if she were
in the act, she sighed a bit, that, by Aphrodite, I was thunderstruck.
Thryallis, nevertheless, did not give up; on the contrary she outdid
Myrrhina in wantonness. 'I certainly am not going to compete behind
a curtain'. . . . So she put off her shift; and, puckering her croup a little,
she said, 'There now, look at the colour, how youthful, Myrrhina,
how pure, how free from blemish; see these rosy hips, how they merge
into the thighs, how there's neither too much plumpness nor any thin-
ness, and the dimples at the tips. But, by Zeus, they don't quiver,' said
she with a sly smile, 'like Myrrhina's.' And then she made her buttocks
vibrate so fast, swaying their whole bulk above the loins this way and
that with such a rippling motion, that we all applauded and declared
that the victory was Thryallis's. . . .

We do not know when Alciphron lived (it seems most likely that he was a Syrian, younger than Lucian, who was born in A.D. 120 and died about 180), but we do know that the series of 'letters' from fishermen, farmers, parasites and courtesans, of which his works consist, are, as his translators mention, 'forged without intent to deceive' (i.e. they are imaginary). None the less, they have deceived Basserman and Henriques, both of whom use them as evidence of conditions in the Athens of the fifth century B.C., some 500 to 600 years before they were written. Alciphron was basically a prose romancer, who drew his inspiration from literature, specifically from the New Comedy of the fourth century (of which Menander, born in 341 B.C., is the most famous exponent); he was not a realist and did not set out to be one. That he occasionally makes an era long bygone in his own day (at least as bygone as Elizabethan England is now) seem to come to life may testify to his literary, but not to his historical skill.

More of Lucian's work has survived, and it is more varied; he was a much more important writer; but he too possessed a nostalgia for the age of the New Comedy: it is hardly less reprehensible to use his writings, more complex though they are, as evidence of conditions in the fourth century B.C. than it is to use Alciphron's.

Krich and Greenwald, however, go one worse. Dating their extract from Lucian's *Dialogues of the Courtesans* 'Second Century [A.D.]', they state that we 'learn from Lucian's sophisticated account' that the *hetairai* were 'the mistresses of Athenians from the best families', and then go on to quote Demosthenes, who really was a fourth-century Greek, as if he was a contemporary. They fail to make clear whether they have in mind the second-century (A.D.) Roman province of Athens, or Demosthenes' Athens; or, indeed, what Athens Lucian himself was writing about. . . . Their chronological confusion is made manifest by a previous remark, in introducing four translations from the Greek from F. A. Wright's *The Girdle of Aphrodite*: 'By the time of the Christian era, the Greek ideal of Eros had become debased into a commercialized promiscuity with various gradations . . .'.

And they go on to designate the classes of prostitute, the *hetairai*, and so on, as though these had come into being during the Christian era.

But the writings of Alciphron and Lucian, whatever their value as natural history, are genuine contributions to the literature of prostitution. Alciphron, as we have seen, is hardly serious, although he has some importance in his literary context and in the development of the prose romance. Such passages as the one already quoted, and the one that follows – extracted from a letter (a fragment) purporting to be from a *hetaira* of the fourth century to her girl-friend – now seem artificial, even 'naughty' in a Victorian sense. They are somewhat frigid, and rather obviously masculine, clever literary imitations rather than seriously realistic. As we read them now, they seem to contain an element of voyeurism; we don't find it hard to imagine Alciphron as a timid man of little sexual experience, dreaming up orgies. But this is not of course a safe inference: we do not know their exact context, and time and translation have largely obscured Alciphron's ripe nostalgia for an earlier era.

[Melissa recently invited us to] her lover's country place, saying that she owed a sacrifice to the Nymphs. It is really a sort of meadow-land or garden; but spreading out at the side of the villa is a little land fit for planting, and the rest is cypresses and myrtle – really the seat of a man of pleasure, my dear, not of a farmer. . . .

At once we busied ourselves with the sacrifice. A little way off from the villa was a rock, its summit shaded by laurels and plane trees; on either side of it are myrtle thickets; and ivy runs around it as though it were interwoven, attaching itself closely to the stone; while from the rock clear water dript. Under its projecting edges are some statues of Nymphs, and a Pan peeped over as if spying on the Naiads. . . .

By that time we were ready for the feast. 'Let's go to the house,' said Melissa, 'and recline at table.' 'No indeed, by the Nymphs and by Pan,' said I, 'just look at him: for you see how mad for love he is. He would be delighted to see us carousing here. No, under the myrtle bushes, come look, how dewy the place is all around and dappled with dainty flowers. I should prefer to lie on this green grass rather than on those rugs and soft coverlets. By Zeus, you know, dinner-parties here, amid the beauty of green fields and under the open sky, are more de-

lightful than in town.' 'Yes, yes, you are right,' said the others. So
straightway some of us broke off branches of yew, others branches of
myrtle, and by spreading our cloaks over them we threw together an
improvised couch. . . .

. . . when Plangon got up and danced, swaying her hips, Pan from
his rock almost leapt upon her buttocks. And at once the music excited
us women, and since we were a bit tipsy our thoughts turned to – you
know what I mean. We stroked the hands of our lovers, gently un-
bending their flexed fingers, and between cups we engaged in amorous
sport. One and another lay back and kissed her lover, letting him feel
her breasts; and as if she were turning away she would actually press
her hips on his groin. And now our passions were rising, and there was
a rising among the men too; so we slipped away and found a shady
thicket a short distance off, a bridal suite suited to this stage of our revel.
Here we quit our drinking and made in haste for our little boudoirs,
doing our act not very convincingly. Then one girl tied together twigs
of myrtle, plaiting them as a wreath for herself, and she cried out, 'See
my dear, if it becomes me'; and another girl came up with violet
blossoms, saying, 'What a lovely fragrance!' and another, taking some
unripe apples from the fold of her garment, showed them and said,
'See these'; and another girl hummed a tune; and another, plucking
leaves from the twigs, nibbled them as if playing coy; and – what was
most ridiculous of all – all of us as we got up for the same purpose
wanted to hide from each other, and those fellows were strolling
around into the thicket the other way. . . .*

This, which is almost certainly influenced by Lucian, if only
in a mechanical way, is to a large extent masculine fantasy. Its
conscious 'naughtiness' assumes the existence of forces that disapproved not merely of individual prostitutes or of frivolous
sexual behaviour but of any kind of 'illicit' sexual activity at all.
Those Athenians who objected to the *hetairai* in the fifth and
fourth centuries did so because they were mostly foreigners from
Asia Minor who were free (although not, by a decree of Pericles,
allowed to bear legitimate sons) in a sense that native-born wives
were not; they would have been perfectly incapable of Alciphron's
almost pornographic attitude.

Lucian's *Dialogues of the Courtesans* are altogether wittier and

* *Alciphron, Aelian and Philostratus,* translated by Benner and Fobes, Heinemann,
London, 1959.

more pointed. He had a sharper mind, and a real sympathy with the oppressed and unrespectable. But of course they are no more historically valuable, for all their shrewdness, than Alciphron's *Letters of Courtesans*. Krich and Greenwald's assertion that the *Dialogues* 'attack the myth of the happy prostitute' is nonsensical, as is their characterization of Lucian as 'a keen observer'. Observer of what?

In fact, *Dialogues of the Courtesans* do not attack any kind of myth about prostitutes; they simply assume their existence. Lucian, who never quoted a Latin author, and who thus appeared to ignore a literature with which he must have been familiar, is in these dialogues nostalgic, mocking, gossipy, sophisticated, ironic, sceptical and gay. Despite the element of nostalgia for the classical age in his writings, Lucian was more of a satirist of the decadence of Greek thought than, so to speak, a participant: he was, after all, an Asiatic. He had no use for the niceties of philo-sophy, and he attacked pederasty; he was interested not in theories but in results. Like John Donne, the Earl of Rochester, and only a very few other writers of the past, he had what the twentieth century may legitimately describe as a 'modern' mind. A practical moralist – who therefore sounds no more like a moralist than Fielding or Swift – he rejected both the abstractions of Greek metaphysics and the later neuroses of Christianity. He attacked all religion. He was interested not in types but in individuals. His dialogues demonstrate no more than his assumption that the Greek prostitutes were human beings of widely varying kinds – an assumption deeply disturbing to lovers of theory.

To a large extent, the dialogues consist of shrewd jokes about women and their attitude towards men and love; that these women happen to be whores is largely immaterial. In 'Melitta and Bacchis' Melitta complains to her friend that her lover, Charinus, has gone off to another girl, Simiche. This is all because mischievous youths have written 'Melitta loves Hermotimus' and 'the shipowner Hermotimus loves Melitta' on the walls at the Ceramicus (the Potters' Quarter and burial area of Athens). Bacchis recommends a certain Syrian witch, who she claims will be able to cause Charinus to return to Melitta. This is no more than a squib at the expense of women's credulity; that Bacchis and Melitta are prostitutes is incidental. 'Leana and Clonarium' is similar in this respect: Leana describes to her lover Clonarium how Megilla seduced her, but refuses to go into the details (which she says are 'not very nice') of the 'substitute' that Megilla employs to turn herself into a man. Nothing here is being said about prostitution, only about women and some of their habits.

In the dialogue between Crobyle and her daughter Corinna, Corinna, urged to imitate a *hetaira* called Lura, protests 'But she's a courtesan', to which her mother replies 'There's nothing terrible in that'. Krich and Greenwald assert that 'Lucian leaves no doubt that Corinna certainly did not embrace the occupation with pleasure, and saw it as a shameful way of life': 'The mother has to spend considerable time convincing her daughter that she should take up the role of a courtesan.'

However, the translation they quote (they do not specify who made it, and I cannot trace it) is inaccurate, and even includes non-authorial stage directions such as 'scandalized' and 'weeps'. The Greek, accurately translated in the Loeb version, does not bear out their contention. Corinna actually offers no more than a token resistance; her curiosity and willingness to learn are much more evident than her reluctance. She has already slept with a client, and this has not worried her. If there is a point, then it is at the expense of mothers-in-general – not of mothers-as-procuresses. Corinna's innocence as to the nature of the trade she has taken up is represented as funny – not, alas, as having anything to do with shame. In the dialogue that follows this one, 'Musarium and her Mother', the same theme is pursued: the mother wants her daughter to do her job properly, and not sentimentally confine her attention to one man; but Musarium is in no way 'ashamed' of being a courtesan. On the contrary, no such feelings are expressed by any prostitute in the *Dialogues*.

Classical and later Greek literature about prostitution tells us that the *hetairai*, and to some extent the dancing-girls, took over for a time part of the function of the wife; in doing so they gained a higher status, in most spheres, than that of the wife. They entered into stable relationships, and provided a counterpart to the attractions of young men. Of the ordinary brothel and street whore we learn little or nothing, beyond the fact that she existed – as she has existed in all societies – and that she existed wretchedly: Xenarchus and Eubulus, dramatists quoted by Athenaeus, describe some aspects of this. It is clear, however, that we can make no psychological or psychoanalytical inferences about modern prostitutes from what we know of the *hetairai*: they were a separate class, existing in a social context unlike anything that now exists. In as much as any class of women may be said to be admirable as a whole, they were admirable: they were witty, intelligent and (so far as we know) good lovers. They performed a useful social function, and were well integrated. They, and not the wife – whose task was to produce children – were the companions of men. Considered, then, in the light of our own time in the West, they were not prostitutes at all. Lucian wrote of them retrospectively, at least aware that their 'innocence' was not accepted in his own day; Alciphron, probably after him and under his influence, used them to create a semi-pornographic literature. It would be interesting to know who his immediate audience was; one would be hardly surprised to learn that his work was surreptitiously passed about amongst early male Christians.

Chapter Three

1

By the beginning of the first century B.C. the Romans had abandoned the sexual rectitude (if that is the right word) to which they might, with justice, earlier have laid claim. Were sex no more than a matter of physical appetite, then they would deserve to be regarded as its realists. Divorce, adultery, prostitution (and even, perhaps, married love) now flourished as they never had in the classical Greek world. Any Roman of means could have whatever kind of sex he wanted without much fear of scandal. Only adultery might lead to serious trouble. However, it is always as well to remember that, as Crane Brinton reminds us in his *History of Western Morals*,★ 'our sources deal almost wholly with the doings of the small group at the top of the social pyramid. . . . A corrupt aristocracy and a sober, steady, virtuous populace seem hardly to go contentedly and in equilibrium together, but the historian cannot close his mind to the possibility that they may, at least in the short term'. We do know of examples of married affection and faithfulness; this may have been more widespread than the histories suggest.

Rome had its *hetairai*, who often assumed Greek names, and its

★ Weidenfeld & Nicolson, London, 1959.

more ordinary whores; unlike Greece, it also had a number of high-ranking married women who behaved like prostitutes. The original Roman women had been stolidly virtuous; the (legendary) behaviour of Lucretia when Tarquinius raped her is typical, and is supposed to reflect this stolid virtue. But such rectitude was a matter of honour, not of morals: the women had to be reliable in order to look after the home while their husbands went out to found an empire. Legally a husband had absolute power over his wife; in practice she probably both accepted his standards and worked in harmony with him. But as Rome began to prosper, so women tended to become more emancipated. The reasons for this are complex – they include, for example, the greed of fathers who did not wish to lose economic control of their daughter's dowry – but there is no doubt that by the first century B.C. the Roman matron enjoyed much more freedom than any Greek woman of the same type had ever known. She might be as well educated as a Greek *hetaira*; if it did not suit her to have children (previously a noble duty), then she could resort to abortion or abandonment. She could divorce her husband with the greatest of ease. It was not surprising in these circumstances that some bored women should lead the life of prostitutes, having every man they fancied and even entering brothels, like Messalina, wife of the Emperor Claudius, to entertain strangers.

Juvenal (c. A.D. 60–c. 130) satirizes, in his capacity as realist and happy prophet of Rome's fall, its sexual licence; he includes the exploits of Messalina:

> look what the Emperor Claudius endured
>   all those long years his wife
> preferred a common mat to his soft chair.
>   Nightly she donned her cowl and with her maid
>   left him to play her shameless masquerade
> using as guise a wig of yellow hair.
>
> She languished in her brothel's stinking covers,
>   seizing that room reserved for her sole use,
>   then went to work under Lycisca's alias.
>   She bared her painted nipples and kept loose
>   those thighs that birthed well-born Britannicus.

> There she received all comers,
> getting top price until the doors shut tight.
> The lust, though, still raged hotly in her bosom.
> Dirt-stained, she left the house and journeyed home
> exhausted, but undaunted by the sweat.
> Thus smeared with lampsoot, she returned unfazed
> to settle odors in the royal pillows.
> So why belabor potions, chants, the poison
> wives brew stepsons, or countless other throes
> wives harbor in, for lust's the mildest reason.*

Like many satirists, Juvenal enjoyed the gusto with which he belaboured his subject; Messalina herself was certainly executed before Juvenal could have known anything about it, probably before he was born. What he attacked, however, was the grossness of her sexuality (rather than the sexuality in itself), and through this the grossness of Roman life. More profoundly, Juvenal was an ironist, a realist, an energetic, cheerful pessimist. He was a moralist least of all; if he was not an antinomian cynic, then this is only because his realism has the uncynical virtue of depicting things as they really are, and because, as a practical tongue-in-cheek poet, he believed in the eventual powers of conscience. He was a natural historian enjoying his job. He saw his age as one in which vice remained supreme; but there is no reason to suppose that his motives were morally virtuous. He enjoyed his disgust, and his disgust at Messalina's lustfulness is not at all the same thing as Christian 'sadness', disapproval, desire to 'save'. His description of Messalina's exploits as a harlot is totally factual, graphic, realistic. The whole of the sixth satire is a deliberately scurrilous attack on women, and Messalina, a paradigm of female lustfulness of over a half-century before he wrote, is employed to demonstrate the general lustfulness of the Roman women of the early second century. Nothing whatever is being said about prostitution itself, which is simply accepted as a fact.

The ninth satire is more specific on the subject, in that it gives an unforgettable portrait of an ageing homosexual prostitute, the

---

* Unless otherwise indicated, translations of Juvenal are from the *Satires*, translated by Jerome Mazzaro, University of Michigan Press, 1965.

sort of man of whom the epigrammatist Martial, Juvenal's older
contemporary, wrote:

> Naevulus, when I see that a boy's
> Prick, and your arse, are sore,
> I don't need to be a psychiatrist
> To know what went before.*

But now the old queer has lost his looks: Juvenal says,

> You've let your black hair knot like thicket points,
> and none of that old sleekness firms your skin.
> Your legs are shot, the hair gone dry and thin
> like an old man's when fever's struck his joints.

And he goes on to mock him, suggesting that he will soon find
new ways to make profits. The old queen replies:

> 'For some a job like that lasts all their lives,
> but me, I only got a raincoat for my sweat,
>
> 'A greasy remnant of some Gallicarts [cheap fabric]
> to keep my clothes respectably one shade.
> Once, too, a piece of silver, low in grade,
> for circumstances rule, even those parts
>
> 'the toga hides, and if the Fates don't bother,
> one's latent sexual powers aren't worth a *sou*
> thou Virro [the speaker's rich lover] sees and takes a
>   shine to you
> and sends you love notes one on top the other.
>
> 'Such men as he lead others into trysts;
> yet what's more shameful, he's a stinking queer.
> "*I gave you so much there, then so much here.*"
> He reckons up his lusts like grocery lists.
>
> 'He sends out for his books: "*Here's what I've paid.
> Now count your services.*" Now is that nice,
> I work my cock in to indulge his vice
> and find the services put down to trade [i.e. "am
> treated as a homosexual prostitute" – which in fact he is].'

> * My translation.

This is just the sort of realism that the conditions of first- and second-century Rome produced from its poets; but Juvenal's attitude is one of humorous, aggressive disgust, not of moral disapproval. The speaker is in no way ashamed; he simply attacks the meanness of his rich lover.

2

The most remarkable of all Roman poets, however, was Catullus, who lived from 87 to about 54 B.C. or perhaps later. Catullus comes into this book because he had a protracted love-affair with a woman whom, although she was not technically a prostitute, most people would agree to describe as a whore. He called her Lesbia; her real name was probably Clodia, the wife of the governor of the province in which Verona, Catullus' birth-place, lay. There is not one convincing reason to suppose that Catullus' lyrics are anything other than a straightforward record of his own experience.

A common interpretation of Catullus is that, for all his tenderness and skill, his experience was not one of love, and that he viewed Lesbia in 'purely genital terms'. But what emerges from an examination of the nature of the relationship he achieved with this quasi-*hetaira*, a woman so promiscuous that she was notorious throughout Rome, tends to challenge this interpretation as an over-simplification based on an assumption that Catullus shared the current Roman view of women and of sex. In his valuable, accurate and readable *The Natural History of Love*,* Morton M. Hunt compares Catullus' view of sex with that of his near-contemporary Lucretius (*c.* 100–*c.* 55 B.C.) as expressed in Book Four of *De Rerum Natura* (*On the Nature of Things*). *De Rerum Natura* was above all intended as a full exposition of the Epicurean philosophy. Thus, '*The one stimulus that evokes human seed from*

* Alfred A. Knopf, New York, 1959.

the human body is a human form': the urge towards ejaculation is
'tyrannical',

. . . when a man is pierced by the shafts of Venus, whether they are
launched by a lad with womanish limbs or a woman radiating love
from her whole body, he strives towards the source of the wound and
craves to be united with it. . . . If you find yourself passionately
enamoured of an individual, you should keep well away from such
images. . . . Vent the seed of love upon other images. . . . [Lovers']
passion is not pure, but they are goaded by an underlying impulse to
hurt the thing . . . that gives rise to these budding shoots of madness. . . .
In the midst of love Venus teases lovers with images. . . . Body clings
greedily to body; moist lips are pressed on lips, and deep breaths are
drawn through clenched teeth. . . . At length, when the spate of lust
is spent, there comes a slight intermission. . . . But not for long. Soon
the same frenzy returns. . . . In aimless bewilderment they waste away,
stricken by an unseen wound. . . . Their wealth slips from them. . . .
Their duties are neglected. . . .*

This is certainly an alarmist view, and one which does see 'love'
in wholly genital terms. The message is, 'Avoid the pangs of
lust'. But such an attitude was really the only one that would fit
into the Epicurean scheme. In this celebrated passage the philosopher Lucretius is concentrating upon the theory of love; the
poet Lucretius, always incidental in the work, gleefully concentrates, in lines Swift must have enjoyed, on the disgust inherent
in sex. Whatever Lucretius' practice or emotional experience may
have been, his intellect certainly rejected love as any kind of
spiritual entity; but then his Epicurean materialism obliged him,
in his writings, to subject everything to the same process.

Does this apply to Catullus? Was Lucretius' formula the same
one, as Morton Hunt insists it was, 'at which poor Catullus arrived
willy nilly'?

To answer this question, we need first to look briefly at the
life of Clodia. For if Catullus' Lesbia was not Clodia, then she was
certainly someone like her – a type of woman not uncommon
in the Rome of the first century B.C.

---

* Lucretius, *On the Nature of Things*, translated by R. E. Latham, Penguin Books,
Harmondsworth, 1951.

The ox-eyed Clodia, wife of Caecilius Metellus Celer (whom she may have murdered) and sister of Clodius Pulcher, politician and rake, was some eight years older than Catullus. She was rich, beautiful, increasingly promiscuous and intellectually talented. She has been described as 'completely lacking in moral principles', but this is to apply latter-day bourgeois standards to an age in which they did not exist. Latter-day horror at her lustful nature has perhaps distracted attention from her other qualities, to which Catullus implicitly paid tribute. However, she was not kind or (ultimately) generous; she was also reckless. When, long after she had tired of Catullus, she was deserted by his friend Caelius Rufus, she accused him of trying to poison her, and of other crimes. One of Rufus' defenders was Cicero, and in the speech now known as 'For Caelius' he destroyed her as a public figure. Nothing more is heard of her. In this speech he called her a prostitute, and not without justice: imitation of prostitution is in itself a kind of prostitution. Clodia not only picked up strangers in the street and went to bed with them (clearly she sometimes did not even bother about a bed), but, like Messalina after her, entertained men in brothels. Thus Catullus wrote, addressing Caelius Rufus,

> Caelius, our Lesbia, Lesbia, that Lesbia
> More loved by Catullus than any besides
> – More than he loves himself and his pleasures –
> Is now, in the alley-ways and even at cross-roads
> Fucked by the noble sons of the Romans.*

And he spoke of her 'who has escaped from my arms', in a place 'Less pub than brothel'; she 'was loved as much, and more than any is loved', but

> You the valueless, corrupt, adulterous all love her;
> You above all Egnatius
> Long-haired son of a rabbit-toothed Celtiberian,
> Only made good by your beard
> Your teeth whitened by Spanish piss.

This suggests that Catullus maintained personal standards that

* Translations of Catullus are from C. H. Sisson, *Catullus*, London, 1966.

were by no means wholly 'genital': there was or had been something in Lesbia that appealed to him as being beyond sexual
promiscuity – even if he, too, wanted her sexually. His railing
against her in xLII, in which she is 'a filthy whore', a 'dirty
bitch', a 'shit', a 'whorehouse', makes it clear that he resented her
decline into prostitution as much as he resented her relationships
with other men, the majority of them riff-raff.

Catullus' poems undoubtedly exhibit a masculine dislike of
female prostitution – one may fairly say, in fact, because of their
frankness, their lack of hypocrisy and their agonized naturalism,
that they exhibit some of the poetic objections, which is to say
the real objections, to prostitution. The point is not that Catullus'
splendid, beautiful and gifted girl is 'immoral' – for so excellent
a poet as Catullus such a notion would have been an irrelevant
abstraction – but that she is demeaning herself for the sake of
sensation. This, rather than a mere obsession with genitality, is
the message of the poems about Lesbia. His candour about lust
has been mistaken for an obsession with it; the accusation that
love was, for him, only a physical act originally arises from bourgeois horror at this candour: a man who can be as honest as that
about sex *must* be obsessed by it. The following (xxxII) is the
sort of poem, actually only the graphic and canny description of
a condition common enough to most men, that has prompted
such reasoning:

> Please darling, dear Ipsithilla,
> All my pleasure, my only attraction,
> Order me to you this afternoon,
> And if you do order me, please arrange also
> That no-one shall get in my way as I enter
> And don't you go off either at the last moment.
> But stay at home and organize for us
> Nine copulations in rapid series.
> If there's anything doing, send round immediately
> For here I am, lying on my bed;
> I have had my lunch, the thing sticks out of my tunic.

But this is only Catullus in a certain mood. It is in a more
romantic mood that he asks Lesbia (LX),

> Did a lioness from the Libyan mountains
> Or Scylla barking out of the mouth of the womb
> Give birth to you? You are so hard and inhuman.
> Your suppliant's voice crying in its last need
> You treat with contempt, so very cruel is your heart.

He knows he will receive no answer. But his supplication is not only to be allowed to love her physically. If he had seen love in 'purely genital terms' – the verdict causes one to wonder whether anyone does, really – then he would have been able to get over his discomfiture without such bitterness and unhappiness. But one of the chief causes of his unhappiness is that Lesbia has genitally degraded herself: Catullus' poems register, however obliquely, what may quite properly be described as a romantic, if highly personal, objection to the indiscriminate genitality that is involved in prostitution. For if we can abuse our mouths and stomachs by over-eating, then it must be admitted that we can abuse our genitals by indiscriminate copulation. In a lighter poem (x), about his friend Vanus' mistress, Catullus makes it clear that he does not wholly share the assumptions of his times. No poets do. Vanus' girl is

> Not at all a bad little whore . . .
> – Quite good looking.

Now the presence of this phrase in a poem, a literary composition, gives it an ironic slant that it could not have had in conversation – it is not merely coarse. No matter how complicated Catullus is, there exists behind all his poetry a system of values: his ironies, subtle, bitter and zestful, spring from his counterpointing of the non-values of his age (and the non-values of himself as a man of his age) with this system. We can most clearly infer this from some of his poems that are not (overtly) about Lesbia, particularly from that dealing with the legend of Attis. If we should try to say something that is really valid about the nature of prostitution, then we should have to take into account the complex motives behind Catullus' 2,000-year-old resentment of Lesbia's whoredom.

3

Horace (58–8 B.C.) was a more typical Roman than Catullus, and one of his satires (1:ii) is rightly described by Henriques as 'the perfect rationalization of prostitution'. It exactly reflects the Roman attitude towards sex – an attitude that Catullus, as we can tell from the bitterness of his tone, rejected.

Horace was an excellent stylist, and is delightful to read; but he became a poet from convenience rather than necessity, and he never felt impelled to go against his times. For the reasons that prostitution flourished in Rome's golden age more than ever before, however, we need not go much beyond this satire. For although the Roman authorities did from time to time try (unsuccessfully) to suppress prostitution, their general attitude was tolerant – tolerant enough for Horace, the Emperor Augustus' 'most immaculate penis', to be able to recommend them, if only in moderation .Horace begins the poem by referring comically to lack of moderation in people's behaviour – one man has long, trailing garments, another goes about with his clothes tucked right up; one man smells sweet, another stinks, and so on. But the essential theme of the poem is 'bad men, when they avoid certain vices, fall into their opposite extremes':

> Some men can only take the married kind
> But others in the stews their pleasures find.
> One, sneaking from a fuckshop in the night
> Found Cato's noble words made guilt seem light:
> 'As soon as filthy lust hoists up your cock,
> Don't fuck a wife: go to the knocking-shop'
> And yet Cupiennius says, 'Don't give me that –
> I like a married cunt for my prick's hat!'
>
> You who want all co-respondent types to fail
> Should listen to my cautionary tale
> Of how there's always more pain than pleasure
> In sniffing out the most dangerous treasure.

One from a desperate roof stark naked leaps;
One writhes to his death beneath slashing whips;
A third is killed, as he flees, by a crook;
A fourth buys his life with his cheque-book;
Yet another is mocked by mere slaves
All for the sake of getting what he craves –
But better be him than have all fucking stopped
By getting your balls and randy penis chopped
(Only Galba says this is really bad luck).
A brothel's the safest place when you must fuck. . . .

For my woman I'll always choose a tart,
Someone to whom I need not 'give my heart'.
So when I'm on the job I have no fear
That the husband will return just near
My climax and smash down the bedroom door.
Then dogs bark, there's a hellish din, the poor
Wife jumps white-faced from bed. I run down the street,
My cock unsatisfied, half-dressed, and with bare feet.
I'll prove it's bloody awful to be caught:
Fabius, you know! Tell us what you thought.*

This is not very profound – clubman's advice, in fact – but in the Latin it is well expressed; in any case, it is mostly done for the fun of the thing. Horace was not a passionate man, and was perhaps for that reason in a good position to give sound advice. There is nothing here about the 'nasty' aspect of sex – the brothel stink that Juvenal says Messalina left on the royal pillows, or the 'quick' disgust of one of Petronius' most famous little poems – only some half-serious observations about the inconveniences of adultery. This is the sort of justification of prostitution that is still made today; but Horace exhibits no hypocrisy. On the whole, we do not find in the Roman writers much evidence of the stigma which attached itself to the prostitutes themselves; Catullus' and other poets' disgust and venom at their mistresses' recourse to whoredom is of a different class altogether: it is deeply personal. But Roman society held prostitutes in as much official abhorrence as our society officially does now. It was tolerant only of the client.

* My rather free adaptation.

This stigmatization of whores, which manifested itself in the laws, seems, however, to have stemmed originally from tribal instincts – the race had to be perpetuated in the correct manner – rather than from moral disapproval. Prostitutes were needed, too, and used: therefore they were, officially at least, taboo. But the notion of them as morally 'fallen women', as opposed to outcasts, arose with Christianity, and in official Christian literature they are never treated except with a kind of solemn – and, from a naturalistic point of view, disastrous – awe.

The episodes concerning prostitution in Petronius' *Satyricon* make a pleasant contrast. They are also instructive, for the author was a typical aristocratic Roman of the early Empire. It is now generally agreed – though with a few dissentients – that the *Saturae*, of which we possess considerable extracts, and which is universally known as the *Satyricon*, was written by the courtier of Nero called Petronius whose downfall Tacitus describes. 'Industry is the usual foundation of success,' says Tacitus,

but with him it was idleness. Unlike most people who throw their money away in dissipation, he was not regarded as an extravagant sensualist, but as one who made luxury a fine art. . . . As consul, he showed himself a vigorous and capable administrator. His subsequent return to his old habits . . . led to his admission to the small circle of Nero's intimates. . . . Nero's jaded appetite regarded nothing as enjoyable . . . unless Petronius had given his sanction to it.*

Petronius was finally, in A.D. 66, forced to commit suicide, since a rival at court had succeeded in turning the Emperor against him. He did not hurry, Tacitus says, but bound up his veins and then re-opened them as the fancy took him; meanwhile he talked to his friends, not about serious matters, but gaily; finally he prepared a full account of Nero's enactments of his bizarre lust, naming names, and sent it to the Emperor.

Clearly Petronius was a remarkable man; more important is the fact that in his surviving literary work, a description of the adventures of a Greek freedman in Italy, he left a picture of the social manners – and, uniquely, a record of the popular speech –

* Quoted by John Sullivan in his translation of *The Satyricon*. See p. 40, footnote.

of his time. And while the *Satyricon* is a satire, partly a parody of episodes in the *Odyssey* and of Greek prose romances, and partly a mockery of provincial manners, it is also a reflection of an aristocratic Roman's attitude towards sex.

The confidence-man narrator, Encolpius, is bisexual. The joke that runs through each episode of his adventures is that, although his intention is to propitiate the god Priapus, whom he has offended by robbing a temple, he accidentally continues to offend him. Priapus was of course the god of fertility, represented as a manikin with a huge phallus, so that the reader who 'confesses an intimate acquaintance with the poem . . . exposes himself to a severe judgement', as a nineteenth-century classical scholar wrote. So far as prostitutes are concerned, the most interesting part of the work is the episode entitled 'Croton' (a town on the toe of Italy, now called Crotone), in which Encolpius becomes involved with Circe, so called because Encolpius is, among other things, a grotesque parody of Odysseus, and Circe was the name of the enchantress who fell in love with Odysseus.

Circe is a whore rather than a prostitute; if she whores for gain, then it is for straightforward sexual, not financial, gain. But she is a type of women that recurs throughout literature – a type that especially, and for reasons that need little explication, fascinates male writers. For the always sexually eager woman, besides being a ubiquitous male fantasy-figure, really can be found. . . . If some women are drawn to prostitution for other than economic reasons – and no one will deny that this is the case – then is Circe's predilection a frequent motive? In his portrait of this type of woman, Petronius may be said to have been realistic, even if he characteristically makes a joke of it.

Encolpius, who is calling himself Polyaenus, and passing himself off as a slave, gets into conversation with Circe's maid, Chrysis. She tells him that her mistress wants him, and continues:

Some women get heated up over the absolute dregs and can't feel any passion unless they see slaves or bare-legged messengers. The arena sets some of them on heat, or a mule-driver covered with dust, or actors displayed on the stage. My mistress is one of this type. She jumps across the first fourteen seats [reserved for aristocrats] from the orchestra and looks for something to love among the lowest of the low.*

Encolpius asks Chrysis if it isn't really she who is in love with him, and she replies that she has never yet been to bed with a slave: 'That's for ladies who kiss the whip-marks'. She only has 'knights' for lovers. Encolpius feels it 'very strange that the maid should cultivate the superior outlook of a lady and the lady the low taste of a maid'.

Soon Chrysis fetches Circe, to whose charms 'No words could do justice'. Encolpius offers to sacrifice his boy-friend, Giton, for her, although she does not demand this. They begin to kiss in the grass, 'as the prelude to more strenuous pleasures'. But apparently Encolpius cannot get an erection, for Circe asks him indignantly:

'What is it?' . . . 'Do my kisses offend you in some way? Does my breath smell through not eating? Have I neglected to wash under my arms? If it's not these, am I to suppose you're somehow frightened of Giton?'

Encolpius, embarrassed, pleads that he has been bewitched. Circe rushes off to examine herself for defects; Encolpius is that night mocked even by Giton, who ironically thanks him for loving him 'in such an honourable platonic way'; Encolpius can only say that the part of his body that once made him 'an Achilles' 'is dead and buried'. Circe writes a letter to him suggesting that he should sleep three nights without Giton; he replies that although he has done 'many bad things' he has 'never till today committed a really deadly sin'. He asks for punishment. If she wishes to kill him, he will bring her his sword; if she only wants to whip him, he will come naked to her. . . .

Chrysis then takes him to an old witch, who performs a spell on him; when she 'tests his virility' with her hands, they are 'filled with a mighty throbbing'. He meets Circe, and all seems to be going well:

Her physical charms were so inviting she impelled me to make love to her. Our lips ground greedily together in kiss after kiss. Our locked

* Translations of Petronius are from *The Satyricon*, translated by John Sullivan, Penguin Books, Harmondsworth, 1965.

hands discovered every possible method of making love. Our bodies
wrapped in a mutual embrace united even our very breaths.

But apparently Encolpius' penis still refused to obey its master's
will; and so, 'Smarting from these open insults, the lady finally
rushed to have her revenge. She called her attendants and had
them beat me.' Then she calls her 'lowest type of servant' to spit
on Encolpius, who agrees that he thoroughly deserves all he is
getting. Chrysis is beaten, too, and the whole household wonders
'who had lowered their mistress' high spirits'.

Encolpius conceals his stripes 'with some doctoring', and pretends to be weary. Then he directs all his anger upon the cause of
his troubles in the following poem:

> Three times I took the murd'rous axe in hand,
> Three times I wavered like a wilting stalk
> And curtsied from the blade, poor instrument
> In trembling hands – I could not what I would.
> From terror colder than the wintry frost,
> It took asylum far within my crotch,
> A thousand wrinkles deep.
> How could I lift its head to punishment?
> Cozened by its whoreson mortal fright
> I fled for aid to words that deeper bite.

He then addresses the offending object, blaming it for dragging
him down to hell when he was in heaven, and so forth. After
this he feels ashamed at 'bandying words' with a part of his body
that 'more dignified people do not even think about'; but this
gives him the opportunity to console himself by the thought,
'There is nothing on earth more misleading than silly prejudice
and nothing sillier than moral hypocrisy'. Finally he prays to the
hostile Priapus. While he is doing this, the old bawd who had
put the spell upon him appears, berates him for putting Priapus
against her (presumably for casting a spell that did not work), and
flogs him – aiming some of the cuts at his groin – until he weeps.

Now Oenothea, an old priestess of Priapus and – we easily
infer – a typical 'temple' prostitute of the time, enters. The old
woman complains to her that Encolpius has a piece of wet

leather for a penis. What can she do? 'I want the young man to sleep a night with me . . . ,' she answers. She then prepares an even more complicated spell to cast on Encolpius, involving beans, an old piece of pig's cheek and other paraphernalia. While she is absent, Encolpius characteristically kills one of the sacred geese in her care, because it attacks him – this is 'Priapus' darling', he is later told, and he might well be crucified if the news of what he has done got round.

Eventually the old woman forgives him, and after the performance of some more mumbo-jumbo, she brings out 'a leather dildo, of the sort whores use, and rubbed it with oil and ground pepper and nettle seed, and began inserting it gradually up my anus'. She soaks his genitals in a brew of cress and other herbs, and proceeds to beat him 'everywhere below the navel' with a green nettle-stalk. Not unnaturally, he runs away.

At this point the text of the original becomes seriously dislocated, and the Circe episode disintegrates into fragments: but it seems that Chrysis, Circe's maid, learns that Encolpius is not a slave. He is told that while she 'detested his earlier position', she now intends to follow him 'for the rest of her life'; she herself tells him that he is now her only pleasure and desire in life. Here we apparently have a further joke at the expense of women and their odd, paradoxical preferences.

The chief interest of the *Satyricon* as a whole, the nature of its relationship to Epicureanism and the effects of its learned parodying, need not detain us here; but Circe is interesting not only because she is a whore but also because of her predilection for lower-class men. It has sometimes been suggested that this type of woman, when her preferences remain unrealized, entertains 'prostitution fantasies'; even that such fantasies may lead women actually to imitate prostitutes' behaviour. This may at least be inferred from the writings of Krich and Greenwald. Furthermore, as John Sullivan points out, the type is very common throughout literature (and history). Possibly Catullus' Clodia liked plebeians, although there are no records of her entering cheap brothels. Certainly both Messalina and she suffered from, or enjoyed, a *nostalgie de la boue*.

Now there is little doubt that some women do indulge themselves in 'prostitution fantasies', either when being made love to, when masturbating, or otherwise. But there are not many authentic records of these by women or even, at second-hand, by men. The most convincing and familiar portrait of a latter-day Messalina is in Luis Buñuel's comic film version of Joseph Kessel's much less distinguished novel, *Belle de Jour*. When shown in Great Britain, it was taken far too seriously by the puzzled film critics. Buñuel directed the not (on the face of it) very intelligent Catherine Deneuve with devastating panache. The wife of a rich, gentle, devoted young man, she has fantasies of being whipped by him, and eventually enters a brothel (in the afternoons only, hence the title) where she can be abused and possessed by all manner of clients. She most desires a repulsive gangster, who eventually shoots and paralyses her husband from the neck down (or is this her fantasy, too? Buñuel lets the viewer decide). This character is a masochist (at one point she imagines herself being pelted with mud; at another she lies in a coffin while a man masturbates beneath it), and she goes to the brothel in order to be degraded: she acts out her fantasy – unless this, too, is fantasy: it does not much matter, since the film is essentially a comic send-up of a certain kind of female sexual make-up, a make-up that men themselves create or exploit in fantasies – with bizarre results. One of Buñuel's many jokes is that men, watching the film, are privately wishing that *they* could find a woman like that. . . .

However, as Mr Sullivan points out in a note, 'one of the latest examples in fiction' is Madame Philibert in Thomas Mann's comic novel *Confessions of Felix Krull, Confidence Man*. Mann must certainly have had 'Croton' in mind when he wrote this episode, and indeed, *Felix Krull* is in certain ways a kind of modern *Satyricon* – at least it has affinities with it.

Krull is working as a lift-boy in a Paris hotel, when he encounters Diane Houpfle, the literary wife of a manufacturer of lavatory-fittings; she writes under her maiden name of Philibert. When she seduces him she offends him 'by her repeated insistence on' his 'humble state'. He asks himself, 'what did she expect to

gain by that?' But it is by this insistence that she gains her gratification, as the description of the seduction makes clear. Having
stripped him of his uniform and herself of her nightdress, she says:

'Oh, sweetheart! Oh, you angel of love, offspring of desire! Ah,
ah, you young devil, naked boy, how can you do it. My husband can
do nothing at all, absolutely nothing. . . . Oh, blessed one, you are
killing me. . . . Call me *tu*,' she groaned suddenly, near the climax.
'Be familiar with me, degrade me! *J'adore d'être humiliée! Je t'adore. Oh,
je t'adore, petit esclave stupide qui me déshonore.* . . . She came. We
came. . . .'*

But Krull is annoyed that she feels humiliated by him, and does
not return her kisses. She asks him to whip her with his braces
until she bleeds, and when he tells her that he has already stolen
her jewel-case expresses delight, and begs him to steal more
from her (which he does). It is her ultimate satisfaction to lie
with a fool, a menial and a thief; to be degraded by him even
while she expatiates upon his foolishness, his 'common' ordinari-
ness – and his naked beauty.

Mann is more sophisticated and explicit than Petronius; but
the type is fundamentally the same. Circe is not credited with any
physically masochistic tendencies, and indeed it is she who has
Encolpius whipped; but doubtless Madame Philibert would have
wished to have the lift-boy whipped, less in pleasure than as con-
firmation of his subordinate position, had he performed as badly
as Encolpius. In both stories it is, technically, the men who are
prostituting themselves, acting as gigolos, although to whores.
Both women desire to be degraded, although Diane Philibert's
masochistic desires are more clearly revealed. 'Sultan' and slave-
girl fantasies are very common indeed in adolescent girls, and
scarcely less so in housewives who like to imagine themselves
chained up, sexually assaulted, and so on. We are all familiar with
television advertisements which coyly exploit this. One would be
surprised, however, if there were any kind of significant corre-
lation between girls who have or have had these fantasies and
girls who become prostitutes.

* *Confessions of Felix Krull, Confidence Man*, translated by Denver Lindley, Secker &
Warburg, London, 1955.

Chapter Four

1

THE non-Christian world, although equivocal in its social attitude to prostitutes, did not regard them as essentially or especially 'fallen women'. Its satirists or older inhabitants may have found prostitution disgusting or unseemly; Catullus implies that indiscriminate whoredom degraded Lesbia; the laws of non-Christian societies almost invariably kept prostitutes from 'respectable' marriages; but they were not specifically 'lost' (and sickly-ripe for 'finding') in the unique Christian sense.

However, the common assertion that the Jewish national movement which came, by an irony unparalleled in history, to be called Christianity – after its tough and fierce founder (self-styled Jewish Messiah, and accepted as such by many Zealots and other rebels against Roman rule) – invented the attitude towards sex that led to this feeling about prostitutes is incorrect.

First, no one can wholly 'invent' an attitude: there has to be something in the air before people can be persuaded to take it up. A number of non-Christian philosophers roughly contemporary with St Paul had denounced all sensual pleasure, including sex, as evil. Secondly, although Jesus and his followers believed him to be the Messiah who would lead the Jews to emancipation

from Roman rule (Jesus' way differed, however, from that of the
Zealots), and to the establishment of Yahweh's Kingdom, their
attitude towards sex was orthodoxly Jewish. But the real Church
of Christ, an essentially Jewish movement with its headquarters at
Jerusalem, was destroyed between A.D. 66 and 70 by the Romans.

The Apostle Saul of Tarsus was, until A.D. 70, regarded with
extreme suspicion by the men who had known Jesus – and who
had shared and understood his motives – as a mentally unstable
transcendentalist: while they were concerned with the historical
rebel and Messiah Jesus, whom they considered would yet
return to deliver them from the yoke and to establish the Kingdom, Paul appealed to Graeco-Roman astralist doctrines in
attributing Jesus' death to demonic forces. Despite his considerable powers of persuasion, the Jerusalem Christians forced him
into retirement for ten years. In his bid for power and influence
he could well afford to play fast and loose with the mere facts of
history: his own 'conversion' had been a notably transcendental
affair.

However, after the destruction of the Temple and the eclipse
of Christ's true Church in A.D. 70, Paul was rehabilitated: the
Christian Church was organized on Jewish lines. As the Rev.
S. G. F. Brandon has lucidly demonstrated in *The Trial of Jesus of
Nazareth*,* the earliest gospel, that of Mark, written in Rome
for a Roman audience just after the Jewish wars in A.D. 71, palters
with the truth: it seeks to disguise the fact that Jesus was executed
by Pilate as a dangerous rebel – and, as Professor Brandon could
have added, therefore further libels the Jews, who have indeed
only recently been exonerated (if anyone can take this belated
apology quite seriously) by the Roman Catholic Church for the
murder of the Son of God. It may here be noted in passing that
in an early version of his *The Brook Kerith*, the most intelligent
and imaginative novel ever written about Jesus (though the
author was no historian), George Moore had Paul murder Jesus –
who has survived the cross by many years, and repudiated his
Messianic past – because living he might be a danger to his, Paul's,
'Christian' cause.

*Batsford, London, 1968.

The real Christians were Jews whose attitude to sex, and therefore to prostitution, may be found in the Old Testament and in the Talmud, not in the New Testament. Had Jesus' own revolutionary and Messianic programme included such a condemnation of sex as, to quote St Augustine, 'a tumult of the senses wherein the world forgetteth Thee its Creator', then the four 'canonical', post-A.D. 70 records of his teachings, distortions though they may be, would have made something of it. But Jesus, who had the establishment of the Kingdom to think of, clearly did not concern himself much with sex; whatever sexual feelings he himself had were doubtless sublimated into his struggle. His only recorded mentions of sexual matters concern hypocrisy (the woman taken in adultery), the resemblance of real to ocular adultery, and several observations on marriage laws. There is no scriptural evidence that Mary Magdalene was an ex-tart; we can confidently attribute this tradition to later, Pauline 'Christianity'.

Paul himself would not have learned, either in Tarsus or from Gamaliel in Jerusalem (if indeed he studied with him: we have only his word for it), the doctrine that even post-nuptial lovemaking is against God and a concession to the flesh. The core of Paul's teaching on sex, which is in I Corinthians, universally accepted as being by him, cunningly and preposterously grafts Greek abstractionism on to Jewish strictness to produce something quite new. The passage is worth quoting without ellipses and in a literal modern version. The language of the Authorized Version is of course incomparable; but what Paul really meant comes across with much more shocking force in Canon Philips' accurate modern version:

As a Christian I *may* do anything, but that does not mean that everything is good for me. I may do everything, but I must not be a slave of anything. Food was meant for the stomach and the stomach for food; but God has no permanent purpose for either. But you cannot say that our physical body was made for sexual promiscuity; it was made for God, and God is the answer to our deepest longings. The God who raised the Lord from the dead will also raise us mortal men by his power. Have you realized the almost incredible fact that your bodies are integral parts of Christ himself? Am I then to take parts of

Christ and join them to a prostitute? Never! Don't you realize that
when a man joins himself to a prostitute he makes with her a physical
unity? For, God says, 'the two shall be one flesh'. On the other hand
the man who joins himself to God is one with him in spirit.

Avoid sexual looseness like the plague! Every other sin that a man
commits is done outside his own body, but this is an offence against
his own body. Have you forgotten that your body is the temple of the
Holy Spirit, who lives in you, and that you are not the owner of your
own body? You have been bought, and at what a price! Therefore
bring glory to God both in your body and your spirit, for they both
belong to him. . . .

It is a good principle for a man to have no physical contact with
women. Nevertheless, because casual liaisons are so prevalent, let every
man have his own wife and every woman her own husband. The
husband should give his wife what is due to her as his wife, and the
wife should be as fair to her husband. The wife has no longer full rights
over her own person, but shares them with her husband. In the same
way the husband shares his personal rights with his wife. Do not cheat
each other of normal sexual intercourse, unless of course you both
decide to abstain temporarily to make special opportunity for fasting
and prayer. But afterwards you should resume relations as before, or
you will expose yourselves to the obvious temptation of the devil.

I give the advice above more as a concession than as a command.
I wish that all men were like myself, but I realize that everyone has
his own particular gift from God, some one thing and some another.
Yet to those who are unmarried or widowed, I say definitely that it is a
good thing to remain unattached, as I am. But if they have not the
gift of self-control in such matters, by all means let them get married.
I think it is far better for them to be married than to be tortured by
unsatisfied desire. . . .

I merely add . . . that each man should live his life with the gifts that
God has given him and in the condition in which God has called him.
This is the rule I lay down in all the churches.

For example, if a man was circumcized when God called him he
should not attempt to remove the signs of his circumcision. If on the
other hand he was uncircumcized he should not become circumcized.
Being circumcized or not being circumcized, what do they matter?
The great thing is to obey the orders of Almighty God. . . .

Now as far as young unmarried women are concerned, I must confess that I have no direct commands from the Lord. Nevertheless, I

give you my considered opinion as of one who is, I think, to be trusted after all his experience of God's mercy.

My opinion is this, that amid all the difficulties of the present time you would do best to remain just as you are. Are you married? Well, don't try to be separated. Are you unattached? Then don't try to get married. But if you, a man, should marry, don't think that you have done anything sinful. And the same applies to a young woman. Yet I do believe that those who take this step are bound to find the married state an extra burden in these critical days, and I should like you to be as unencumbered as possible. All our futures are so foreshortened, indeed, that those who have wives should live, so to speak, as though they had none! There is no time to indulge in sorrow, no time for enjoying our joys; those who buy have no time to enjoy their possessions, and indeed their every contact with the world must be as light as possible, for the present scheme of things is rapidly passing away. That is why I should like you to be as free from worldly entanglements as possible. . . .

But if any man feels he is not behaving honourably towards the woman he loves, especially as she is beginning to lose her first youth and the emotional strain is considerable, let him do what his heart tells him to do – let them be married, there is no sin in that. Yet for the man of steadfast purpose who is able to bear the strain and has his own desires well under control, if he decides not to marry the young woman, he too will be doing the right thing. Both of them are right, one in marrying and the other in refraining from marriage, but the latter has chosen the better of two right courses.

A woman is bound to her husband while he is alive, but if he dies she is free to marry whom she likes – but let her be guided by the Lord. In my opinion she would be happier to remain as she is, unmarried. And I think I am expressing here not only my opinion, but the will of the Spirit as well.*

We see from this, which is not perhaps as familiar as we think it is – especially in such a straightforwardly intelligible form – that while Paul may, if he was not possessed by the spirit of God, have been fundamentally unstable, he was a most convincing propagandist for his cause. He was not merely not a naturalist, but was explicitly an anti-naturalist. One false assumption –

* *The New Testament in Modern English*, translated by J. B. Phillips, Bles, London, 1960.

unless Paul had a curious idea of time – underlies this teaching
about sex as it does all Paul's teaching: 'these days' are 'critical':
'All our futures are . . . foreshortened': the Kingdom of God –
something very different from Jesus' kingdom – is literally at
hand. But in that assumption lay exactly the appeal that Paul's
new religion had: the poor, the slaves, the oppressed – all these
could hope not only for an alleviation of their sufferings but also
for revenge on the rich and powerful, their oppressors, who would
of course not be able to enter into the promised Kingdom. However, Paul was always clever enough – or inspired enough – in
his transformation of a nationalistic religious movement led by a
Messiah into an apolitical one, to go along with just as many
worldly facts as were necessary for its survival. Paul, it will be
noted, permits enough not to put any converts off: he wishes
(of course) that all men were like him, but those who lack his
self-control may marry rather than burn with desire.

But his argument, although it is calculated to win converts by
showing how they can reject the sexual cake and yet eat it without
too serious consequences, is not sound: it demonstrates his own
diseased thinking on the subject of sex, although it is impossible
in our ignorance, at this distance of time, to give the personal
reasons for his rejection of pleasure.

The argument is: God will raise all of us just as he raised Jesus;
therefore your bodies, since they will be raised as Christ's was
raised, are parts of Christ; therefore we must not join our bodies
to prostitutes' bodies: for when any two people fuck, they make
one flesh, since God said of man and wife that they 'shall make
one flesh'.

This shows that Paul actually thought of all women as 'prostitutes', since he chooses to illustrate his point about the wrongness
of love-making by asking the question, Should I join my body,
a part of Christ's, to a *prostitute's*? As I have pointed out, the
personal reasons for Paul's masculine fantasy about women (for,
in naturalistic terms, they are not all prostitutes) must remain
obscure. Then he quotes a dictum about *marriage* to prove that
this terrible activity really does mean 'joining'. (No wonder the
Anglo-Saxon admonition to a bride to be 'buxom and bonny

(*Left*) The excursion of Mr Lovelace and Clarissa to Hampstead, from an early-nineteenth-century edition of Samuel Richardson's *Clarissa* (*Radio Times Hulton Picture Library*)

(*Right*) Harriette Wilson, from a print published in 1825 (*British Museum*)

Two seventeenth-century ladies of pleasure, from a series of prints   (*Mansell Collection*)

Launching a frigate, by Thomas Rowlandson, 1809   (*Mansell Collection*)

in bed and at board' – true, it should have been addressed to the groom, too – was cut out of the marriage-service when it was realized how it clashed with Paul's teaching.) Apart from this argument, in which all sexual activity is equated with experience with a prostitute – to give full force to the anti-sexual teaching – Paul simply cannot make up his mind. He knows sex is wrong, and like many men before and after him, he knows exactly what the Lord has and has not commanded (although, with exquisite cunning, he at one point confesses that he has not actually had anything direct from the Lord on the subject of young un-married women); but he is not going to prohibit sex, even in the present eschatological atmosphere, because this might lose him converts.

Obviously Paul feared women – he seems to have been what Gordon Rattray Taylor calls in his Freudian account, *Sex in History*, 'father-attached' – and so he rationalized this fear, at the same time revenging himself upon what disturbed him, by in effect describing them all as prostitutes. But there were many women in his Church, so he took care to wrap his essentially anti-female feelings up: only by referring carefully to his initial reasons for regarding sex as no more than 'a concession' can we discern that actually he made no distinction whatever between prostitutes and wives.

The prostitute, however, her position having always been *socially* dubious, was a most appropriate Christian symbol for sex: for men such as Eusebius Sophronius Hieronymous (c. 340–420), known as St Jerome, who obtained his sexual gratification by the practice of a sadistically aggressive asceticism, all sexual activity must seem wrong (as Paul had preached); so that any wife who opened her legs even only to her husband was really no better than a scarlet temptress, a whore like the 'MOTHER OF HARLOTS AND ABOMINATIONS OF THE EARTH' of Revelations. In his *Eros Denied*,* Wayland Young, sparing us the 'routine quotations', conveniently cites one medieval Latin couplet that sums them all up: 'Woman pollutes the body, drains the resources, kills the soul, uproots the strength, blinds the eye and embitters the voice'.

* Weidenfeld and Nicolson, London, 1965.

Pauline Christianity and its startling success, culminating in its adoption by the Emperor Constantine, was the result of many things; but sexually there is a good case for saying that it was in one sense homosexually motivated – or at least, strongly anti-feminine, which is really saying the same thing. Women were only safe when they had been defused: desexualized. Meanwhile the fantasy that all women are 'hot' – prostitutes – was fascinating. Thus the cloistered whore soon became a Christian favourite: here was the perfect symbol of woman's essence. her rampant sexuality, subdued and imprisoned.

Shakespeare wrote:

> Th' expense of spirit in a waste of shame
> Is lust in action. . . . *

lines in which the words 'spirit' and 'waste' are clearly puns, playing on the respective senses of 'semen' and 'waist' (i.e. cunt). His subject, in general terms, was the tension set up in the male human psyche by sexual activity; the experience that occasioned this poem seems to have been his liaison with a whore – or a woman, the so-called 'Dark Lady of the Sonnets', whom he regarded as and called a whore. The savage bitterness of his attitude towards this woman and towards his sexual enjoyment of her might seem comparable to that of St Jerome, or to the similar sentiments expressed in the medieval couplet quoted by Wayland Young. But it is not; and this is an appropriate place to examine the contrast between the early Christian approach to sex, which still survives, and Shakespeare's. As we have seen, to the first Christians (tactics apart) women were essentially prostitutes: Paul's argument against all sexual relations, even marital (his concession, as we have seen, is only grudging), is based on the premise that when a man does it he is joining Christ's body to that of a prostitute. . . . To Shakespeare – there can be no doubt about this – the woman represented in Sonnets 127 to 152 is,

---

* Sonnet 129. My own edition of the Sonnets, Heinemann, 1963, in the notes of which I give a much fuller commentary on the poems to the 'Dark Lady' than is possible here, is in old spelling; here – as in the section on *Measure for Measure* – I quote from the modernized text of Peter Alexander, *Complete Works of William Shakespeare*, Collins, London, 1951, 1966.

so far as he is concerned, a prostitute. No comparison, I think, reveals so well the difference between an essentially neurotic, programmatic approach to prostitution, and an exploratory one, ultimately dedicated to the discovery of the true nature of the tensions that lust and its fulfilment set up.

At the same time, while Shakespeare's approach incidentally demonstrates that the Pauline solution to the problem is a failure – 'none knows well / To shun the heaven that leads men to this hell', in which some emphasis may be put on 'well', for in Shakespeare's poetry every word carries the weight of all its meanings – it also makes it clear, if such needs making clear, that there is a problem to solve. Those who most vehemently reject the solution of the problem by means of enforced chastity may do so for psychological reasons, and not because they attach no value to chastity or because they advocate total sexual freedom. But complete abstinence from physical sexual activity may well lead to sexual indulgence that is extremely harmful and cruel, as at least those who have been flogged by monks in contemporary Roman Catholic boarding-schools know very well.

Shakespeare describes his mistress as being fascinating rather than beautiful. She is dark – possibly very dark-skinned, but more probably a brunette in an age when the blonde was held up as the type of beauty; and he refuses –'My mistress' eyes are nothing like the sun' (Sonnet 130) – to indulge in fashionable love-conceits about her beauty; but his love for her, he insists, is as 'rare', unique, as any man's is for a woman praised with such conceits. However (Sonnet 135), her 'will', here meaning both 'desire' and 'vagina', is 'large and spacious': will she, he ironically asks, now that she has betrayed him with his friend, 'not once vouchsafe to hide my will [penis] in thine'? Clearly Shakespeare is repelled, but he is as repelled by his own lust for this unfaithful creature as he is by her lust and sexual promiscuity. In certain limited respects his mood recalls that of Catullus. The Pauline Christians tried to solve the problem crudely: by the *exclusion* of sex. Shakespeare never does this, even if he records the sort of despairing, lust-ridden moods, when sexual desire is loathed, which can lead to the practice of that asceticism now familiarly

known as Christian. Because he has been disappointed and made
unhappy by his mistress, he does not pretend to himself that his
feelings for her are merely lustful and therefore base: that what is
wrong is only his sensuality. He does not, he says in Sonnet 141,
love her with his eyes or with any other of his senses: it is his
'foolish heart' that makes him her slave. The twenty-five sonnets to
the mistress (Sonnet 146 does not mention her, even if it arises
from Shakespeare's experiences with her) are extremely complex;
too much so to discuss at any further length in this context. But
one thing is certain: he never takes the simplistic, Pauline approach
of simply rejecting sex.

The sexual hell Shakespeare described in the Sonnets is the hell
of selfish possession, of lust, of the sort of desire visited upon
prostitutes by their fantasy-inspired clients, But it is not the hell of
all possible sex: as we have seen, the hellish act is defined at the
outset as 'th' expense of spirit in a waste of shame'. Such poetry
as Sonnet 129 means many things; it may most appropriately be
taken as a description of the type of guilt that assails many sensitive
men when they have reluctant or obsessive recourse to prostitutes:

> Th' expense of spirit in a waste of shame
> Is lust in action; and till action, lust
> Is perjur'd, murd'rous, bloody, full of blame,
> Savage, extreme, rude, cruel, not to trust;
> Enjoy'd no sooner but despised straight;
> Past reason hunted, and, no sooner had,
> Past reason hated, as a swallowed bait,
> On purpose laid to make the taker mad—
> Mad in pursuit, and in possession so;
> Had, having, and in quest to have, extreme;
> A bliss in proof, and prov'd, a very woe;
> Before, a joy propos'd; behind, a dream.
>> All this the world well knows; yet none knows well
>> To shun the heaven that leads men to this hell.

To understand this is to understand, sympathetically, why the
asceticism of the Christian Church held out such a wide appeal.
Gradually the Church, using Paul's grudging and wholly propagandist concession as a basis for 'Christian marriage', has ceased

to insist on chastity: it has been too bad for business, and besides, the world has not quite come to an end. But Paul's equation of all sexually active women with prostitutes did not make the lot of whores, which had never been very easy, any easier – unless, of course, they would agree to be poor, but saved.

Chapter Five

1

THERE have been certain, very rare, non-primitive societies in which there was no prostitution. One of them, the Muria of Bastar State in Central India, was reported by the late Verrier Elwin in his classic *The Muria and their Ghotul*,* but most Westerners would consider the ghotul too immoral an institution to be officially tolerated by society, and would prefer their own unofficial institution of prostitution. The ghotul, as well as being a guest house for visiting officials, was a communal dormitory for young people, and in it they experienced sex with each other from puberty onwards. This was common to all the ghotuls, though Elwin distinguished between different types. Later the young people married in the ordinary way.

But in the first thousand or so years of Christian supremacy in the West, prostitution, despite individual reports of 'saved' women, continued to flourish. At the Council of Elvira in Spain, at which celibacy was enforced on the clergy for the first time, prostitutes were excommunicated unless they had married Christians (that is, only Christian ex-whores could be members of the Church); pimps, always treated by moralists with great

* Oxford University Press, 1947. The Muria have since wound up this institution.

(perhaps often jealous) savagery, were denied absolution. But St Augustine, despite his famous pronouncement that 'by continence are we bound together and brought back into that unity from which we were dissipated into a plurality', believed that prostitution was an essential protection against universal lust. Presumably, like the ancient Jewish legislators, he hoped that the whores would be 'foreign', non-Christian. The story is a familiar one, and prostitutes crop up in the literature of the Dark and the Middle Ages as often as they do in that of other ages. One of the most revealing accounts is by Procopius, the sixth-century author of the *Anecdota* ('unpublished things', because posthumous), or *Secret History*.

2

Procopius (*c.* 500–*c.* 565), born at Caesarea in Palestine, practised law in Byzantium before becoming private secretary to Belisarius, whom he accompanied on some of his early campaigns. Later he was an official historian so much in favour with the Emperor Justinian that in 560 he seems to have been prefect of Byzantium. During his lifetime he published a long, accurate and impeccably official history of the wars – and other matters – and a highly flattering account of the buildings with which Justinian had enriched Byzantium. But Procopius was not such an admirer of Justinian and his wife Theodora as he made out, or was forced to make out; he possessed some of the impulses of a natural historian. After we have taken into account his susceptibility to the superstitions of his time, there is no reason to doubt the essential truth of the story he told. What is open to question, however, is the degree of balance he shows: were his villains so much more villainous than the rest of their society? The prostitute of whose life he gave such a vivid account was the Empress Theodora.

Theodora was the middle of the three daughters of a bear-keeper in Byzantium. After her father died, her mother put all three of her daughters on the stage. The eldest, Comito, soon became 'one of the most popular harlots of the day'.* Theodora was 'still too undeveloped to be capable of . . . having inter-course'; but until she was she allowed 'customers of the lowest type' to bugger her, and, we may infer, she sucked them off. She soon became famous for exhausting her lovers; Procopius says that she could not 'satisfy her lust' even when she had ex-hausted 'ten young men' and, after that, their thirty 'menials'. And though she brought 'three openings into service [i.e. vagina, anus and mouth] she often found fault with Nature, grumbling because Nature had not made the openings in her nipples wider . . . so that she could devise another variety of intercourse in that region'. This audacity, which might only secretly have appealed to the officials of the Christian Church to which Theodora even then nominally belonged (she was, indeed, later, in 543, to use her influence with her husband on behalf of the Monophysites against the eventually victorious Nestorians), anticipates that of the son of an eighteenth-century Archbishop of Canterbury, Thomas Potter, who wittily declared Fanny Murray, a well-known whore, 'a better piece than the Virgin Mary for never having borne a child'.

One of the tricks of which Theodora was particularly proud was to order barley grains to be scattered on her 'private parts', while she lay on the theatre floor, so that specially trained geese might pick them off. By such means, and by 'constantly playing about with novel methods of intercourse', she 'could always bring the lascivious to her feet'. She 'appeared to have her private parts . . . in her face!' It is evident that as a teenage girl she was already notorious, 'a bird of ill omen' for people 'of any decency' and a malicious termagant among her fellow actresses.

Later she went to Libya as the mistress of one Hecebolus, who soon threw her out without a penny. She then made a kind of grand tour of the East, 'following an occupation', says Procopius

---

* The best translation of *The Secret History*, from which I have quoted, is by G. A. Williamson, Penguin Books, Harmondsworth, 1966.

with a sudden incongruous piety, 'which a man had better not name . . . if he hopes ever to enjoy the favour of God'.

On her return to Byzantium she managed, in some way not specified by Procopius, to attract the attention of Justinian, then still heir to his senile uncle's throne. Justinian at this time seemed to be 'a convinced believer in Christ', but he soon 'conceived an overwhelming passion' for Theodora, and made her his mistress. The old Roman law forbidding any one of senatorial rank or higher to marry a prostitute still operated in Byzantium, but as soon as his mother died Justinian married Theodora, 'thereby enabling everyone else to get engaged to a courtesan'. Procopius then goes on to attribute all Justinian's evil and irresponsible deeds to this step: 'this marriage would be quite enough to reveal only too clearly his moral sickness'. No one, he adds, dared to oppose Theodora. During the whole of their joint reign (527-47; Justinian died in 565), 'neither did anything apart from the other', although with considerable cunning they continually pretended to be on opposite sides, thus keeping 'the factions at logger-heads'.

From her marriage onwards Theodora, with one possible exception, seems to have confined her sexual activities to her husband's bed, a fact which suggests that the diagnosis of 'nymphomania' made by both Henriques and Benjamin and Masters may be incorrect, unless Justinian had quite extraordinary sexual powers; at all events, fulfilment of ambition seems to have cured it. True, she was guilty of atrocious (although then not at all unusual) cruelties and acts of ruthlessness. But she and Justinian evidently understood each other, and led a congenial life together. Procopius' explanation that she kept her husband under her influence by the use of sorcery is not, of course, adequate; possibly both shared a villainous sense of humour. Justinian enacted laws against pagans, who often 'decided to assume for appearance's sake the name of Christian', and penalized such male seducers of boys as had politically offended him by having them castrated and 'exposed to public ribaldry'. Theodora rounded up all the poorer Byzantine prostitutes and confined them 'in the Convent known as Repentance in an attempt to force them into a better way of life. However, some of them from time to time threw themselves down from the parapet during the night, and so escaped being transmogrified against their will.'

It has been said that *The Secret History* is a 'horrid' book; and so it is – as horrid as life. But the behaviour of these two Christian monarchs was not, perhaps, so different from that of others of their age. As I have said, there is no reason to dispute the main facts of Procopius' account, although none of his charges are repeated by other historians.

But we have to remember that he was writing in order to compensate himself for having had to keep to official limits in his much longer, published history. The explanation of the lives of most of the powerful men in Byzantium may have revealed a similar pattern; but Procopius concentrated on Justinian and Theodora, and chose – at least by implication – to attribute Justinian's demonic behaviour to his marriage with a whore. That the Empress Theodora outdid the other women of her century in wickedness we may be prepared to believe. But was this because she had been a prostitute – or was it, more simply, because she was an empress, and possessed comparatively unlimited power? Did her perverted, capricious and cruel sense of humour, which caused her to make an attempt to 'reform' her own kind, originate in her extreme sexuality? Or in the circumstances of her time? Procopius provides no evidence that her sexuality caused her wickedness. All we can know is that she was as intense in the one activity as in the other. In this instance Procopius is writing as a moralist and not as a naturalist. Perhaps, since Theodora seems to have had an unstable – or at least a capricious – personality, her gesture in incarcerating all the whores of Byzantium 'in the Convent known as Repentance' arose from a genuinely charitable impulse; we cannot project the values of our own age on to her. She gave much to the poor, and possessed high courage. Her husband's reign was one of the most brilliant the world has known, although his heir was not able to consolidate the territorial gains he had made. But his legal code survived. The Justinian–Theodora concern flourished and, whether demonic or not, it acted with intelligence – which, while it does not prove that prostitutes and those who admire them are good, does suggest that extensive sexual experience does not necessarily soften the brain.

3

The Byzantium of Justinian and Theodora was not a pornocracy (government by prostitutes), if only because the Empress apparently gave up her trade on marriage. But the Rome of the late ninth and early tenth centuries was. The period is not well documented, and few historians have tried to give an account of it. Gibbon writes, with his incomparable irony:

The influence of two sister prostitutes, Marozia and Theodora, was founded on their wealth and beauty, their political and amorous intrigues: the most strenuous of their lovers were rewarded with the Roman mitre. . . . The bastard son, the grandson and the great grandson of Marozia, a rare genealogy, were seated in the chair of St Peter, and it was at the age of nineteen years that the second of these became the head of the Latin Church. . . . As John XII had renounced the dress and decencies of his profession, the *soldier* may not perhaps be dishonoured by the wine which he drank, the blood that he spilt, the flames that he kindled, or the licentious pursuits of gaming and hunting. His open simony might be the consequence of distress; and his blasphemous invocation of Jupiter and Venus, if it be true, could not possibly be serious. But we read with some surprise that the worthy grandson of Marozia lived in public adultery with the matrons of Rome; that the Lateran palace was turned into a school for prostitution; and that his rapes of virgins and widows had deterred the female pilgrims from visiting the tomb of St Peter, lest, in the devout act, they should be violated by his successor. The Protestants have dwelt with malicious pleasure on these characters of antichrist; but to a philosophic eye the vices of the clergy are less dangerous than their virtues. After a long series of scandals, the apostolic see was reformed and exalted by . . . Gregory VII. That ambitious monk. . . .*

To this one would not, I think, wish to add a word.

* Edward Gibbon, *The Rise and Fall of the Roman Empire.*

4

Accounts of prostitution before the beginning of the seventeenth century are abundant, and may conveniently be found quoted in W. W. Sanger's *The History of Prostitution*★ and in Henriques. The story of how the saintly but foolish Louis IX of France tried to ban prostitution, and utterly failed, is a familiar one. But most rulers accepted, and often took advantage of, the inevitable. With a few exceptions, writings about whores were monotonous: the writers provided the dreary anecdotes that fill the pages of such works as Sanger's, or simply took whores for granted, or held up their hands in horror. Wayland Young says in *Eros Denied* that *La Puttana Errante* (*The Wandering Whore*) of Lorenzo Veniero, which I have not seen, is dull: 'a convulsive declaration of horror and fascination'. 'Veniero cannot come to terms with the fact that a whore is promiscuous. . . . He is . . . delighted by the fact that she is old and smelly.'

The most vivid writer on the subject, however, is François Villon, who did not preach or theorize about it because he knew it too well. Krich and Greenwald, in quoting him, state that he was 'reared in houses of ill-fame'. This is untrue. He was born of poor parents called Montcorbier in Paris in 1431; his father died when he was a small boy. However, he was taken into the care of a chaplain called Villon (whose name he later adopted as his own) when he was seven or eight, and was thus able to obtain a good education. At the age of twenty-one he received the humblest of the degrees offered by the University of Paris, the Master of Arts, which gave him a half-clerical status. He soon got into bad, or at any rate unrespectable, company – two of his friends were later hanged – and may have acquired a reputation for cadging. He also fell in love with a girl called Katherine de Vausselles, who rejected him – probably because her family considered that he was a bad character – and later caused him trouble. He killed a

★ Harper, New York, 1858.

priest in circumstances that remain obscure, fled, was pardoned, got in with a secret society called the Coquille who used peddling as a front for their criminal activities – which probably included pimping – and from then on was never out of trouble on account of robberies or brawling. In 1462 he was sentenced to death, and when in 1463 this was quashed, and a sentence of ten years' exile from Paris substituted, he disappeared from history. He is as likely to have survived as a tramp for the next ten or twenty years as to have died.

Villon's poetry was scurrilous, direct, technically skilful, capable of lyrical flights of great beauty, and, above all, highly personal. He tells all about his life, names real names, and does not try to disguise his immediate emotions of hatred for his various enemies: Katherine de Vausselles, who rejected him, the officials who pursued and punished him for his crimes, and others. He was an educated man who fell on very hard times indeed – doubtless through his own recklessness as well as through bad luck. But he was no more corrupt or wicked, of course, than the hypocrites who controlled his fate, and he saw this clearly; he could afford to speak the truth. As well as being a lyrical poet, he was a natural historian – not by any particular conviction, but simply by habit. He is never concerned to portray things except exactly as they are. His poems about prostitution, notably 'The Lament of the Fair Heaulmière'* and 'The Ballad of Fat Margie', taken in their context of the whole of his work, show that it was no more than a part of the squalid part of an age, most of whose aspects Villon faithfully recorded. Those who are more distressed by the idea of women selling their bodies for money than by the idea of poverty and suffering in general may not, of course, agree. But that was how Villon saw it; his sympathies were with the oppressed and the exploited because he was one of them. Savage though he was in his disappointment and disgust with his age and with himself, the unsentimental Villon could be compassionate, as he is in the words he puts into the mouth of the helmet-maker's girl:

* Helmet-maker's girl: whores were often called by the names of the trades at which they worked or had once worked.

Methinks I hear the harlot wail
Who was the helmet-maker's lass,
Wishing herself still young and hale,
And crying in her woe: 'Alas!
Old Age, so cruel and so crass,
Why hast thou struck me down so soon?
What holds me back that, in this pass,
I do not seek death's final boon. . . .

'There's many a man I could have had,
But flouted, in my foolishness,
For love of a sharp-witted lad
On whom I shower'd my largesse.
Others might buy a feign'd caress:
'Twas he I lov'd, more than myself,
Whom he did cruelly oppress,
And lov'd me only for my pelf.

'And yet his bitterest attack
Could never cause my love to die.
He could have dragg'd me on my back
Or trampled me – did he but cry
"Kiss me!" away my woe would fly.
That beast, that slimy manikin,
Would cuddle me. . . . And what have I
Left for it all? Disgrace and sin!

'Well, thirty years ago he died,
And I am left here, old and hoar. . . .

'Where are the shoulders neat and slender;
Those long, soft arms; those fingers brent [unwrinkled];
Those little breasts; those haunches tender,
High-rais'd and smooth and plainly meant
For riders in love's tournament;
Those ample loins, firm thighs, and twat
Set like a graceful monument
Within its handsome garden-plot. . . .

'Aye, such is human beauty's lot!
The arms are short; the hands clench tight;
The shoulders tangle in a knot;
The breasts, in shame they shrink from sight;
Nipple and haunch, they share their plight;
The twat – ah bah! The thighs are thin
As wither'd hams, and have a blight
Of freckles, like a sausage-skin.

' 'Tis thus we mourn for good old days,
Perch'd on our buttocks, wretched crones,
Huddled together by the blaze
Of some poor fire of forest cones,
That dies as quickly as our moans,
A briefly-lit, brief-living flame—
We who have sat on lovers' thrones!
With many a man 'tis just the same.'*

Christianity gave the (repentant) whore the opportunity to
possess a soul, but not a heart. What is notable about these lines
of Villon's is that he treats the woman speaking them as wholly
human. She has loved, been ill-treated, and turned tart (probably
to sustain her lover); yet, as her last remark demonstrates, she
does not even hate men – her view of life is bitter, but it is none
the less warm, generous and uncomplicated. Villon displays an
understanding of and sympathy with women that is extremely
unusual in any French poet; in the fifteenth century no one
achieved anything like the same degree of realism.

The disgust expressed in 'The Ballad of Fat Margie' is not disgust against whores in particular, or against women at all – it is
self-disgust of a universal kind; but Villon, reduced to criminality,
could feel it more easily than the luckier, more law-abiding but
not less morally reprehensible torturers, officials and dignitaries
who made his life so difficult. The fact that the initial letters of
the first six lines of the last stanza of the original French form an
acrostic on VILLON confirms that the situation described closely
resembled Villon's own. It is usually supposed that 'La Grosse

* Translations of Villon are by Norman Cameron: *Poems of François Villon*, Jonathan
Cape, London, 1952.

Margot' ('Fat Margie') was the name of a whore; in fact it was
the name of a Paris tavern that has been identified. What 'The
Ballad of Fat Margie' describes is life in a Paris brothel. Many
Paris criminals lodged in brothels. Villon is describing the emotions of a sensitive man turned pimp. No doubt he himself had
done his share of pimping. But it is important to note that this
poem neither expresses nor implies any moral objection to
brothel-life: it merely realistically accepts the fact that it is a life
from which beauty and peace of mind (which are realized in
other of Villon's poems) are tragically absent:

> If I do serve my love with all my heart,
> Must you, then, take me for a rogue or sot?
> For certain charms she hath no counterpart.
> With her I am a very Lancelot:
> When people come, I run to drink a pot,
> I 'go for wine' with soft and nimble tread,
> I fetch them water, cheese and fruit and bread,
> If they pay well, I cry them: '*Bene stat*;
> Pray come again, when you've a load to shed,
> To this bordel where we are thron'd in state!'
>
> But afterwards a bitter brawl may start,
> When Margie comes back home without a groat.
> Then hatred of her stabs me like a dart;
> I seize her gown, her girdle and her coat
> And swear I'll sell them all to pay her scot;
> Whereat she screams; with arms akimbo spread,
> And swears, by all the living and the dead,
> It shall not be! And then I seize a slat
> And score her face with notches fiery red,
> In this bordel where we are thron'd in state.
>
> Then peace is made and she lets flee a fart,
> Like an envenom'd beetle all a-bloat,
> And lays her hand upon my privy part.
> 'Go, go!' she cries, and smites my tender spot.
> Both drunk, we slumber like a worn-out boot.
> At dawn her rumbling stomach wakes her greed;
> She mounts me, eager not to waste my seed.

The Haymarket, London: a Victorian scene (*Radio Times Hulton Picture Library*)

A street corner in Barcelona, *c.* 1951 (*Radio Times Hulton Picture Library*)

The Empress Theodora: detail from a mosaic in San Vitale, Ravenna (*Radio Times Hulton Picture Library*)

Jane Shore, depicted in a late-eighteenth-century print (*British Museum*)

A Renaissance courtesan: a painting by Bartolommeo Veneto, *c.* 1520 (*Städelsches Kunstinstituts, Frankfurt-on-Main*)

Catherine Sedley, after a portrait by Wissing (*British Museum*)

I groan beneath her, flatten'd by her weight,
Until the very life of me is sped,
In this bordel where we are thron'd in state.

Come wind, come hail, come frost, I've bak'd my bread.
A lecher to a lecheress is wed.
Which is the worse? There's little to be said.
Like unto like: 'Bad cat for a bad rat.'
We love the mire, and miry is our bed;
We flee from honour, honour now is fled,
In this bordel where we are thron'd in state.

In the work of the most outspoken and least formal of the poets of the Middle Ages, then, prostitution is simply a part of a generally squalid context. The point is worth emphasizing. It is not 'criminal' in itself, like thieving; but of course prostitutes associated with criminals and formed a part of the texture of criminal life – as they still do. And Villon's poetry stands out because it represents them as individual human beings – which, like criminals, they still are.

5

The successful courtesans of the Italian Renaissance were personalities in their own right, who, like their Greek counterparts, were often educated and wrote prose and poetry. However, they were rather more vulnerable – because of the Christian attitude – than the Greek *hetairai*, and probably more of them ended their lives in poverty. A pope such as Paul III (1468–1549; Pope from 1534) could make things miserable for them. Although the father of bastards whose interests he always laboured to advance, Paul forced the remarkable Tullia d'Aragona, daughter of another successful courtesan, Giula Ferrarese, and a talented and learned woman, to wear the official prostitute's veil – thus causing her to die in poverty.

It is a relief to turn from this kind of behaviour to the writings

of Michel de Montaigne (1533–92). Montaigne was an utterly
different kind of man from Villon, but in his essays we find the
same appreciation of the humanity of prostitutes and women.
Unlike Villon, Montaigne was born of a Gascon family who were
rising into the aristocracy; he was never in trouble – in fact he
was a (not very efficient or ordinarily ferocious) judge, a mayor
and an intermediary between the Catholic and Protestant factions.
Although he respected the externals of his nominal Roman Catholicism (receiving, for example, the last rites of his Church),
he was actually a pyrrhonist, an extreme sceptic ('*Que sais-je?*' he
asked), who wrote his essays primarily in order to find out more
about himself (he invented the term in French *essai*, and meant
by it a 'trial': a 'test' of his opinions about given subjects or circumstances). He was rewarded for his courageous scepticism by
a final ripeness, apparent in his later essays. In an age nearly as
brutal and cruel as Villon's a hundred years before, in which the
lives of ordinary French people were torn apart by senseless religious dissension, he shines out. Montaigne was so humane and
sensible that he could even oppose the corporal punishment of
children; he was as straightforwardly honest with himself and his
readers about his sexual philanderings as any man ever has been;
he tried to effect a compromise between Catholicism and Pro-
testantism, seeing it as the best means of avoiding bloodshed;
he was, surely, the only man of his century who could give a fair
appraisal of Julian the Apostate (the Master of the Sacred Palace
referred it to Montaigne's 'conscience to alter it'; he refused).

The main part of Montaigne's thinking on the subject of sex is
contained in a long essay, one of his finest, called 'On Some Lines
of Virgil'. (But we know from his *Journal de Voyage*, an account
of his travels in Germany, Switzerland and Italy, that he met and
admired the writings of the Viennese courtesan Veronica Franco.)
Characteristically, he begins by saying that since he is old he is
now 'on the defensive against temperance, as I was once against
sensuality'.* He feels that women are treated inconsiderately by

* Quotations from Montaigne's works are from the translation of E. J. Trechman,
Oxford University Press, 1929; Florio's Montaigne (1603) is a marvellous and influential
book in its own right, but is inaccurate as translation.

men, since 'After knowing that they are incomparably more capable and ardent in the sexual act than we' (here he teasingly gives the example of the Roman Emperor, Proculus, who had ten virgins in one night, and Messalina, who had twenty-five men in the same time), men censure lust in them but not in themselves. Here Montaigne is comically demonstrating male hypocrisy – that he is being comic is shown by his remark that 'six per diem' is not enough for the needs of a woman. . . . This is no grimly homosexual hostility to the 'insatiability' of women, but a gently ironic means of pointing out that they, like men, possess sexual desire. He goes on to tell a story of his daughter's governess, who interrupted her when she came to a word, *fouteau*, meaning beech-tree. She 'made her pass over the danger spot' (*foutre* means, of course, to fuck). 'But, if I am not mistaken, the conversation of twenty lackeys could not, in six months, have implanted in her imagination, the meaning and use and all the consequences of the sound of those criminating syllables. . . .' This, it should be remembered, was not written by an opponent of such people as Mary Whitehouse, Cyril Black, or David Holbrook in our own day – but five hundred years ago.

As will have become apparent, Montaigne's reasoning about sex in general is cool and pragmatic rather than moral. His observations on prostitution are similarly level-headed:

'And the people we fear least are perhaps the most to be feared; their silent sins are the worst:

I confess
A simple prostitute offends me less [Martial].

There are acts which, without immodesty on their [women's] part, may cost them their virginity, and, what is more, without their intention. *Sometimes a midwife, on pretence of examining a virgin's integrity, by evil-mindedness, unskilfulness or accident, has destroyed it* [St Augustine]. . . . The very idea we create of their chastity is ridiculous for among the extreme patterns I have [is] . . . the wife of Hiero, who did not realize that her husband had a stinking breath, thinking it was a characteristic of all men. . . . Now we must confess that our difficulty in estimating this duty [chastity within marriage] lies chiefly in the disposition. . . . Many a woman there has been who, though she loved honour more than life, has prostituted herself to the furious appetite of a deadly enemy, to save her husband's life; doing for him what she would never have done for herself.

It is necessary to appreciate that Montaigne was a humorist and an ironist, as indeed a man of his stamp in such an age had to be. His main argument he states directly, 'The very idea we create of their chastity is ridiculous'; but his chosen examples are ironically or comically presented. The notion, slipped quietly in, that the estimation of a woman's own sexual 'duty' is a matter of temperament was then preposterous. And the careful reader will note that the faithful wife who, in the cliché, 'loved honour more than life', nevertheless loves it less than her husband's life. . . . When Montaigne continues, 'But for examples of more common-place distinction, are there not women amongst us who every day lend themselves out for their husband's benefit, and by their express command . . . ?' he is not simply being reasonable, but drawing attention to male hypocrisy, since the very men who most condemned prostitution and adultery often indulged in it. One has only to think of Paul III, pope when Montaigne was a boy, who excommunicated Henry VIII and officially instituted the Jesuits: he was (see p. 67) an enemy of prostitutes, and worked to advance his bastards. Montaigne goes on:

This woman may be of loose conduct, and yet of a more moral disposition than that other whose behaviour appears more correct. As we hear some lamenting the fact that they had made a vow of chastity before the age of discretion, I have also heard others truly complain of having been given over to a dissolute life before the age of discretion. . . . In the East Indies, although chastity was there held in singular esteem, yet custom permitted a married woman to abandon herself to any man who presented her with an elephant; and it reflected a certain glory to have been valued at so high a price.

But Montaigne did not over-simplify sexual matters. He recognized that the absurdity or perversity of most social and religious attitudes towards sex and prostitution originate in a genuinely mysterious situation, in which man, having lost his animal capacity for innocence, has in some way become 'unnatural'. As he says:

The sexual act . . . absorbs and dissipates [the mental faculties]. Truly it is a mark not only of our original corruption [this is good orthodox Catholic thinking and is not part of Montaigne's argument] but also of our inanity and deformity. On the one hand Nature pushes us on to it, having connected with this desire the noblest, most useful, and pleasant of all her operations; and on the other hand she allows us to condemn and fly from it as from a shameless and immodest action, to blush at it and recommend abstinence. Are we not indeed brutes to call brutish the operation that makes us? . . . Every one avoids seeing a man born; every one runs to see him die. For his destruction they seek out a spacious field, in the full light of day; for his construction they creep into some dark little corner. It is a duty to hide and blush while making him; and it is a glory . . . to be able to unmake him. The one is offence, the other is grace. . . . we regard our being as a sin. . . . What an unnatural animal to be a horror to himself, to grieve at his pleasures, to regard himself as a misfortune!

This paradox, as we shall see, is the essential subject of *Measure for Measure*.

On one aspect of Italian prostitution, or rather the Italian clientele of prostitutes, Montaigne is interesting:

In Italy they act the part of the languishing suitor even with the ladies who are for sale, and defend this practice as follows: 'that there are degrees in enjoyment, and that by paying them homage we try to procure for ourselves the most complete. For these ladies sell only their bodies; their good will cannot be on sale, it is too free and too much at its own disposal.' Hence they say that it is the will they lay siege to; and they are right. It is the will we must serve and win by our attention. To me it is a horrible idea that a body void of affection should belong to me. . . . I say that we love a body without a soul, or without feeling, when we love a body without its consent and desire.

This attitude on the part of Italian men was shared in part by 'Walter', the Victorian author of *My Secret Life*, with the important difference that Walter sought to elicit, and according to himself in most cases obtained, a physical – and not at all an emotional – response from the hundreds of whores he paid. Montaigne here is not arguing against the fact of prostitution – he was far too much a man of the world for that – but pleading, with admirable realism, that relations with whores should be humanized: the *will*, the mind, of the woman who sells her body, he insists, can never be for sale.

Finally, Montaigne seems to anticipate the findings of some modern sexual researchers, when he concludes that 'I say that male and female are cast in the same mould; saving education and habits, the difference is not great'. This may or may not be true in a psychological sense, but in the physiological sense in which Montaigne meant it, it was a great humanizing thought in his century. One has only to compare Montaigne's writings about women to the offensive, cynical-naïve remarks of the equally sophisticated Brantôme ('. . . women who have been free cannot be kept from breaking out of confinement, no matter how closely they are watched, whenever they hear the tinkle of gold') to realize just how important the former's contribution to the cause of sexual equality was.

Chapter Six

1

THE Elizabethan and Jacobean treatment of prostitution had, above all, zest; both Puritan and other writers wrote of the seamy side of life with an uninhibited energy that has not been equalled since. The background against which they wrote is well described by Thomas Nashe in *Pierce Penniless his Supplication to the Devil* (1692), a fantastical satiric reply to the Martin Marprelate pamphlets, which were Puritan in inspiration. The work, like most of Nashe, is a heady mixture of disparate elements; but in this passage the author, while parodying the Puritan style, imparts a certain amount of valuable information:

The child of Sloth is Lechery, which I have placed last in my order of handling: a sin that is able to make a man wicked that should describe it; for it hath more starting-holes than a sieve hath holes, more clients than Westminster Hall, more diseases than Newgate. Call a leet at Bishopsgate, and examine how every second house in Shoreditch is maintained; make a privy search in Southwark, and tell me how many she-inmates you find – nay, go where you will in the suburbs and bring me two virgins that have vowed chastity, and I'll build a nunnery.

The Court I dare not touch, but surely there, as in the heavens, be many falling stars and but one true Diana. *Consuetudo peccandi tollit sensum peccati.* Custom is a law, and lust holds it for a law to live without law. Lais, that had so many poets to her lovers, could not always preserve her beauty with their praises. Marble will wear away with much rain; gold will rust with moist keeping; and the richest garments are subject to time's moth-frets. Clytemnestra, that slew her husband to enjoy the adulterer Aegisthus, and bathed herself in milk every day to make her young again, had a time when she was ashamed to view herself in a looking-glass; and her body withered, her mind being green. The people pointed at her for a murderer, young children hooted at her as a strumpet: shame, misery, sickness, beggary is the best end of uncleanness.

Lais, Cleopatra, Helen – if our clime hath any such, noble Lord Warden of the witches and jugglers, I commend them with the rest of our unclean sisters in Shoreditch, the Spital, Southwark, Westminster, and Turnbull Street to the protection of your Portership, hoping you will speedily carry them to hell, there to keep open house for all young devils that come, and not let our air be contaminated with their sixpenny damnation any longer.

There would, of course, be more 'vice', and in particular more prostitutes, in proportion to the total population, until social conditions were improved and poverty reduced. Poverty exposed women to the temptation to sell their bodies without regard to the future consequences, which were often grim; when, however, over a period of some hundreds of years, poverty was gradually reduced, the prostitution of the very poor doubtless became the adultery, or 'promiscuity', or 'vice', of the comparatively comfortable lower classes. There are no statistics available. But there is no reason to suppose that better living conditions and more money to spend actually improved 'morals' (adultery is usually less sordid than prostitution; but this is a matter of taste, not morals); the conditions for non-marital sex were improved and brothel-life became partially absorbed by bourgeois 'immorality' – but sex itself obstinately refused to be eliminated.

However, in the time of Nashe and his contemporaries, and right up to the beginning of the nineteenth century (with the exception of the short Commonwealth and Protectorate period) little serious attempt was made to disguise or suppress the seamy side. Prostitution and seaminess went together, for reasons which are obvious enough. Today the least fortunate or least young prostitutes, or those who happen to be the most psychopathic, still live in sordid circumstances; but 'promiscuity', which is morally as reprehensible (or otherwise) as prostitution, thrives (presumably) in non-sordid situations.

The Elizabethan dramatists depicted the lives of the criminal classes with varying good humour. There is a savage, nearly puritanical edge to some of the many plays of London life, most particularly in Middleton; but all are zestful and realistic. They humanized their material by partaking of its immense vitality – the vitality, courage, wit and directness that always characterize the poor and the oppressed (except when they are turned into something else by demagogues, as Shakespeare demonstrated to such effect).

The happiest of all plays of London life, 'a celebration of a rite of summer', as Maurice Hussey has called it, is Ben Jonson's *Bartholomew Fair* (1614), with its good-humoured but remorseless satire on Puritanism and its comically sympathetic picture of the Falstaffian Ursula, Pig-Woman and bawd.

Ursula has been before Justice Overdo, he tells the audience, as a 'punk [whore], pinnace [procurer; but an obvious pun], and baud'; her naturalness is contrasted, throughout the play, with the Puritan Zeal-of-the-Land-Busy, who is presented with Jonson's usual but not always fully acknowledged insight and subtlety, as ignorant and sexually prurient. We learn here, as from other sources, that London prostitutes frequently wore green gowns and crimson petticoats. Knockem, the horsetrader, says to Ursula:

Ursula, take them [a whore and a putative whore] in, open thy wardrobe, and fit them to their calling. Green gowns, crimson petticoats, green women, my Lord Mayor's green women! Guests o' the game, true bred. . . .

(Green, of course, is the colour a girl gets on her gown when she has been lying on the grass; but it has many other associations, which are obvious enough.)

But while the Elizabethan writers took some pleasure in describing the low life of London, it was to Italy, particularly Venice, that they usually turned when they wanted to depict real vice. Plays dealing with serious villainy were most often set in Italy. In the first part of *The Pleasant History of the Gentle Craft* (registered 1597) the Norfolk pamphleteer and ballad-writer Thomas Deloney, who began as a silk-weaver, re-tells the old tale of St Hugh and St Winifred. Deloney, although almost certainly educated at a grammar school, was no intellectual, but wrote directly and intelligently in the folk-tradition; his work is valuable for its description of the attitudes of the middle classes of his time (the last years of the sixteenth century). When Hugh in his miraculous journeyings is tormented by 'deceiving sirens', 'a crew of Courtlike Dames richly attired', they sing him *The Courtesan's Song of Venice* ('Oh Venice', wrote another Elizabethan, Barnabe Rich, 'a wonder it is, that the sea swalloweth thee not up for thy sin, which retainest so many brothel houses, and wicked Bawds'):

LADIES: Welcome to Venice, gentle courteous Knight,
   Cast off care, and entertain content.
 If any here be gracious in thy sight,
   Do but request, and she shall soon content:
 Love's wings are swift, then be not thou so slow:
HUGH: Oh that fair *Winifred* would once say so.

LADIES: Within my lap lay down thy comely head,
   And let me stroke those golden locks of thine, –
 Look on the tears that for thy sake I shed,
   And be thou Lord of any thing is mine, –
 One gentle look upon thy *Love* bestow.
HUGH: Oh that fair *Winifred* would once say so.

LADIES: Embrace with joy thy lady in thine arms,
   And with all pleasures pass to thy delight:
 If thou dost think the light will work our harms,
   Come, come to bed, and welcome all the night,
 There shalt thou find what Lovers ought to know.
HUGH: Oh that fair *Winifred* would once say so.

LADIES: Give me those pearls as pledges of thy love,
    And with those pearls the favour of thy heart, –
Do not from me thy sugar'd breath remove,
    That double comfort gives to every part:
Nay stay Sir Knight, from hence thou shalt not go.
HUGH: Oh that fair *Winifred* would once say so.

Deloney, although an anti-Catholic of politically Puritan tendencies whose main purpose is to celebrate the high moral qualities of his tradesman hero, certainly goes out of his way to make his harlots delightful and graceful. Typical of him, too, and of the generously straightforward way the middle classes for whom he wrote could feel in the reign of Elizabeth, is his touching ballad about Jane Shore, Edward IV's mistress: *A New Sonnet, containing the Lamentation of Shore's wife, who was sometime concubine to King Edward the fourth, setting forth her great fall, and withal her most miserable and wretched end.*

Jane Shore, who did not die until about 1617, was much written about in the sixteenth century. She married a goldsmith when very young, and was first noticed by Edward in about 1570. On his death she may have been kept by the Marquis of Dorset. But the Lord Protector, Duke of Gloucester, soon afterwards Richard III, fined her and caused her to do open penance in Paul's Churchyard, 'not', wrote Michael Drayton, 'so much for his hatred to sin, but that by making his brother's life odious, he might cover his horrible treasons the more cunningly': sexual misdemeanours frequently offer tyrants and statesmen their best excuses. After this Jane Shore, who had never misused her influence – Thomas More said, in her lifetime, that 'she beggeth of many at this day living, that at this day had begged, if she had not been' – lived out her long life in abject poverty.

    Shore's wife I am,
    So known by name:
    And at the *Flower-de-Luce* in *Cheapside*
      Was my dwelling:
    The only daughter of a wealthy merchant man,
    Against whose counsel evermore,
      I was rebelling.

Young was I loved;
No affection moved
My heart or mind to give or yield
　To their consenting.
My Parents thinking richly for to wed me,
Forcing me to that which caused
　My repenting.

Then being wedded,
I was quickly tempted,
My beauty caused many Gallants
　To salute me.
The King commanding, I straight obeyed:
For his chiefest jewel then,
　He did repute me. . . .

When the King died,
My grief I tried:
From the Court I was expelled
　With despite.
The Duke of Gloucester being Lord Protector,
Took away my goods, against
　All law and right.

In a Procession
For my transgression,
Bare foot he made me go,
　For to shame me.
A Cross before me there was carried plainly,
As a penance for my former life,
　So to tame me. . . .

Wherefore, Fair Ladies,
With your sweet babies,
My grievous fall bear in your mind,
　And behold me:
How strange a thing, that the love of a King
Should come to die under a stall,
　As I told ye.

There is here at least a hint, in the last stanza, that Jane Shore
got her deserts for being a whore; but in general the ballad is
much more in the gentle spirit with which More wrote about its
heroine – the emphasis is upon the tragedy and pathos of her
plight, upon the caprices of fortunes rather than the results of
sexual wickedness. Thomas Churchyard's uninspired version of
the story, in one of the later editions of the *Mirror For Magistrates*,
is more moralistic, but not with any real conviction. But a much
later (eighteenth-century) ballad version, included by Bishop
Percy in his *Reliques of Ancient Poetry*, provides an unpleasant
contrast: all the sympathy is gone, its place taken by a mechanical and meaningless moralizing, as is shown in the following
extracts:

> Thus was I scorn'd of maid and wife,
> For leading such a wicked life. . . .

> The which now since my dying day,
> Is Shoreditch called, as writers say [a quite incorrect derivation];
> Which is a witness of my sin,
> For being concubine to a king

> You wanton wives, that fall to lust,
> Be you assur'd that God is just;
> Whoredome shall not escape his hand

> If God to me such shame did bring,
> That yielded only to a king,
> How shall they scape that daily run
> To practise sin with every one?

The habit of moralizing without reference to natural history
had fully developed by Percy's time.

I have already given a brief outline of Shakespeare's highly
complex personal attitude to sex as evinced in his sonnets.* In
his plays he shared his contemporaries' undisguised zest in the
depiction of bawds and prostitutes, particularly in his portrayal
of Mistress Quickly and Doll Tearsheet in *King Henry IV*. The

* See pp. 52–5.

famous brothel scene in *Pericles* does not evince disgust at prostitution, but is a celebration of the chastity of the witty and resourceful Marina, and simultaneously contrasts the coarseness and sordidity of the brothel environment with the deliberate – and markedly non-ignorant – sexual innocence of a royal princess. But it was in *Measure for Measure* that he most specifically examined the question of prostitution and of sex in general.

2

Measure for Measure (written, it is now widely assumed, in 1604) explores the human sexual paradox so lucidly set forth by Montaigne in the passage I have already quoted.* Shakespeare's sources were a prose tale in a collection called the *Hecatommithi*, by an Italian, Cinthio, and an unactable ten-act play, *Promos and Cassandra*, by George Whetstone. The plot combines three themes, all of which (particularly the last) were commonplace in the period. J. W. Lever (to whose scrupulous edition of the play† I am indebted, although I differ sharply from him about its meaning) describes them as: The Corrupt Magistrate, The Disguised Ruler and The Substituted Bedmate. The three really important changes that Shakespeare made were: to make his corrupt magistrate, Angelo, into a repressive puritan – in Cinthio he is a mere boy, in Whetstone a romantically infatuated old fellow; to turn his heroine, Isabella – sister of the man condemned for fornication, Claudio – into a novice-nun, who at the beginning of the action is just about to enter a convent and who believes that the rules of her chosen order should be stricter; and to provide a new character, a libertine wit, the 'fantastic', Lucio.

A brief reminder of the plot: the Duke of Vienna – which is transparently London – decides that he has been ruling too leniently. Not wishing to discredit his authority by an admission of

* See p. 71.   † Methuen, London, 1965.

this, he puts Angelo – a deputy whom he knows to be severe, and believes to be just – in charge while he absents himself. Secretly, he remains in the country, disguised as a friar, to observe his subjects' (and Angelo's) behaviour. Angelo immediately proceeds to sentence a young man, Claudio, to death for the 'crime' of getting his girl with child before he had been officially married to her (although it is clear that Claudio had already entered into a contract that would have fully satisfied the susceptibilities of Shakespeare's audience, if not of some Puritans). Isabella, Claudio's sister, about to enter a nunnery, is persuaded by Lucio – who advises her – to plead with Angelo for her brother's life. Angelo, after a brief struggle with himself, agrees to spare the young man if Isabella will surrender her virginity to him. She says that she would prefer Claudio to die.

The Duke, now disguised as a friar, arranges for Mariana, a girl whom Angelo had jilted because of the loss of her dowry at sea, to take Isabella's place in the dark. Angelo enjoys her, imagining that it is Isabella; he then treacherously sends instructions for Claudio to be executed before the appointed time, and asks for his head. By the Duke's machinations, the head of a dead pirate resembling Claudio is sent instead. The Duke eventually reveals himself, and after allowing all the culprits to imagine that they are to be doomed, spares everyone (including Lucio, who has libelled him to the 'friar'). Angelo marries Mariana, Lucio is made to marry the mother of his bastard, and the Duke instructs Isabella to marry him (she does not reply to his proposal).

The sub-plot, which is important, concerns the fortunes of the brothel-keepers Pompey and Mistress Overdone – they are 'closed down' under Angelo's régime – and a comically obscene dispute between Elbow, an illiterate constable, and Froth, 'a foolish gentleman', about the former's wife.

Measure for Measure, often described as a 'problem play', has been interpreted in widely differing ways. A brief account of the main interpretations is a necessary preliminary to any discussion of it.

The usual view of Shakespearean critics in the first part of this century was that it was a 'brutal' and 'cynical' play, reflecting

Shakespeare's general disgust with the world – and with the sexual aspect of it in particular. Holders of this view see Isabella as a repulsively cold and limited character, possessed only by self-righteousness, and unwilling to save her brother's life at the expense of her chastity.

A newer view of the play is that it is an allegory of the Divine Atonement: the Duke is the Incarnate Lord, Lucio the Eternal Adversary, and Isabella the soul of man (elected to be the Bride of Christ). This rather foolish view I shall not consider: it has been convincingly refuted,* its proponents are not above tampering with the Folio text in order to further their point,† and – last but not least – Shakespeare was a busy playwright, not the author of church services. That an allegory of the Divine Atonement should contain so strong an undercurrent of bawdiness has not been explained.

The third, and currently most fashionable interpretation of the play, an almost exclusively academic one, rejects the 'cynical view' (best expressed by Quiller Couch in his New Cambridge edition of the play), and modifies the 'Christian' view. It endorses the opinion of the late C. J. Sisson that the play is 'sound to the core, and profoundly Christian in spirit' – illusory qualities, however, that are more likely to have been aspirations of the simplistic critic than properties of the non-Victorian playwright. The play is seen as optimistic rather than pessimistic, an account of 'the wise ruler' (the Duke, it is generally conceded, is a weakly conceived character who seldom comes to life), of a 'sensual' youth (Claudio), who has 'sinned' – but lightly – and of a girl, Isabella, who lacks self-knowledge at the beginning of the play but gains in it as she gains in experience. It is assumed, in this donnish interpretation, that Shakespeare's thinking is typical of that of an orthodox middle-of-the-road Anglican of his time; certainly it is regarded (rather tamely, some may think) as conventionally Christian.

The most unsatisfactory feature of much modern Shakespearean interpretation is that it denies Shakespeare any real

---

* By J. W. Lever, for example, and by Patrick Murray, *The Shakespearean Scene*, Longmans, Green, London, 1969.   † Radio production of 27 March 1955.

originality. Confusing his expression of himself in contemporary terms with acceptance of those terms, critics are shocked at the notion that Shakespeare did not believe in 'the system'. Thus, because the time of James I's accession to the throne (1603) was a generally hopeful one (in the sense that people talked hopefully, and were glad to see the last of an old Queen who had become tiresome), it has been assumed that Shakespeare himself would not have been 'cynical' – or written 'cynical' plays – in the period 1603–5!

While it would be foolish to try to make an Elizabethan gentleman into a twentieth-century libertarian, it is equally foolish to deny him independence of thought. That Shakespeare wrote in terms his audiences could understand, and therefore in terms of ideas that were in the air at the time, goes without saying: he could not have been a successful playwright if he had not done so. But modern critics tend to assume both that his audience never differed among themselves, and that he was a spokesman for the values of his age. Those who think that Shakespeare really believed in these values should read his Sonnet 66 ('Tired with all these, for restful death I cry'); the fact is that although poets are representatives of their age, they are not – in their poetry – *spokesmen* for it. Shakespeare did not, like most of his fellow dramatists at one time or another, get put into prison for offending the authorities; but his caution should not lead us to suppose that he was any less subversive. A reading of *Measure for Measure* that makes due allowance for Shakespeare's independence of mind reveals that he was concerned with a theme quite beyond the scope of the public thinking of his time.

It may safely be guessed that *Measure for Measure* came into being because Shakespeare's interest in a story by Cinthio coincided with his company's requirement for a comedy that would flatter, or at least please, the new King, who was the author of a book – *Basilicon Doron* (Edinburgh, 1599), which dealt with political ethics and his own aims in particular – and who certainly regarded himself as a 'wise ruler'. The story by Cinthio might first have represented itself to Shakespeare as the subject for a tragedy; in the event he made it into a sour, ironic comedy: as it stands, it is a mixture of bitterly intelligent parody of a romance plot, unobtrusive natural history, poetic satire and politically unexceptionable material (to be taken as ironic only by the initiated). Certainly, from the standpoint of official good spirits, the play is 'bitter', 'cynical' and therefore 'irresponsible' (hence the modern need to turn it into a 'sound' Christian drama: the Victorians and their successors had their own, external respectability, and could afford admiringly to allow Shakespeare to be beastly); but 'comic' is a much more appropriate term to apply to the play – at least for those who can consider these matters for themselves. It is a frequent mistake of literary critics to confuse natural history with 'cynicism' and 'brutality'.

The character of the Duke fails because the audience would have taken him not 'as', but as a deliberate tribute to, James I – and James, for all his good intentions and talk about morality, was a bisexual whose behaviour was ridiculous as well as, in his own terms, 'bad'. Shakespeare pokes some very discreet fun at James's especial dislike of any kind of criticism, and cleverly gets the audience on Lucio's side when the latter recklessly attacks his reputation and wisdom. Lucio tells the Duke, disguised as a friar (but does Lucio know who he is?), that the absent ruler is 'very superficial, ignorant and unweighing', 'he had some feeling for the sport [of sex]', 'he knew the service'; he is also often drunk, and eats mutton on Fridays.

The point is that the Duke (in the play) is *not* guilty of any kind of womanizing, brothel-touring or stupidity – but it was known fairly well that the cowardly, slobbering James's behaviour within his Court was not above official reproach, and even better known that he was a pedantic fool whose wisdom was wholly theoretical. However, since the Duke in the play is plainly represented as not guilty, James (or his representatives) could hardly complain. . . . Shakespeare may have been more cautious than his contemporaries; he was not less critical.

The essentially ironic nature of the play is most clearly seen in the character of Lucio, who although he is selfishly dissolute (he refuses to marry the mother of his child), vicious in effect, and may be guilty of gratuitous treachery (if the accusation of his procuress, who also cares for his bastard, is to be believed), is consistently presented as a realist. Pompey, the bawd, and Mistress Overdone – who go to prison on information that the latter insists was given by Lucio – are certainly realistic; but they are non-literate. Lucio's brand of cynical pragmatism is literate: educated and highly articulate. He is also unmitigated natural history: inconsistent, as human beings, despite literary critics, are: sexually free, irresponsible, cynical, a true friend to Isabella and Claudio in their troubles, and yet viciously casual towards those beneath him in the social scale upon whom he (in part at least) relies for his sexual escapades.

As I have suggested, the circumstances surrounding the composition of this play seriously inhibited Shakespeare's desire to present things as they actually are: so, apart from Lucio, his naturalism resides in his depiction of the plebeian characters and, above all, in his language – which teems with sexual *double-entendre*. The presence of this richly sexual language, together with the zestful realism of the plebeians and the gloating insistences of Lucio, continually undermine the fairy-tale pretensions of the main plot, in which two people whose sexual rectitude is repulsive – in that it is life-denying in a literal sense – are supposedly 'educated'. This plot even undermines itself. Nothing could be more ridiculous than the Duke's final speeches, in which he pardons Claudio and adds to Isabella:

> and for your lovely sake,
> Give me your hand and say you will be mine,
> He [Claudio] is my brother too.

It is surely significant that Shakespeare gives no short speech to Isabella so that she may welcome this sudden proposition. Would we be wrong in seeing in all this a reference to the well-known impulsive absurdity of King James I, whose most idle whims nevertheless carried great weight?

The Duke tells Angelo to love his wife,

> I have confess'd her, and I know her virtue.

This is doubly ironic: for the sake of getting married to Angelo,

Mariana has given him her 'virtue' – and we know of course that it is precisely 'virtue', virginity, that most sexually excites Angelo. Testing out Isabella before putting his proposal before her he has said:

> Which had you rather – that the most just law
> Now took your brother's life; or, to redeem him,
> Give up your body to such sweet uncleanness
> As she that he hath stain'd?

Clearly for Angelo the thrill is as much sadistic, as much involved in the illicit exercise of his power for sexual ends, as in what he is going to 'get'. But because he is convinced that sex is 'unclean', while he concedes that it is 'sweet', it is a virginity that he wants: his blinkered vision can see sexual pleasure only as a thrillingly illicit *corruption* of that of which he imagines virtue to consist: virtuous virginity. Thus when the Duke tells him that he knows Mariana's 'virtue' it implies both that Angelo's tastes have not changed and that, alas, the real thrill has already been had. . . .

Ironically, the only character in the play whose sexuality is presented as 'natural', responsible and non-neurotic (if we do not include the Duke, whose functions are to serve as chorus, manipulator and vehicle for discreet satire against the King; but even he states, in reference to himself – amusingly, in view of his parodic 'happy ending', marriage to Isabella – that 'the dribbling dart of love' cannot 'pierce a complete [whole, perfect] bosom') is Claudio. But Claudio, bewildered, stands condemned for a natural act – that it was natural, unexceptionable, responsible, loving, is made absolutely clear by its being represented as socially acceptable to Sheakespeare's audience.* Angelo's condemnation of him may legitimately be seen as a jealous condemnation of impulses in himself which he feels he must not indulge, for he is one whose blood (Lucio shrewdly tells Isabella)

> Is very snow-broth, one who never feels
> The wanton stings and motions of the sense,
> But doth rebate and blunt his natural edge
> With profits of the mind, study and fast.

* For the fullest details of this, see J. W. Lever's edition.

Angelo is immediately attracted by Isabella, who causes him to give way to temptation (his proneness to which he has openly acknowledged, telling his fellow-deputy Escalus that it is one thing to be tempted, another to fall: 'I have had such faults', he admits, as Claudio, but if I 'do so offend / Let mine own judgement pattern out my death'), *because* she is 'virtuous', has his own ability to be cold, to deny physical passion. In both these characters we are presented not with people who are immune from sexual passion, but who regard it as evil (because they are afraid of it). In fairness to such an attitude we may recall some words of the anthropologist Bronislav Malinowski: 'I maintain that sex is regarded as dangerous by the savage . . . for the simple reason that *sex really is dangerous.*'

Angelo regards sexual pleasure as wrong; Isabella does not merely value her chastity, which is understandable – the decision to allow one's body to be enjoyed, and to give it in enjoyment, is a crucial and important one – but she overvalues it. The 'measure for measure' of the title implies, among other things, that to just the extent we deny our physical needs, so those physical needs will assert themselves.

The supreme irony of the two lengthy exchanges between Angelo and Isabella is the nature of the language they use to each other. This not only links up with and (all ignorantly) echoes the down-to-earth language of the plebeians, but also demonstrates how fierce a sexuality lies at the heart of their puritanism.

When Isabella first goes to plead with Angelo for her brother's life she is accompanied by Lucio (who treats her, throughout the play, with great respect) as an advisor. Lucio shrewdly sees that Isabella's only way to gain Angelo's attention is to appeal to him sexually. When she first comes into his presence she can only tell him that she agrees with him that Claudio's 'vice' is abhorrent, and begs Angelo to spare the man but not his 'fault'. Angelo expostulates that the 'actor' of a fault must not go unpunished, and Isabella – in deep sympathy with him – turns to leave, with a pleasant salutation that is full of dramatic irony, 'heaven keep your honour'.

In my quotations I have italicized what Victorian editors used

to call the 'equivoques', and added a footnote where necessary.
Lucio quickly tells Isabella not to give in so easily,

> Kneel down before him, hang upon his gown;
> You are too *cold*. If you should need a *pin*,
> You could not with more tame a *tongue* desire it.
> *To him, I say.*

When Isabella, heeding this advice, performing metaphorical
fellatio, asks Angelo 'Must he needs *die*?' she utters a pun that is
central to the meaning of the play, for 'die' of course meant 'to
come' (sexually) as well as to cease to live. This pun was and is an
important one, linking together as it does the potent and disturbing theme of love in its connection with what is in many ways
its opposite: dissolution. It is no accident that the bawd Pompey,
in prison for sexual offences, becomes assistant to Abhorson, the
executioner (specifically, cutter-off of people's *heads*★).

Angelo again refuses to consider a pardon, and Lucio – seeing
that he is becoming affected, tells Isabella, 'You are too cold'.
She begins to prevail a little, and Lucio exclaims, 'Ay, *touch*
him . . .'. Isabella continues in the same style, referring not for one
moment to the notion that Claudio's 'sin' may not be very
great, but appealing to Angelo's mercy. This 'virtue' so excites
Angelo that he shows signs of giving way, and Lucio urges her
on: '. . . He's *coming*, I perceive't'. At last, stunned by the girl's
eloquent tirade of moralistic commonplaces – the sort of thing
that is exactly to his taste – Angelo says to himself:

> She speaks, and 'tis such *sense*†
> That my *sense*† *breeds* with it.

In the second exchange, when Angelo actually asks Isabella to
go to bed with him in exchange for her brother's life, it is Isabella
who reveals the sexuality teeming beneath her rigidly moralistic
exterior. On being admitted to Angelo, she says,

> I am come to know your *pleasure*.

★ A pun on 'penis' that recurs throughout the play.
† (1) Common sense, (2) sensuality: lust.

Angelo reacts to this with an aside,

> That you might *know* it, would much better please me
> Than to demand what 'tis. . . .

and Isabella immediately repeats 'Heaven keep your honour'.
Angelo shifts his ground: Claudio 'may live', 'yet he must *die*'.

When Angelo has made his proposition almost crystal clear,
Isabella, who identifies her 'soul' with her chastity, immediately
reacts in strongly sexual imagery:

> Were I under the terms of death
> The impression of *keen whips* I'd wear as rubies,
> And *strip* myself to *death* as to a *bed*
> That *longing* have been sick for, ere I'd yield
> My body up to shame.

Angelo, now working for his lust's goal and nothing else,
tries to tempt her with abstract legal arguments, including the
(then) commonplace belief that 'compelled' sins were no sins.
She is confused and dismayed, because it is in such abstractions
that sexual puritans eagerly take refuge. But Isabella's own sexual
gratification is totally narcissistic. She exclaims

> Men their creation mar
> In profiting by them.

This means not only that men mar their (proverbial) creation
in God's image by taking advantage of women, but also that
those who have sexual connection with women 'profit' by them:
Isabella is a novice nun because she does not believe in any sex
at all. She ends, refusing the bargain, by expressing her belief
that Claudio is so honourable that even if he had twenty 'heads'
he would lose them rather than that his sister 'should her body
stoop / To such abhorr'd pollution':

> Then, Isabel live chaste, and brother, die:
> More than our brother is our chastity.

There is no evidence whatever that Isabella ever changes her
attitude. She is prepared to prostitute Mariana to Angelo (on a
friar's authority) to save her brother. It is an additional irony, of

course, that Isabella is happy to parallel the behaviour of Mistress Overdone and Pompey by allowing Mariana to take her place. But she will not give up her own chastity – and she lies to the revealed Duke when she pretends that she has 'yielded' to Angelo; she accepts the Duke's proposal of marriage – but says not a word. Yet this is not 'cynical', but merely realistic: people seldom drastically change their sexual natures.

It may well be asked, at this point, what the play has to do with prostitution. The answer is that it is a comic account of unrespectable plebeian sexual life – of prostitution – that Shakespeare counterpoints against the ostensible anti-sexuality of his 'noble' characters. Even recent critics of the play have solemnly assumed that Pompey the bawd, Mistress Overdone, and the rest, are 'immoral', and representative of the situation which the Duke absents himself to cure. This is based on the assumption that Shakespeare believed in their own latter-day morality (not likely, if only on historical grounds); critics usually fail to allow for the fact that *poetry*, as distinct from the poets who write it, is naturally subversive: i.e. subscribes to values independent of 'the system', such as, for example, the objectivity of true naturalism, a luxury that can never be afforded by those in power.

Actually the Duke, describing the motives for his deception to Friar Thomas, does not allude specifically to sexual vice in his description of the situation:

> our decrees
> Dead to infliction, to themselves are dead;
> And liberty plucks justice by the nose;
> The baby beats the nurse, and quite athwart
> Goes all decorum.

True, the unbridled ease with which Pompey and Co. manage their brothel-affairs is symptomatic of this situation; but there is no evidence in the text that 'bawdry' is deliberately being presented as 'sinful'; it is presented, however, realistically, and as genuinely comic – hardly the kind of presentation to be expected from a moralist. Just as symptomatic of the generally 'lax' situation is the irresponsible warmongering of Lucio and his friends,

who are hoping for war and not peace ('patriotic' killing is invariably regarded by the public mind as more 'honourable' than
sexual licence; but Shakespeare did not have an official mind).

The language used by Angelo and Isabella (there is more of it
in the scene where she angrily tells her brother Claudio that he
ought to be prepared to die rather than even think of submitting
her to dishonour) is unconsciously sexual; its sexual nature is
emphasized by and contrasted with the consciously bawdy language employed by the plebeians. The language of Lucio and his
friends is something in between the two: it is consciously bawdy,
but elegantly and slyly so. It has its disgusting elements, too,
chiefly its obsessive dwelling upon sexual disease, and its tiredness
– it quite lacks the thrilling energy of Mercutio's bawdiness in
Romeo and Juliet.

The first Angelo-Isabella exchange is immediately preceded
by the courtroom scene between Pompey, Elbow the 'simple
constable' and Froth the 'foolish gentleman'. The deliberate
comedy of this scene – the sheer fun – make critics' lugubrious insistence on Pompey and the rest's being 'true sinners' rather hard
to sustain. It is simply not enough to take the commonplaces of
contemporary moral thinking and then apply them to Shakespeare's play, as if Shakespeare himself shared them.

Elbow is a typical low-grade policeman: sure of the correctness
of the 'law', but incapable of understanding it or even of using the
correct words: leading Pompey and Elbow in as prisoners, he
refers to them as 'notorious benefactors', and when corrected by
Angelo confesses that he does not really know what they are,
except that they are 'precise villains' (exactly what Angelo is: he
has already been described as 'precise' (puritanical) by the Duke)
'void of all profanation in the world, that good Christians ought
to have'. This forms not only 'an ironic commentary on Angelo's
principles' (as Lever says), but also a subversive commentary on
the nature of Christian authority itself;* we see the same strand
of irony appear when Pompey becomes assistant executioner:

* It should probably be pointed out that even the most severe critics of authority do
not necessarily advocate its immediate overthrow: there is every reason to believe that
Shakespeare remained unconcerned with all kinds of political action.

the man put in prison as a 'sinner' is soon put to another 'use'. Pompey mocks Elbow, in the manner in which the brighter (if not intellectually brilliant) members of the criminal fraternity usually do bait the slower upholders of the law, and Elbow retaliates by describing him to the justices as a 'parcel [part-time] bawd' who serves a 'bad woman; whose house . . . was . . . plucked down in the suburbs; and now she professes a hot-house'. This means that Mistress Overdone has become proprietress of a bathhouse, merely another brothel. So much for Angelo's clean-up campaign: the remark echoes Pompey's consolatory words to Mistress Overdone when he tells her the news, 'though you change your place, you need not change your trade', and anticipates Lucio's observation that 'it is impossible to extirp it [vice] quite . . . till eating and drinking be put down'.

Elbow's wife, whom he 'detests' (he means that he 'protests', swears), has been approached by Mistress Overdone's pimp, and has (according to Elbow) defied him. Pompey denies this, and launches into a rambling story whose humour, as Lever says, depends on 'its run of equivocal words and phrases';

Sir, she [Elbow's wife] came in great with child; and longing . . . for *stewed prunes*; sir, we had *but two* in the house, which at that very distant time *stood* as it were in a *fruit dish*, a dish of some three pence. . .

and so he goes on, with puns on 'pin', 'cracking the stones', and so on. Clearly Elbow's wife has been procured for Froth; what has actually occurred is obscure. But this whole scene serves as a background for the main plot: the crude but 'natural' attitude of the folk towards sex serves as a contrast to the more intellectual, orthodox, inhibited moralistic approach of Angelo and Isabella, whose language none the less shows them to be as much subject to sexual drives as their social inferiors.

Measure for Measure shows all the members of a society, except its semi-real ruler, at the mercy of sex (and, in Lucio's case, sexual disease). Only Claudio is healthy and honourable, and he has been condemned to die for it. The plebeians are comic and harmless, but crude and inarticulate; their ignorance may become treachery, and is at best humanly insensitive. Lucio is shrewd and

amusing, but vicious. Angelo and Isabella are the prisoners of
their own 'virtue', their denial of their own sexual needs. And the
world of lower-class prostitution emerges exactly as it is: the
product of society's hypocritical attitude towards sex. Since it
is in no way idealized, it is perfect natural history.

3

The position of the high-class prostitute, or courtesan (the word
originally meant 'of the court': hence the 1607 example cited by
the *Oxford Dictionary*: 'Your whore is for every rascal, but your
Courtesan is for your Courtier'), was insecure. Society's toleration
of prostitution of all sorts did not preserve individual women
from calumniation on the grounds of unchastity, a charge against
women that males, in particular, have always jealousy reserved
the right to bring. Few men of good family were prepared to
marry a woman who was notorious as a courtesan, though the
actual sexual behaviour of their wives was quite another matter.
Kenelm Digby (1603–65), a typically eccentric seventeenth-
century gentleman, was a notable exception. Some parts of
Private Memoirs, or 'loose fantasies', which were not published
until 1827, and then in an expurgated edition, are relevant to the
literature of prostitution.

Kenelm Digby was the son of Sir Everard Digby, who was
executed for his part in the Gunpowder Plot. Handsome and very
well off, he was one of the most versatile men of his age: diplo-
mat, scientist, poetaster, plotter, philosopher, cook, sailor,
astrologer, Roman Catholic, Anglican – and perhaps above all,
lover.* Described by the Puritan Philip Stubbes as 'the very
Pliny of our age for lying', Digby was a friend of Descartes, and
won a sea-battle. He was as capable as he was superstitious.

* See Robert Torsten Petersson, *Sir Kenelm Digby*, Jonathan Cape, London, 1955.

The chief woman in his life was Venetia Stanley, who, John Aubrey wrote in his life of her:

... was the daughter of Sir Edward Stanley. She was a most beautiful desirable Creature, and being matura viro was left by her father to live with tenants and servants at Euston Abbey in Oxfordshire: but as private as that place was, it seems her Beauty could not lie hid. The young Eagles [of the Court] had espied her, and she was sanguine and tractable, and of much Suavity (which to abuse was great pity).

In those days, Richard, Earl of Dorset (eldest son and heir to the Lord Treasurer) lived in the greatest splendour of any nobleman in England. Among other pleasures that he enjoyed, Venus was not the least. This pretty creature's fame quickly came to his Lordship's ears, who made no delay to catch at such an opportunity. . . . The Earl of Dorset . . . was her greatest Gallant, who was extremely enamoured of her, and had one, if not more children by her.

Apart from the fact that Venetia was probably mistress not only to Richard Sackville but also to his brother (Aubrey also mentions a Sir Edmund Wyld), there is no reason to doubt the truth of this account: Venetia was an accomplished and beautiful courtesan. In his life of Kenelm Digby, Aubrey described her as 'that celebrated beauty and Courtesan'. But in his (separate) life of her he added that she 'redeemed her Honour by strict living' after her marriage to Digby. She is even said to have worn a hair shirt.

In 1620 Digby fell in love with her, but his mother objected violently, tried to marry him off elsewhere, and in some way arranged for him to go off on a grand tour of more than three years. While he was abroad his letters to Venetia miscarried or were stolen by his mother; apparently she continued her successful career, and he tried to forget her. When he returned, he determined to have nothing to do with her – until he saw her accidentally one day. Cleverly (and, as seems likely, lovingly), she refused to allow Digby the privileges she had more easily granted to others. She was a woman of extraordinary personality: vain, elegant, graceful, aloof, and yet loving – and generally more liberal with sexual favours than many women who were less aloof. Digby pressed his suit, and secretly married her in 1625.

Their marriage was happy, and when Venetia died of consumption in 1633 he was inconsolable.

Digby's *Private Memoirs* or 'loose fantasies' is a unique book, in that it anticipates the English allegorical romance by some thirty years (John Barclay's *Argenis*, 1621, usually mentioned as the first of this particular genre, was published in Paris – and Barclay himself was born in France). What is interesting about it from the point of view of the subject of this book is Digby's treatment of Venetia's reputation. He called himself Theagenes and her Stelliana. He said:

And the sweetness of her disposition is such, that through the virulent malice of this age, it hath been the only cause of her misfortunes. . . . her good parts are such as may be expected to be harboured in a worthy lady that is born with all the advantages of nature. . . .

Digby's attitude has been well summed up by Robert Petersson: '. . . he prefers to prove on paper that Stelliana has an innocence of soul superior to mere chastity'; 'It is . . . trust in [a woman's] goodness of heart and soul, that will make a good wife of her'. As Digby wrote: 'a wise man should not confine himself to what may be said of the past actions of his wife'. And while Havelock Ellis was wise to point out that Digby's attitude, particularly his sexual attitude, represented 'the final efflorescence of the pagan English Renaissance', it is worth remembering that it is still a valid one. Venetia was a whore who married well and made a 'good wife'; from the point of view of natural history, it is well to remember that she was rich, probably careful in her choices, and that she left the profession while still young.

4

The impact on the lives of prostitutes of the twelve years of Puritan rule in England would make an interesting short study. Early Puritans such as Thomas Lupton and Phillip Stubbes (author of

the *Anatomy of Abuses*) had prescribed Draconian penalties, including death, for prostitution; but with no hope of seeing them
carried out. But under the actual rule of the Puritans, whores do
not seem to have been particularly singled out. The Puritans only
thought of the Puritan poor as deserving; most of their prohibi-
tions were directed against the old aristocratic class against whom
they had triumphed in revolt. Like gambling and 'lewdness',
whatever this is (certainly, for the Puritan, it did not mean marital
fornication, since he remained singularly untroubled about this
aspect of Paul's teaching), prostitution simply went underground – to emerge again into the open with the Restoration of
Charles II. In as much as the Puritans destroyed 'Merry England',
they destroyed a certain zestful and natural attitude towards prostitution; but they inveighed no more against whores than against
any other 'abominations'. One who was deeply influenced by
their seriousness and sense of responsibility, Andrew Marvell,
seems to share (in his later satirical verse) the Jacobean attitude.
The Puritans, even at their least tolerant, would never have indulged in the 'necessary evil' view of prostitution, for they were
not, on the whole, hypocrites. They were sternly patriarchal –
even Milton cynically employed the arguments of the Alsatian
Protestant reformer Martin Bucer (1491–1551), which advocated
the equality of men and women, to plead for the right of divorce
for dissatisfied husbands – but they were consistent in seeing
prostitution as merely a part of 'lewdness': they would have condemned a prostitute's customer quite as severely as a prostitute.
Their equation, in their writings, of Rome with whorishness was
traditional and rhetorical; it shows no particular obsession with
contemporary prostitution.

George Wither (1588–1667) was not a typical Puritan. He
began as a moderate Anglican and a satirical pamphleteer, as
well as poet; but supported the parliamentary party before the
Civil War and subsequently fought against the King. He certainly
embraced Puritanism with what looked like fervour, and became
Cromwell's Major-General for Surrey. But his behaviour was
mainly opportunist, so that his *Hallelujah* (1641), a collection of
not very good hymns for almost all people and occasions, is

quite useful as a guide to what an astute man (doubtless convinced of his own sincerity) thought would go down well with a Puritan audience.

Wither has a number of hymns for such as innkeepers, to help to defend them from 'disorderliness', but nothing for whores. Virgins are exhorted, in Wither's own headnote, not to strive 'for the godsend of perpetual virginity beyond their power, nor [to shun] it, being made capable there of'.

Chapter Seven

1

THE period lasting from 1660 until towards the end of the
eighteenth century, when the social and moral attitudes that led
to Victorianism began to make themselves felt, has often, and
justifiably, been described as 'the century of the courtesan'.
By the end of the seventeenth century it was estimated (though
hardly reliably) that there were altogether 50,000 prostitutes in
London alone, twice the number in Paris. There is an extensive
account of eighteenth-century London prostitution in the second
volume of Henriques's history, although some readers may feel
that such 'price lists' as that contained in *Nocturnal Revels: or the
History of King's Place, and other Modern Nunneries, etc.* 'by a Monk
of the Order of St Francis', are taken rather literally. In the entry,
'A young girl for Alderman Drybones. Nelly Blossom, about
19 years old, who has had no one for four days, and who is a
virgin: 20 guineas', not only 'Drybones' is fictitious, as Henriques
concedes, but so may be the price. . . . The jokes about old men's
impotence and the trade in 'virgins' became distinctly tedious in
this period. They were abundant because the upper classes had
sublimated most of their sexual drive in the quest for power and
money. We do not hear any stories of lower-class impotency.

The fashion for having virgins seems to have something to do with the desire for 'treasure' and 'private property', as well as sex: an odd case of economic drives 'sublimating' themselves in sex.

In seventeenth-century literature prostitution is never studied truly objectively – although it may be described, as by the traveller D'Archenholz, quoted by Henriques – but it is accepted.

At the beginning of the period Charles II may be said to have set the tone for the rest of the country. But even his brother, the Duke of York, the future James II, who was more serious-minded, as well as more obstinate (he totally lacked humour), had mistresses. He was said to have syphilis, and Macaulay points out that his taste in women was not as 'nice' as his brother's. At the time he ascended the throne, his chief mistress was Sir Charles Sedley's daughter, Catherine, by whom he was irresistibly attracted. When he became King 'a sense of the new responsibility which lay on him made his mind for a time peculiarly open to religious impressions', says Macaulay, and so he promised his wife not to see Catherine Sedley again. But he soon did, and with typical rashness decided to make her Countess of Dorchester. Before she would accept she made James promise that he would never desert her. But the 'warm blood of Italy boiled in the veins of the Queen', Mary of Modena: she wept and remonstrated, and James alternated between sin and repentence. To the end of her life Mary 'treasured . . . the scourge with which [James] had vigorously avenged her wrongs upon his own shoulders' – something on which Freud might have had a comment. Eventually she bequeathed it to a convent, which was doubtless the right place for it. Ultimately Catherine was bribed to leave for Ireland.

This episode, perhaps unexpected in the life of a King who has usually been regarded as a disastrous ruler, but one of 'moral probity', casts light upon what Malcolm Muggeridge or L. P. Hartley might call the exceedingly 'permissive' standards of society at the time. Even the bisexually inclined William of Orange had a mistress whom he had to buy off with an Irish estate worth £26,000 a year. She was Elizabeth Villiers, who, Swift told Stella, 'squinted like a dragon'; but she did not suffer,

like Jane Shore, from having been a royal mistress. Her husband,
the Duke of Hamilton, was killed in a duel in 1712, and she survived him by thirty-two years, inviting this tribute from Lord
Landsdowne:

> Villiers, for wisdom and deep judgement famed,
> Of a high race, victorious beauty brings
> To grace our Courts, and captivate our Kings.

Some of the most amusing and revealing accounts of upper-
class prostitution in the eighteenth century are to be found in
Horace Walpole's *Memoirs*. Every king from Charles II to George
II had mistresses; but George III did not. Walpole seems to censure him for this: he was 'unfeeling, insincere, cunning and
trifling'; he 'feared the influence of a mistress and her connections';
he 'had none of the vices that fall under the censure of those who
are past enjoying themselves'. The excesses of his successors are
well known. Apart from his long reign and Anne's much shorter
one, all the monarchs of the period 1660–1837, one spanning
nearly two centuries, had – and, one must hope, enjoyed – mistresses. Almost all George III's ministers, however, more than
made up for his sexual restraint.

One of his potentially most able ministers, the Duke of Grafton
– a descendant of Charles II – suffered from an incapacity to perform his duties owing to his 'weakness for the fair sex and the
turf'. His wife, says Walpole, 'had thought to govern him by
spirit'; but he left her, and 'openly attended his mistress'. This
mistress, Nancy Parsons, 'distinguished by an uncommon degree
of prostitution', was one of the more remarkable women of her
age. She had been, like many successful whores of the seventeenth,
eighteenth and nineteenth centuries, an actress. She once boasted
of having raised one hundred guineas in a week at a guinea a head.
After this, possibly for a rest, she married a Mr Haughton of
Jamaica, who conveniently died. When it became known that
she was Grafton's mistress, she began to be referred to as 'Mrs
Haughton'; before 'she had only been known to the public by
her former name of Nancy Parsons'. The public anticipated, in
fact, that she might soon become the Duchess, since Grafton was

in process of divorcing his wife, but 'it was . . . extraordinary that a woman of her vocation should have sacrificed [this prospect] to a real inclination. . . .' For Nancy, a busy woman, was also the mistress of the Duke of Dorset, and after Grafton had dismissed her with a pension of £400 a year, lived openly with him. Subsequently she married the young Lord Maynard, 'whom she still had charms or art enough to captivate'.

Of course, from Charles II onwards, those who kept mistresses were censured for it when it suited the aims of the censurers: the age never lost consciousness of the existence of the opinion that – as Boswell once put it in his *London Journal* (to which we shall be returning), having just enjoyed a whore – 'in strict morality, illicit love is always wrong'. Even Walpole himself wrote, in a letter of 1749, 'I think . . . flagrancy was never more in fashion'. But when Andrew Marvell, who had served under a Puritan administration, in an anonymous satire of 1674, wrote of Charles,

> He spends all his days
> In running to plays
> When in his shop he should be poring;
> And wastes all his nights
> In his constant delights
> Of revelling, drinking and whoring

he was criticizing him for not attending to his duties rather than for the nature of his amusements. Again, when he wrote (the satire, *The History of the Insipid*, although once attributed to Rochester, is probably Marvell's),

> New upstarts, pimps, bastards, whores,
>   That locust-like devour the land,
> By shutting up th' Exchequer doors
>   When thither our money was trepann'd,
> Have render'd, Charles, thy restoration
> A curse and plague unto the nation

he was complaining about misuse of public money. It took over a century, as we shall see, for Puritan moral indignation to re-assert itself to any practical effect.

This was an age remarkably flagrant, as well as brutal and

corrupt; but it could also be honest. The Victorians could say of
George II that his 'worst vice' was mistresses, and at the same time
keep quiet about the behaviour of the Prince of Wales (later
Edward VII), whom they poker-facedly described as 'much
interested in sport'; George II's own age could never have described his propensity for mistresses as his 'worst' vice. They would
do no more than allow, if pressed, that it was a vice. Walpole
could be quite straightforward: 'His . . . passions were Germany,
the Army and women. Both the latter had a mixture of parade in
his pursuit of them; he kept my lady Suffolk, and afterwards Lady
Yarmouth, as his mistresses, while he admired only the Queen.'

2

It was almost in the exact middle of the eighteenth century
(1748-9) that John Cleland published, in two volumes, his classic
of prostitution, *Fanny Hill*, whose actual title is *Memoirs of a
Woman of Pleasure*. This is a *tour de force* because it studiously
avoids every 'coarse' word, i.e. its author does not titillate himself,
or attempt to appeal to others, through the use of terms that
have become erotically overcharged through repression. The
book was written for money, but although it is in one sense
cynically and satirically pornographic in intention, it is not
characterized by that painful, strained solemnity that pervades
the words of the so-called 'hard-core' pornographers. It got
Cleland into trouble because he made no attempt to keep it
underground: even that age could not tolerate such a straightforward celebration of sexual pleasure. In this light, his eschewal
of 'dirty' words and the ironically 'moral' structure of the book –
Fanny is only 'forced' into prostitution, and eventually marries
the man she loves – are seen to be impertinent, a snook cocked
at the establishment.

Fanny Hill – though not too much should be made of it – is a clever and delightful book, composed with a relaxed skill. When Wayland Young speaks of its 'devious and florid malapropism', he underestimates Cleland's intelligence and misunderstands his intentions. The book is not sick (or devious), but written in a consistently amused state of mind; it correctly gauges the degrees of eighteenth-century sexual hypocrisy, and exploits and satirizes it. It meant much more to the over-repressed nineteenth-century male than it did to anyone of its own century; it sells well, too, in the century of Sir Cyril Black. We tend to consider it only in terms of its sexual content, perhaps because we are continually forced into the false position of defending it against the humourless legal onslaughts of unenlightened officials. The late (celibate) Sir Robert Blundell, Bow Street magistrate, took only a very short time to order its destruction within the area of his jurisdiction; this act doubtless meant a good deal to him – but neither it nor the elaborate defence put forward by the publishers, with the help of many witnesses, had much to do with a consideration of the book itself.

Eberhard and Phyllis Kronhausen in *Pornography and the Law** point out that *Fanny Hill* differs in many ways from the kind of straightforward hard-core pornography that became popular in the following century. It is not 'pornographically structured': there are many realistic passages describing sexual acts, but no 'build-up of erotic tension' throughout; there is little exaggeration – one of the writer's aims is to represent sexual contact as it actually occurs, that is, naturalistically; there is no element of fantasy, such as almost inevitably characterizes purely pornographic works.

'Hard-core' pornography has its origins in the seventeenth century, and its development from then until the nineteenth century has been in an anti-literary, anti-realistic direction. It was given its real impetus in the eighteenth century by the rise of that middle-class morality which in due course came to characterize the public society of the Victorians. Written by men for men, pornography caters mainly for the unimaginative. Its basic feature, as has frequently been pointed out, is its 'circularity', its

* Revised edition, New English Library, London, 1967.

inability to lead to any real conclusion: its action may be defined as 'impossibility', both because sexual organs are personified, and because the pretence of total gratification is maintained in situations that do not allow of this. If anything is diametrically opposed to natural history then it is pornography.

Wayland Young calls *Fanny Hill* 'eighty per cent' pornographic; Steven Marcus in *The Other Victorians** says it 'is of course a pornographic novel'. Now although both Young and Marcus (particularly) are consistently more scholarly and critically more acute than the Kronhausens, I am inclined to agree, here, with the latter writers in their assertion that *Fanny Hill* cannot ultimately be classed as truly pornographic. We can call it pornographic only if we apply this term to all sexually stimulating writing; but a book cannot be described as pornographic simply on the grounds that it gives men an erection when they read it. However, in their enthusiasm about its 'realism', the Kronhausens miss its subtlety and its irony, and quite fail to consider the context in which it was written.

I have already pointed out that although the eighteenth century was, in Walpole's word, an age of 'flagrancy', some lip-service was paid, even by libertines, to the notions of 'morality' and 'decency' – not in the sense of how human beings treat one another, but in an exclusively sexual sense. In the eighteenth century a society that for centuries had been directed by tradition was in its final efflorescence. With the beginning of an industrial period that would create a type of 'inner-directed' (rather than 'tradition-directed'†) person, there was bound to be an assertion of the values of 'public morality'.

Furthermore, the moral movement we think of as 'Victorianism' actually had its origins in the period just after the Revolution of 1688. The Society for the Reformation of Manners was founded in London in as early as 1692, and it achieved some success in enforcing certain sumptuary laws that had fallen into disuse, including ones against whores. Quite solidly supported by wealthy

---

* Weidenfeld & Nicolson, London, 1966; paperback edition, Corgi Books, London, 1969.

† These terms are, of course, those of the American sociologist David Riesmann, from his book *The Lonely Crowd*, Yale University Press, 1950.

people of the middle classes, it is significant that the society did not dare to publish the names of its members. This society, and its many imitators that soon sprang up throughout Great Britain, could of course achieve only very limited successes, and these exclusively amongst people who were poorer than themselves. They were denounced by such writers as Swift and Defoe, and their members described as hypocrites, which a number of them probably were. Defoe thought that their efforts were 'as futile as preaching the Gospel to a kettle-drum'. But the influence of such thinking, whether it was hypocritical or not, was considerable. Thus the bookseller Edmund Curll, Pope's enemy and dupe, was prosecuted by the Attorney-General and convicted, for publishing a book called *Venus in a Cloyster*. Sir Philip Yorke, Baron of Hardwicke, who was the Attorney-General at the time, based his case on the premise that any work that tended to corrupt the morals of His Majesty's subjects constituted an obscene libel; any act prejudicial to morals was also a breach of the peace. (Hardwicke, incidentally, was described by Walpole, with justification, as 'a man of low birth and of lower principles'.)

   Cleland was aware of how far it was possible to go, and so he devised an unimpeachable framework for his book: Fanny, who tells her own story in the form of two long letters, writes as a woman who has 'climbed up again'. Ironically exploiting this 'fact', transparently a device, together with his eschewal of coarse language, Cleland confidently went ahead. His first three paragraphs are worth consideration:

I sit down to give you an undeniable proof of my considering your desires as indispensable orders. Ungracious then as the task may be, I shall recall to view those scandalous stages of my life, out of which I emerg'd, at length, to the enjoyment of every blessing in the power of love, health, and fortune to bestow; whilst yet in the flower of youth, and not too late to employ the leisure afforded me by great ease and affluence, to cultivate an understanding, naturally not a despicable one, and which had, even amidst the whirl of loose pleasures I had been tost in, exerted more observation on the characters and manners of the world than what is common to those of my unhappy profession, who

looking on all thought or reflection as their capital enemy, keep it at
as great a distance as they can, or destroy it without mercy.

Hating, as I mortally do, all long unnecessary prefaces, I shall give
you good quarter in this, and use no further apology than to prepare
you for seeing the loose part of my life, wrote with the same liberty
that I led it.

Truth! stark, naked truth, is the word; and I will not so much as
take the pains to bestow the strip of a gauzewrapper on it, but paint
situations such as they actually rose to me in nature, careless of violating
those laws of decency that were never made for such unreserved intimacies as ours; and you have too much sense, too much knowledge
of the ORIGINALS themselves, to sniff prudishly and out of character
at the PICTURES of them. The greatest men, those of the first and most
leading taste, will not scruple adorning their private closets with nudi-
ties, though, in compliance with vulgar prejudices, they may not think
them decent decorations of the staircase, or saloon.

There can be no doubt of Cleland's irony or intelligence:
Fanny's task is 'ungracious', her whoredom was 'scandalous', an
'unhappy profession'; furthermore, since she is writing to another
woman, she cannot be accused of 'violating' 'the laws of decency'.
In the concluding sentence Cleland smuggles in – in a manner
common to ironists of the time, who adopted a mask or viewpoint
not necessarily their own – a personal observation: hypocrisy is
dismissed as 'vulgar' prejudice. . . .

Cleland was, we may be sure, writing to make money (he
made £21, while his publisher, Fenton, made £10,000); but his
aggressive and satirical effrontery happened to amount to something else. True pornography, written solely to produce prolonged erection followed by masturbation, is utterly humourless.
Humour pervades *Fanny Hill*; it is never solemn. Its central
'theme' is, admittedly, to stimulate sexually. But that is treated as
a joke: in the process of raising the penis it humanizes the mechanical aspect of sex, partly by virtue of the ingenious literacy of the
style and partly by virtue of the author's outlook. As I shall show
in a later chapter, pornography – a male product – usually treats
its female components as prostitutes (although they are never
represented as being prostitutes in the 'story'): these 'females'
are really masculine fantasies, puppets. Fanny is a whore, but she

is also endowed with genuinely feminine characteristics. It is, after all, although it is kept as close an official secret as possible, true that women take as much pleasure from sexual activity as men (actually, in terms of orgasm, they have a capacity for more prolonged pleasure). That so 'unfortunate' a woman as Fanny should have so zestfully enjoyed her work-play doubtless officially offended such men as Lord Hardwicke (if he read the book; he did not die until 1764) even in mid-erection. The notion that women should actually enjoy sex, and have an enjoyment of it with a man, removes one of the most delicious elements of all from the fantasy-objects of the publically censorious, who are frequently sadistic.

No serious reader of fiction will pretend that Fanny is a triumphant feat of characterization, or that *Fanny Hill* is a masterpiece of natural history. But she is not a machine, nor is she the mere sex-object familiar in true pornography. She is consistently represented as possessing emotions. Let us consider part of the famous passage in which Fanny, concealed, watches a couple fucking. She conceals herself in a closet, while the no longer young madam of the brothel in which she is employed prepares to entertain a young man:

Oh! how still and hush did I keep at my stand, lest any noise should baulk my curiosity, or bring Madam into the closet!

But I had not much reason to fear either, for she was so entirely taken up with her present great concern, that she had no sense of attention to spare to anything else.

Droll was it to see that clumsy fat figure of hers flop down on the foot of the bed, opposite to the closet-door, so that I had a full front-view of all her charms.

Her paramour sat down by her: he seemed to be a man of very few words, and a great stomach; for proceeding instantly to essentials, he gave her some hearty smacks, and thrusting his hands into her breasts, disengag'd them from her stays, in scorn of whose confinement they broke loose, and swagged down, navel-low at least. A more enormous pair did my eyes never behold, nor of a worse colour, flagging-soft, and most lovingly contiguous: yet such as they were, this neck-beef eater seem'd to paw them with a most uninvitable lust, seeking in vain to confine or cover one of them with a hand scarce less than a shoulder of mutton. After toying with them thus some time, as if they had been worth it, he laid her down pretty briskly, and canting up her petticoats, made barely a mask of them to her broad red face, that blush'd with nothing but brandy.

As he stood on one side, for a minute or so, unbuttoning his waist-coat and breeches, her fat brawny thighs hung down, and the whole greasy landscape lay fairly open to my view; a wide open-mouth'd gap, overshaded with a grizzly bush, seemed held out like a beggar's wallet for its provision.

But I soon had my eyes called off by a more striking object, that entirely engross'd them.

Her sturdy stallion had now unbutton'd, and produced naked, stiff, and erect, that wonderful machine, which I had never seen before, and which, for the interest my own seat of pleasure began to take furiously in it, I star'd at with all the eyes I had: however, my senses were too much flurried, too much concentred in that now burning spot of mine, to observe anything more than in general the make and turn of that instrument, from which the instinct of nature, yet more than all I had heard of it, now strongly informed me I was to expect that supreme pleasure which she had placed in the meeting of those parts so admir-ably fitted for each other.

Fanny then goes off to masturbate.

It will be noted that at the beginning of the quoted extract a short paragraph is devoted to a description of Fanny's incidental (non-sexual) emotion: her fear of discovery. This never happens in true pornography, in which the writer is totally unaware of any non-sexual aspect of his protagonists. Such asides as this show that Cleland had a real woman in his mind as he wrote, even if he is not very interested in her characteristics: he is not, like the pornographer, enacting a sexual fantasy; a controlling intelligence is always at work.

The description of the preliminaries to the actual act is not pornographic, but comic. The Kronhausens rightly call it 'anti-erotic' in conventional pornographic terms. Fanny finds the fat, clumsy figure of 'the venerable mother Abbess', with her great pendulous breasts, 'wide open-mouth'd gap' and 'grizzly bush', more comic than anything else; the pornographer can never afford to be amused in this way, for the centre of his attention is invariably the personified, utterly unridiculous, solemnized erect penis or direly threatened cunt.

However, Fanny is sexually excited when the 'sturdy stallion ... unbutton'd', for she has never seen a prick – let alone a stiff one – before. Nevertheless, while Cleland's account does proper psychological justice to this excitement, and never seeks to dehumanize it, it remains comic with regard to the old woman – just as comic, but no more, as it might properly be were it concerned with her greed or some other non-sexual gratification. It has been suggested that the passage is not realistic, but deliberately pornographic, because women are not aroused by watching sexual acts, and would not in any case be led to masturbation. This is not true of all women, however – in fact, it is true of rather less women than some men would like to think. Kinsey reported that very few women indeed admitted to pleasure from witnessing sexual acts; but he did not confine his enquiries to young virgins achingly curious about sex, and eagerly awaiting to experience it. . . .

However, it is no part of my case to suggest that Cleland is not seeking to arouse his readers sexually: of course he is – and why not? Nevertheless, he is doing it in an unusual way: it is as if he were continually saying, 'This is really pornographic isn't it? You aren't fooled by my bluff about "naked truth", are you? But have you seen what else I am doing? Observing female psychology; ironically representing the whore who is my subject as a putative human being – which is what you devourers of pornography don't want; and showing that sex isn't really dirty by using "clean" words to describe it . . . ; laughing at our strained attitude to sexual pleasure, releasing tension, by being relaxed.'

One must not, though, make too much of this frolic with language, in which the florid and devious prose of the period is mischievously parodied by being applied in an unexpectedly direct way to the subject of sexual pleasure. Fanny's character is in no sense developed. We see her as a human being only incidentally – because Cleland himself could not help seeing her as one. *Fanny Hill*, like *opera seria*, is made up of detachable 'numbers' – in its case erotic numbers. Naturally, there is something of everything: straight fucking, homosexuality, flagellation, hair-fetishism, and so on. But the psychology is always good, and the attitude is sympathetic. Nothing is more sensitive than the flagellation episode, although it is certainly pornographic about Fanny's sensations upon being birched.

Fanny has just birched Mr Barville, who cannot get an erection or an orgasm unless he is treated in this way. Now it is her turn:

All my back parts, naked half-way up, were now fully at his mercy: and first, he stood at a convenient distance, delighting himself with a gloating survey of the attitude I lay in, and of all the secret stores I thus expos'd to him in fair display. Then, springing eagerly towards me, he cover'd all those naked parts with a fond profusion of kisses; and now, taking hold of the rod, rather wanton'd with me, in gentle inflictions on those tender trembling masses of my flesh behind, than in any way hurt them, till by degrees, he began to tingle them with smarter lashes, so as to provoke a red colour into them, which I knew, as well by the flagrant glow I felt there, as by his telling me, they now emulated the native roses of my other cheeks. When he had thus amus'd himself with admiring, and toying with them, he went on to strike harder, and more hard; so that I needed all my patience not to cry out, or complain at least. At last, he twigg'd me so smartly as to fetch blood in more than one lash: at sight of which he flung down the rod, flew to me, kissed away the starting drops, and, sucking the wounds, eased a good deal of my pain. But now raising me on my knees, and making me kneel with them straddling wide, that tender part of me, naturally the province of pleasure, not of pain, came in for its share of suffering: for now, eyeing it wistfully, he directed the rod so that the sharp ends of the twigs lighted there, so sensibly, that I could not help wincing, and writhing my limbs with pain; so that my contortions of body must necessarily throw it into infinite variety of postures and points of view, fit to feast the luxury of the eye. But still I bore everything without crying out: when presently, giving me another pause, he rush'd, as it were, on that part whose lips, and round-about, had felt this cruelty, and by way of reparation, glues his own to them; then he opened, shut, squeez'd them, pluck'd softly the over-growing moss, and all this in a style of wild passionate rapture and enthusiasm, that express'd excess of pleasure; till, betaking himself to the rod again, encourag'd by my passiveness and infuriated with this strange taste of delight, he made my poor posteriors pay for the ungovernableness of it; for now showing them no quarter, the traitor cut me so that I wanted but little of fainting away, when he gave over. And yet I did not utter one groan, or make any angry expostulation; but in heart I resolv'd never to expose myself again to the like severities.

This is remarkable for its sympathy and accuracy, and for its emphasis on the natural chivalry of Fanny, who is clearly not herself sexually stimulated by flagellation, although she becomes excited afterwards. If no criticism is made of Mr Barville's predilection, neither – as we see from a later paragraph – is it praised; it is simply observed.

Fanny Hill is an anti-moralistic novel, concerned with sexual pleasure as an end in itself, and not with the psychology of prostitution. It is highly realistic in its treatment of sexual details – such as semen; therefore it never seeks to invest such details with a 'filthy' appeal. Run-of-the-mill pornography avidly seizes upon such facts as, for example, semen deposited on clothes or thighs, because they are officially regarded as 'beastly'. Cleland is absolutely relaxed about them.

But by laughing at sex, and representing a whore as a human being who enjoyed her work, *Fanny Hill* cleverly challenged the official line – as represented by Hardwicke – on prostitution. It is a playful and generally liberating book, which should be given to young people to read as soon as they show an interest in sex. Had it been dreary, sad or 'naughty', like the vast mass of pornographic literature circulated since its time, it would not have survived. That it has done so is a tribute to its vitality and its humanity – as well as to its capacity to produce oddly unguilty erections.

One more feature of *Fanny Hill* remains to be considered, and this is its relationship to Richardson's *Pamela, or Virtue Rewarded*, published in 1740 but dated 1741, and to the same author's *Clarissa* (1748–7). Both these novels are in letter-form, and the heroines of both are the opposite of Fanny in that they are possessed of absolute sexual virtue – that is to say, they are abstractions arising from eighteenth-century middle-class neuroses, and not real. Richardson, as has often been pointed out, is obliquely pornographic because of his technique of 'procrastinated rape'; he is of course a much more important writer than Cleland – but

this is because his characters, particularly Mr B. of *Pamela* and
the rake Lovelace of *Clarissa*, arose directly from his unconscious-
ness. (There is nothing of Cleland's unconscious in *Fanny Hill*,
which is as contrived a book as any in the language.) The passage
describing the prostitutes round the bed of the dying bawd Mrs
Sinclair, from *Clarissa*, has been quoted by Walter Allen, in his
The English Novel, as an apt illustration of Richardson's power:

The other seven seemed to have been just up, risen perhaps from
their customers in the fore house, and their nocturnal orgies, with faces,
three or four of them, that had run, the paint lying in streaky seams
not half blowzed off, discovering coarse wrinkled skins: the hair of
some of them of divers colours, obliged to the blacklead comb where
black was affected; the artificial jet, however, yielding place to the
natural brindle: that of others plastered with oil and powder; the oil
predominating: but every one's hanging about her ears and neck in
broken curls or ragged ends; and each at my entrance taken with one
motion, stroking their matted locks with both hands under their coifs,
mobs, or pinners, every one of which was awry. They were all slip-
shoed; stockingless some; only under-petticoated all; their gowns,
made to cover straddling hoops, hanging trollopy, and tangling about
their heels; but hastily wrapped round them as soon as I came in. And
half of them (unpadded, shoulder-bent, pallid-lipped, limber-jointed
wretches) appearing, from a blooming nineteen or twenty perhaps
over night, haggard well-worn strumpets of thirty-eight or forty.

This is incomparably more powerful and authentic (although
Cleland supposedly had more acquaintance with the insides of
brothels than the worthier Richardson: Richardson's novels were
his substitutes for brothel-visits) than anything in *Fanny Hill* or,
indeed, in Cleland's other rather weak novel, *Memoirs of a Cox-
comb* (1751). Cleland is certainly realistic, but only humorously
and casually so. Richardson's description emphasizes an aspect of
prostitution that Cleland never really touches: the ugliness,
squalor and degradation which are so frequently its environment.

Nevertheless, Cleland was not unintelligent to parody the
overtly simplistic notion of virtue that Richardson had put forward in *Pamela*. Richardson was a good novelist in spite of himself; Cleland was cleverer.

There is a considerable paradox involved in comparing the authenticity of *Fanny Hill* and *Clarissa* as truthful portraits of prostitution. (In *Clarissa*, Lovelace carries Clarissa off to a brothel; after several attempts on her virtue, he eventually rapes her while she is drugged; she still refuses to marry him, and in due course wastes away and dies.) Cleland, the believer in sexual pleasure, presents a less authentic picture; Richardson, who gets (and conveys) a more oblique sexual pleasure by taking up a moral attitude, and exaggerating the virtues of virtue, is nearer to the generally sordid truth. But Cleland's book is really a plea for sexual delight cast in the form of a whore's memoirs: as a polemicist he is more enlightened, but as a novelist less interesting because so unconfused. Had society operated in accordance with Cleland's values his own wilfully idyllic picture of prostitution might have been a truer one; Richardson's conscious values helped to perpetuate the misery and the squalor he so well describes. And, even if Richardson is the more rewarding as well as the more influential novelist – which he very clearly is – then it must also be allowed that he is infinitely the more obscene one. Cleland, his tricks with language apart, is infinitely more straightforward. Richardson did not know what Defoe had known and ironically stated about Moll Flanders:

[that though] the moral 'tis hoped will keep the reader serious . . . there cannot be the same brightness and beauty, in relating the penitent part as is in the criminal part. . . . It is too true that the difference lies not in the real worth of the subject so much as in the gust and palate of the reader.

Richardson's own gust and palate, and those of the third-rate ladies who worshipped him, gained special powers because their precise natures remained hidden from the sight of their possessors. The famous sadistic passage in *Pamela* when Mr B. is trying to get Pamela's private papers (and for 'private papers' read, of course, 'private parts' – all the more thrilling for being wrapped up in 'virtue'), which she has stitched into her underclothes, gains all its snide pornographic power from the fact that Richardson did not know what he was doing. We can see just how salacious

Richardson is from another passage: his description of Clarissa's appearance, contained in a letter by Lovelace:

Her morning-gown was a pale primrose-coloured paduasoy; the cuffs and robings curiously embroidered by the fingers of this ever-charming Arachne, in a running pattern of violets and their leaves; the light in the flowers silver; gold in the leaves. A pair of diamond snaps in her ears. A white handkerchief wrought by the same inimitable fingers, concealed – O Belford! what still more inimitable beauties did it not conceal! – And I saw, all the way we rode, the bounding heart (by its throbbing motions I saw it!) dancing beneath the charming umbrage.

Her ruffles were the same as her mob. Her apron a flowered lawn. Her coat white satin, quilted: blue satin her shoes, braided with the same colour, without lace; for what need has the prettiest foot in the world of ornament? Neat buckles in them: and on her charming arms a pair of black velvet glovelike muffs, of her own invention; for she makes and gives fashion as she pleases. – Her hands velvet of themselves, thus uncovered the freer to be grasped by those of her adorer. . . .

Thou hast often heard me launch out in praise of her complexion. I never beheld in my life a skin so illustriously fair. The lily and the driven snow it is nonsense to talk of: her lawn and her laces one might indeed compare to those: but what a whited wall would a woman appear to be, who had a complexion which would justify such un-natural comparisons? But this lady is all glowing, all charming flesh and blood; yet so clear, that every meandering vein is to be seen, in all the lovely parts of her which custom permits to be visible.

Thou hast heard me also describe the wavy ringlets of her shiny hair, needing neither art nor powder; of itself an ornament, defying all other ornaments; wantoning in and about a neck that is beautiful beyond description.

Her head-dress as a Brussels-lace mob, peculiarly adapted to the charming air and turn of her features. A sky-blue riband illustrated that. But, although the weather was somewhat sharp, she had not on either hat or hood. . . .

Without pretending, then, that the quality of Cleland's creative imagination was in any sense equal to Richardson's, one may still admire the comparative honesty of his prose as judged from a polemical or sociological viewpoint. Cleland could hardly have

been parodying the particular passage quoted above (it was published in the same year as the first part of *Fanny Hill*); but we can
easily see how Richardson's sentimental obscenity (in *Pamela* at
least) affected him, and how he has deliberately mocked it in
his prose style. One must remember that *Pamela* was in its day
universally talked of; church bells were rung to celebrate the
heroine's escape from threatened chastity into sexually satisfied
marriage. . . . Sex is not dispensed with, but is tamed and made
captive by 'marriage'; the triumph achieved by the book is a
testament to the developing strength of bourgeois values in its
century.

Coleridge, who admired Richardson's work, rightly called
him 'vile . . . oozy . . . hypocritical, praise-mad, canting, envious,
concupiscent!'; quoting this well-known judgement, Lionel
Stevenson in his *The English Novel* continues: 'It was this side
of . . . Richardson that degenerated into the sewage of John
Cleland . . .'. But what Stevenson calls 'sewage' is, alas, no more
than straightforward sexual pleasure. Cleland was quite certain
that it is not sewage, and his novel remains a persuasive argument
for his point of view.

3

It is difficult to dislike James Boswell, especially since the publication of his transparently honest journals, with their details of his
sexual wanderings. During his first stay in London, recorded in
his *London Journal 1762–1763*,★ Boswell lodged in Downing
Street. Near by was St James's Park, the gates of which were
locked at night – but 6,500 people had official keys, and there
were many more unofficial ones. Here he looked for pleasure.
On 11 December 1762 he had breakfasted with James Mac-
Pherson, then at the height of his fame as the 'translator' of

★ Heinemann, London, 1950.

Fingal; he seems to have taken comfort from the Scottish forger's philosophy of love:

He told me that he was very susceptible of tormenting love. But that London was the best place in the world to cure it. 'In the country,' said he, 'we see a beautiful woman; we conceive an idea that it would be heaven to be in her arms. We think that impossible almost for us to attain. We sigh. We are dejected. Whereas here we behold as fine women as ever were created. Are we fond of one of them? For a guinea we get the full enjoyment of her, and when that is over we find that it is not so amazing a matter as we fancied. Indeed, after a moderate share of the pleasures of London, a man has a much better chance to make a rational unprejudiced marriage.'

This is the way Boswell, as well as MacPherson, thought, and it is characteristic of the enlightened later eighteenth century, which on the whole rejected the tensions generated by love, though not the more easily and quickly relieved ones of lust. A case might even be made for asserting that eighteenth-century men dissolved their romantic proclivities in lust: it is certainly true of Boswell, and Boswell was in most ways typical of his age. And of course, all that is wrong – if it is wrong – with a 'rational un-prejudiced marriage' is that it is not a marriage based on romantic ideals. Eighteenth-century 'passion' was not unlike eighteenth-century beauty: its 'wildness' was severely and reassuringly lim-ited. Boswell said of MacPherson that he had 'strong and nice' feelings, and was thus 'easily made miserable or happy'. 'But then' (Boswell quotes MacPherson himself as saying) 'nothing will make me either happy or the reverse above a day. It is hard that we tire of everything.' But MacPherson and Boswell did not seriously regret or find 'hard' their emotionally superficial sexuality. Boswell, in his *London Journal* a true naïf (he was only twenty-two when he wrote it), was also curious and shrewd. To a certain extent he turned his curiosity on himself and his own often extravagant behaviour, although his self-analysis stopped short at the point when it might have caused him serious disturb-ance. Typical are his reflections of the same day as that upon which he breakfasted with MacPherson: he is 'pushing' to get into the Guards, but if he fails or even if he is 'cut off':

GOD is good; He will take care of me. O happy situation of mind which I now have! All things look well. I hope I shall be very happy. Let my mind be never so much distempered, I have devotion towards GOD and benevolence towards mankind. I have an honest mind and a warm friendship. Upon my soul, not a bad specimen of a man. However my particular notions may alter, I always preserve those great and worthy qualities.

Curiously, we are inclined to agree, upon our souls – not a bad specimen of a man. He was concerned to be 'nice', in the peculiarly eighteenth-century sense of that word, and always to be 'nicely' 'strong' when being 'strong' at all. It did not take very much to keep Boswell happy in God's goodness; and so, on that evening, he sat 'calm and indulgent', with a fire in both his upstairs rooms, drinking tea by himself 'for a long time'. Then he had his feet washed with 'milk-warm water', had his bed warmed, 'and went to sleep soft and contented'.

On the Tuesday (14 December) Boswell is 'very curious' to note that he has been 'in London several weeks without ever enjoying the delightful sex'. Actually, he had come very near to it on the previous 24 November, when he records:

I picked up a girl in the Strand; went into a court with intention to enjoy her in armour [i.e. a linen sheath, in order to protect himself from pox or clap – not the girl from pregnancy]. But she had none. I toyed with her. She wondered at my size, and said if I ever took a girl's maidenhead, I would make her squeak. I gave her a shilling, and had command enough of myself to go without touching her. I afterwards trembled at the danger I had escaped.

Now, however, Boswell was getting very impatient for some kind of a lady – if possible, not a 'free-hearted' one. He was, he said, surrounded with numbers of these,

. . . from the splendid Madam at fifty guineas a night, down to the civil nymph with white-thread stockings who tramps along the Strand and will resign her engaging person to your honour for a pint of wine and a shilling.

This is interesting about eighteenth-century prices. The modern equivalent of 1s. and a pint of wine was, until Butler's Act put whores off the streets and out of the parks, 10s. and a glass of Guinness (if the girl was lucky) – so, taking into account the change in the value of money, the modern Hyde Park girl was doing rather less well than her eighteenth-century counterpart. But this was the price asked by whores of the lowest rank. The 'models' of Soho, up whose stairs the client walks, may nowadays ask anything from 30s. to £3 or £4, depending on the way business has been going and, sometimes, whether they like the man. The ordinary as opposed to the highly exclusive whore has usually charged an economic rate for the job, and its value in terms of its relationship to the income of the client has remained fairly constant.

Boswell would have quickly yielded to his impulses, in spite of his opinion that 'there cannot be higher felicity on earth enjoyed by man than the participation of genuine reciprocal amorous affection with an amiable women', but – as he said – 'the surgeons' fees in this city come very high' (he had been clapped previously). He was thus more easily enabled to write that he really could not 'think of stooping so far as to make a most intimate companion of a grovelling-minded, ill-bred, worthless creature, nor can my delicacy be pleased with the gross voluptuousness of the stews'.

Only in his honesty with himself was Boswell an atypical client. When in his fine and prophylactic 'delicacy' he told himself that he was 'walking about . . . in search of a woman worthy' of his love, he meant that he was looking for an altogether 'nicer' as well as safer lay than he would have been likely to get in St James's Park. If he had to be 'a single man for the whole winter', he would be happy because he had had so much elegant pleasure. 'However', he continues,

I hope to be more successful. In this view, I had now called several times for a handsome actress of Covent Garden Theatre, whom I was a little acquainted with, and whom I shall distinguish in this my journal by the name of LOUISA [all we know of her apart from what Boswell tells us is that her name was Mrs Lewis, and that she played in two Shakespeare plays at Covent Garden in the autumn of 1762]. This lady had been indisposed . . . but today I was admitted. She was in a

pleasing undress and looked very pretty. . . . We were not easy –
there was a constraint upon us – we did not sit straight on our chairs,
and we were unwilling to look at one another. . . .

Nevertheless, she asked Boswell to call upon her again, 'without ceremony', on the following Thursday; he recorded that he
'left her, very satisfied' with his first visit. There is no doubt that
this young man wanted not only sex but also romantic elegance.
Not for him a grovelling creature with whose voluptuousness
his delicacy could not be pleased.

But what kind of woman was Louisa? The not seldom quite
foolish young Boswell seems to have had an inkling as early as that
following Thursday. He speaks of her 'pretty fine artful speech'.
But he wanted her (or sex in the form of her) rather urgently;
however, his form of urgency, if one may say so with admiration
rather than offensiveness, was somewhat Scottish in its post-
poning, not to say self-disciplined, shrewdness:

In the afternoon I went to Louisa's. A little black young fellow, her
brother, came in. I could have wished him at the Bay of Honduras.
However, I found him a good quiet obliging being who gave us no
disturbance. She talked on a man's liking a woman's company, and
of the injustice people treated them with in suspecting anything bad.
This was a fine artful pretty speech. We talked of French manners,
and how they studied to make one another happy. 'The English,' said
I, 'accuse them of being false, because they misunderstand them. When
a Frenchman makes warm professions of regard, he does it only to
please you for the time. It is words of course. There is no more of it.
But the English, who are cold and phlegmatic in their address, take all
these fine speeches in earnest, and are confounded to find them otherwise, and exclaim against the perfidious Gaul most unjustly. For when
Frenchmen put a thing home seriously and vow fidelity, they have the
strictest honour. O they are the people who enjoy time; so lively,
pleasant, and gay. You never hear of madness or self-murder among
them. Heat of fancy evaporates in fine brisk clear vapour with them,
but amongst the English often falls heavy upon the brain.'

We chatted pretty easily. We talked of love as a thing that could not
be controlled by reason, as a fine passion. I could not clearly discern
how she meant to behave to me. She told me that a gentleman had
come to her and offered her £50, but that her brother knocked at the

door and the man ran out of the house without saying a word. I said I
wished he had left his money. We joked much about the £50. I said
I expected some night to be surprised with such an offer from some
decent elderly gentlewomen. I made just a comic parody to her story.

We may reasonably suspect, as Boswell did, the 'little black
young' 'brother'.

By the next day Boswell's urgency had become a little less
native:

I engaged in this amour just with a view of convenient pleasure but
the god of pleasing anguish now seriously seized my breast. I felt the
fine delirium of love. I waited on Louisa at one, found her alone, told
her that her goodness in hoping to see me soon had brought me back:
that it appeared long to me since I saw her. I was a little bashful. However, I took a good heart and talked with ease and dignity. 'I hope,
Madam, you are at present a single woman.' 'Yes, sir.' 'And your
affections are not engaged?' 'They are not, Sir.' 'But this is leading me
into a strange confession. I assure you, Madam, my affections are
engaged.' 'Are they, Sir?' 'Yes, Madam, they are engaged to you.'
(She looked soft and beautiful.) 'I hope we shall be better acquainted
and like one another better.' 'Come, Sir, let us talk no more of that
now.' 'No, Madam, I will not. It is like giving the book in the preface.'
'Just so, Sir, telling in the preface what should be in the middle of
the book.' (I think such conversations are best written in the dialogue
way.) 'Madam, I was very happy to find you. From the first time that
I saw you, I admired you.' 'O, Sir.' 'I did, indeed. What I like beyond
everything is an agreeable female companion, where I can be at home
and have tea and genteel conversation. I was quite happy to be here.'
'Sir, you are welcome here as often as you please. Every evening, if
you please.' 'Madam I am infinitely obliged to you.'

On the Saturday he of course again went to Louisa's:

I talked on love very freely. 'Madam,' said I, 'I can never think of
having a connection with women that I don't love.' 'That, Sir,' said
she, 'is only having a satisfaction in common with the brutes. But when
there is a union of minds, that is indeed estimable. But don't think
Sir, that I am a Platonist. I am not indeed.' (This hint gave me courage.)
... (I thought it honest and proper to let her know that she must
not depend on me for giving her much money.) 'Madam,' said I,

'don't think too highly of me. Nor give me the respect which men of great fortune get by custom. I am here upon a very moderate allowance. I am upon honour to make it serve me, and I am obliged to live with great economy.' She received this very well.

It is by now clear that Boswell, like so many men before and after him, was trying to have it both ways, and at the same time preserve his money. Love is one thing, money another, as Boswell began to discover on Monday, 20 December:

I went to Louisa's after breakfast. 'Indeed,' said I, 'it was hard upon me to leave you so soon yesterday. I am quite happy in your company.' 'Sir,' she said, 'you are very obliging. But,' said she, 'I am in bad humour this morning. There was a person who professed the greatest friendship for me; I now applied for their assistance, but was shifted. It was such a trifle that I am sure they could have granted it. So I have been railing against my fellow-creatures.' 'Nay, dear Madam, don't abuse them all on account of an individual. But pray what was this favour? Might I know?' (She blushed.) 'Why, Sir, there is a person has sent to me for a trifling debt. I sent back word that it was not convenient for me to let them have it just now, but in six weeks I should pay it.'

I was a little confounded and embarrassed here. I dreaded bringing myself into a scrape. I did not know what she might call a trifling sum. I half-resolved to say no more. However, I thought that she might now be trying my generosity and regard for her, and truly this was the real test. I thought I would see if it was in my power to assist her.

'Pray, Madam, what was the sum?' 'Only two guineas, Sir.' Amazed and pleased, I pulled out my purse. 'Madam,' said I, 'if I can do you any service, you may command me. Two guineas is at present all that I have, but a trifle more. There they are for you. I told you that I had very little, but yet I hope to live. Let us just be honest with one another. Tell me when you are in any little distress, and I will tell you what I can do.' She took the guineas. 'Sir, I am infinitely obliged to you. As soon as it is in my power, I shall return them. Indeed I could not have expected this from you.' Her gratitude warmed my heart. 'Madam! though I have little, yet as far as ten guineas, you may apply to me. I would live upon nothing to serve one that I regarded.'

On the next day he realized that by letting Louisa have 2 guineas he had only 13s. to last him for seventeen days, so he was forced to buy cheese at a cheesemongers, and to eat it with a half-penny roll. He could not dine. However, 'I comforted myself by thinking that I suffered in the service of my Mistress'. At the same time he was 'romantically amused to think' that he was now obliged to his wits. Anticipation even caused him, in the evening, to give 6d. (which he characteristically describes as 'the twenty-sixth part of my little store') to a child gingerbread nut-seller who protested he had been given a farthing for 6d. by a customer. He could not help 'valuing' this 'as a specimen of my own tenderness and willingness to relieve my fellow-creatures'.

This mixture of parsimony, lust and 'nice' romanticism is charming, but it is also revealing. Boswell cannily knew the sort of sexual adventure upon which he had embarked, but for all that he was determined to extract from it the maximum of what he would have called delicacy, elegance and passion. He was walking on eggs in the matter of whether he would eventually be able to purchase Louisa's body, and he even enjoyed this aspect of the affair; but he was not quite prepared to starve. Such mild suffering as he does endure is comfortingly elegant. Louisa was ultimately not real to him as a human being: onto her he determinedly, if always with delicacy, projected a fantasy-image, of what was to him the romanticized beloved he wanted to enjoy. He was remarkably well, if not exactly truthfully, adjusted.

On the following morning he rushed to Louisa's 'in full expectation of consummate bliss', with concomitant fears of impotence. For a time they spoke of religion, Louisa telling him that although she was not a Roman Catholic she liked confession. Then Boswell's 'powers' became 'excited':

'You know, Madam, you said you was not a Platonist. I beg it of you to be so kind. You said you are above the finesse of your sex.' (Be sure always to make a woman better than her sex.) 'I adore you.' 'Nay, dear Sir' (I pressing her to me and kissing her now and then), 'pray be quiet. Such a thing requires time to consider of.' 'Madam, I own this would be very necessary for any man but me. But you must take my character from myself. I am very good-tempered, very honest, and have little money. I should have some reward for my particular honesty.'

However, at this stage Louisa played her cards in this essentially
prostitute-client relationship with more skill than Boswell. While
not actually refusing him, she told him to come back on Friday.
But when he arrived she affected to be 'very unhappy': she was
anxious about what might happen if any 'connection' they might
form were to become known. She had been having 'many dis-
agreeable apprehensions'. And so she continued to work Boswell
up to the necessary pitch. She was not one to give anything away
for nothing. He was forced to go away, this time to call back on
Sunday, and to dine 'in dejection'. On Sunday he failed again;
but this time Louisa told him that if, within a week, he should be
'of the same opinion', 'she would then make me blessed'.

He survived well enough during the next week: he sold his
old laced hat and sharp penknife for 6d., listened to MacPherson
denounce Gray's *Elegy* – 'Hoot! . . . to write panegyrics upon a
parcel of damned rascals that did nething but plough the land
and saw corn' – and called on Louisa a couple of times, but did not
– by agreement – press her.

On the Saturday he sold a suit of old clothes for 11s. and then
called again at Louisa's. He informed her of the consistency of
his feelings and simultaneously made 'a sweet elevation of the
charming petticoat'. Louisa permitted him to embrace her, and
exclaimed 'O Mr Boswell!' Finally she surrendered – but, still
cleverly, not immediately: he was to call after three on the next
day, while her landlady, of whom she was 'most afraid', would be
at church.

At three, having had an early dinner, he hastened to 'his
charmer':

The time of church was almost elapsed when I began to feel that I
was still a man. I fanned the flame by pressing her alabaster breasts and
kissing her delicious lips. I then barred the door of her dining-room,
led her all fluttering into her bedchamber, and was just making a
triumphal entry when we heard her landlady coming up. 'O Fortune
why did it happen thus?' would have been the exclamation of a
roman bard. We were stopped most suddenly and cruelly from the
fruition of each other. She ran out and stopped the landlady from
coming up. Then returned to me in the dining-room. We fell into

each other's arms, sighing and panting, 'O dear, how hard this is.' 'O Madam, see what you can contrive for me.' 'Lord Sir, I am so frightened.'

Louisa, as is now evident, had reduced Boswell to a state of considerable anxiety. In a phrase, she had him where she wanted him. Such fear of impotence and lack of amorous self-confidence in so pawky a man as Boswell is a tribute to her skill. So far, we must remember, she had 2 guineas from him and he had nothing from her.

On Tuesday, 4 January, Boswell went to a good friend, Hayward, who kept the Black Lion, and told him that he had just got married, that he and his wife would stay there until they found lodgings:

In this instance we could not be admitted to any decent house except as man and wife. Indeed, we are so if union of hearts be the principal requisite. We are so, at least for a time. In Scotland it is impossible. We should be married with a vengeance [Boswell thought, not quite accurately, that no more was necessary to establish a legal marriage in Scotland than for a marriageable couple to acknowledge themselves man and wife before two witnesses, e.g. by registering at a hotel as a married couple]. . . . This afternoon I became very low-spirited. . . . I hated all things. . . . I could see nothing in a good light.

Boswell could not take Louisa into an 'indecent' house, of which there were hundreds, and in any case he did not, 'romantically', want to; but while he was content to acknowledge a 'union of hearts', he was deadly afraid of marriage. Few less essentially romantic lovers can have existed. However, frustrated sexual desire combined (probably) with generalized guilt caused him to lapse into melancholy.

On Friday, 7 January, he was told by Louisa that Saturday 'could not be the hoped-for time to bestow perfect felicity' upon him.

'Not,' said she, 'that I have changed my mind. But it cannot be.' In short, I understood that Nature's periodical effects on the human, or more properly female, constitution forbade it. I was a little uneasy at this, though it could not be helped. It kept me longer anxious till my ability was known. I have, together with my vivacity and good-humour, a great anxiety of temper which often renders me uneasy. My grandafther had it in a very strong degree.

By now Louisa had worked Boswell to a pitch were he was probably as anxious about his 'ability' as he was about making his 'triumphal entry' into her. He was in fact put into such a state by Louisa's period (or 'period' – who knows?) that he actually forgot to record on that day that his allowance had been paid to him. He was only able to record this, and his amazement at having forgotten to mention it, on Tuesday, 11 January – by which time Louisa had finally promised to spend the following night with him.

On the Wednesday night he at last had – and enjoyed – her. She was no disappointment to him in this respect. 'Five times was I fairly lost in supreme rapture.' Nevertheless, he could not help 'roving in fancy to the embraces of some other ladies which my lively imagination strongly pictured. I don't know if this was altogether fair.'

The next morning, after parting from Louisa, Boswell was extremely pleased with himself, a state of mind from which he was seldom distant. 'I really conducted this affair with a manliness and prudence that pleased me very much. The whole expense was just eighteen shillings.' But Boswell had forgotten the 2 guineas – and he could not foresee the future. Meanwhile he was toying with a 'Lady Mirabel', perhaps Lady Mary Coke, and quotes the following piece of conversation he had with her:

BOSWELL: You must know, Madam, I run up and down this town just like a wild colt.
LADY MIRABEL: Why, Sir, then, don't you stray into my stable, amongst others?
BOSWELL: Madam, I shall certainly have that pleasure.

On the next Saturday Louisa, true to form, refused 'what I most desired'. On the Sunday he was, however, 'permitted the rites of love with great complacency; yet I felt my passion for Louisa much gone. I felt a degree of coldness for her and I observed an affectation about her which disgusted me.' On the

Monday he had her again, but found his real enthusiasm was over
(because, indeed – although he does not say so – he had her).
It was not until 18 January, however, that he began to flirt with
'Lady Mirabel':

> I then called for Lady Mirabel. She seemed to like me a good deal.
> I was lively, and I looked like the game. As it was my first visit, I was
> very quiet. However, it was agreed that I should visit her often. This
> elated me, as it afforded a fine, snug, and agreeable prospect of gal-
> lantry. Yet I could not think of being unfaithful to Louisa. . . .
> I this day began to feel an unaccountable alarm of unexpected evil:
> a little heat in the members of my body sacred to Cupid, very like a
> symptom of that distemper with which Venus, when cross, takes it
> into her head to plague her votaries. But then I had run no risks. I
> had been with no woman but Louisa; and sure she could not have
> such a thing. Away then with such idle fears, such groundless, uneasy
> apprehensions!

Two days later he 'rose very disconsolate',

> . . . having rested very ill by the poisonous infection raging in my
> veins and anxiety and vexation boiling in my breast. I could scarcely
> credit my own senses. What! thought I, can this beautiful, this sensible,
> and this agreeable woman be so sadly defiled? Can corruption lodge
> beneath so fair a form? Can she who professed delicacy of sentiment
> and sincere regard for me, use me so very basely and so very cruelly?
> No, it is impossible. I have just got a gleet by irritating the parts too
> much with excessive venery. And yet these damned twinges, that scald-
> ing heat, and that deep-tinged loathsome matter are the strongest
> proofs of an infection. But she certainly must think that I would soon
> discover her falsehood. But perhaps she was ignorant of her being ill.
> A pretty conjecture indeed! No, she could not be ignorant. Yes, yes, she
> intended to make the most of me. And now I recollect that the day we
> went to Hayward's, she showed me a bill of thirty shillings about which
> she was in some uneasiness, and no doubt expected that I would pay it.

After getting treatment he went straight to Louisa's:

> With excellent address did I carry on this interview as the following
> scene, I trust, will make appear.
> LOUISA: My dear Sir! I hope you are well today.
> BOSWELL: Excessively well, I thank you. I hope I find you so.

LOUISA: No, really, Sir. I am distressed with a thousand things. (Cunning jade, her circumstances!) I really don't know what to do.

BOSWELL: Do you know that I have been very unhappy since I saw you?

LOUISA: How so, Sir? . . .

BOSWELL: Pray, Madam, in what state of health have you been in for some time?

LOUISA: Sir, you amaze me.

BOSWELL: I have but too strong, too plain reason to doubt of your regard. I have for some days observed the symptoms of disease, but was unwilling to believe you so very ungenerous. But now, Madam, I am thoroughly convinced.

LOUISA: Sir, you have terrified me. I protest I know nothing of the matter.

BOSWELL: Madam, I have had no connection with any woman but you these two months. I was with my surgeon this morning, who declared I had got a strong infection, and that she from whom I had it could not be ignorant of it. Madam, such a thing in this case is worse than from a woman of the town, as from her you may expect it. You have used me very ill. I did not deserve it. You know you said where there was no confidence, there was no breach of trust. But surely I placed some confidence in you. I am sorry that I was mistaken.

LOUISA: Sir, I will confess to you that about three years ago I was very bad. But for these fifteen months I have been quite well. I appeal to God Almighty that I am speaking true; and for these six months I have had to do with no man but yourself.

BOSWELL: But by G–d, Madam, I have been with none but you, and here am I very bad.

LOUISA: Well, Sir, by the same solemn oath I protest that I was ignorant of it.

BOSWELL: Madam, I wish much to believe you. But I own I cannot upon this occasion believe a miracle.

LOUISA: Sir, I cannot say more to you. But you will leave me in the greatest misery. I shall lose your esteem. I shall be hurt in the opinion of everybody, and in my circumstances.

BOSWELL (to himself): What the devil does the confounded jilt mean by being hurt in her circumstances? This is the grossest cunning. But I won't take notice of that at all. – Madam, as to the opinion of everybody, you need not be afraid. I was going to joke and say that I never boast of a lady's *favours*. But I give you my word of honour that you shall not be discovered.

LOUISA: Sir, this is being more generous than I could expect.
BOSWELL: I hope, Madam, you will own that since I have been with
you I have always behaved like a man of honour.
LOUISA: You have indeed, Sir.
BOSWELL: (rising): Madam, your most obedient servant.

During all this conversation I really behaved with a manly com-
posure and polite dignity that could not fail to inspire an awe, and she
was pale as ashes and trembled and faltered. . . . As I was going, said
she, 'I hope, Sir, you will give me leave to inquire after your health.'
'Madam,' said I, archly, 'I fancy it will be needless for some weeks.' . . .
There is scarcely a possibility that she could be innocent of the crime
of horrid imposition. And yet her positive asseverations really stunned
me. She is in all probability a most consummate dissembling whore.

So in a sense Louisa had, at this stage, won; but of course she
did not get the 30s. So her victory was really a Pyrrhic one.
After all, what a professional wants above all is fees. Still, it
doubtless pleased her to think of Boswell's surgeon's bill.

But this is not quite the end of the story: on the morning of
13 February, not yet cured of his clap, Boswell awoke to a conviction that 'the treacherous Louisa deserved to suffer for her
depravity'. He therefore sent her the following letter:

Madam: – My surgeon will soon have a demand upon me of five
guineas for curing the disease which you have given me. I must therefore remind you of the little sum which you had of me some time ago.
You cannot have forgot upon what footing I let you have it. I neither
paid it for prostitution nor *gave* it in charity. It was fairly borrowed, and
you promised to return it. I give you notice that I expect to have it
before Saturday sennight.

I have been very bad, but I scorn to upbraid you. I think it below
me. If you are not rendered callous by a long course of disguised wickedness, I should think the consideration of your deceit and baseness,
your corruption both of body and mind, would be a very severe
punishment. Call not that a misfortune which is the consequence of
your own unworthiness. I desire no mean evasions. I want no letters.
Send the money sealed up. I have nothing more to say to you.

He had some qualms, however, for he confided to himself:

This, I thought, might be a pretty bitter potion to her. Yet I thought to mention the money was not so genteel. However, if I get it (which is not probable), it will be of real service to me; and to such a creature as her a pecuniary punishment will give most pain. Am not I too vindictive? It appears so; but upon better consideration I am only sacrificing at the shrine of Justice; and sure I have chosen a victim that deserves it.

The last mention of Louisa in Boswell's journal is part of the entry for 10 February:

This forenoon a maid from Louisa left a packet for me. It was most carefully sealed up, 'by the hands of attention', but was not addressed to me. I opened it up and found my two guineas returned, without a single word written. I felt a strange kind of mixed confusion. My tender heart relented. I thought I had acted too harshly to her. I imagined she might – perhaps – have been ignorant of her situation. I was so foolish as to think of returning her the money and writing her a letter of atonement. I have too much of what Shakespeare calls 'the milk of human kindness'. I mentioned the thing to Dempster. He said it was just a piece of deep artifice in her. I resolved to think no more on the matter, and was glad that I had come off two guineas better than I expected.

Honours were about even, I suppose, in this most charming of all the non-fictions about whores and their clients. But who was the original owner of the returned 2 guineas? Did he get clap? We may at least safely conclude that he was nothing like as tough a customer as the romantic James Boswell, who can be considered as a prototype for the tough, no-nonsense client. The story of Louisa may begin as a romance, but it soon descends into natural history.

4

While prostitution of all sorts continued to flourish, the public attitude towards it changed considerably. This change took place between about 1790 and 1825, the year of the publication of the *Memoirs of Harriette Wilson*. This was, to its public, a scandalous book: it was also considered to be libellous. But Harriette knew how far she could go, for she was determined on a bestseller (it sold thirty editions in a year): there is not a scrap of 'grossness' in it: it is, that is to say, in no way physically frank or graphic. She set the tone with her first paragraph:

> I shall not say why and how I became, at the age of fifteen, the mistress of the Earl of Craven. Whether it was love, or the severity of my father, the depravity of my own heart, or the winning arts of the noble Lord, which induced me to leave my paternal roof and place myself under his protection, does not now much signify: or if it does, I am not in the humour to gratify curiosity in this matter.

She could not have got away with it if she had been 'in the humour'.

Harriette Dubouchet was one of the children of a Swiss clockmaker, John Dubouchet. She was born in Shepherd Market (at 2 Carrington Street), which made a good beginning. Her father was dreary and poor, and took it out on his children by not allowing them to address him and making them speak amongst themselves in whispers. Two of her sisters became high-class whores, and one of them became Lady Berwick – upon which she cut off her ties with Harriette.

The beginning of Harriette's memoirs gives a pleasing foretaste of their entertainment value. As a writer, she was artless; but she possessed a vigorous, irreverent and emancipated personality, had broken from an intolerable parental yoke at an early age, and had done it alone. She personifies a certain kind of female freedom – she quickly and efficiently took the only road to independence that was available to her, and, being tough, she cashed in on it before it was too late. We can thoroughly admire her. In the *Memoirs* her fresh, bright personality – she was forthright, naturally sceptical about the pretensions of males when in the grip of physical desire, and solidly common-sensical rather than gifted or intelligent – is delightfully expressed through her artlessness:

> I resided on the Marine Parade, at Brighton; and I remember that

Entertaining the client: sixteenth-century houses in Belgium (*above*) and Germany (*British Museum*)

A CHAMPION WIFE.—A LADY FOLLOWS HER HUSBAND INTO A NIGHT-HOUSE, AND TAKES HIM HOME.

JANE SHORE

(*Above*) A champion wife reclaims her husband from a 'night-house', *c.* 1870 (*Mansell Collection*)

(*Left*) Jane Shore penitent, after a drawing by W. S. Lethbridge (*British Museum*)

Lord Craven used to draw cocoa trees, and his fellows, as he called them, on the best vellum paper, for my amusement. Here stood the enemy, he would say; and here, my love, are my fellows: there the cocoa trees, etc. It was, in fact, a dead bore. All these cocoa trees and fellows, at past eleven o'clock at night, would have no peculiar interest for a child like myself, so lately in the habit of retiring early to rest. One night, I recollect, I fell asleep; and, as I often dream, I said, yawning, and half awake, Oh, Lord! oh, Lord! Craven has got me into the West Indies again. In short, I soon found that I had made but a bad speculation by going from my father to Lord Craven. I was even more afraid of the latter than I had been of the former; not that there was any particular harm in the man beyond his cocoa trees; but we never suited nor understood each other.

I was not depraved enough to determine immediately on a new choice, and yet I often thought about it. How, indeed, could I do otherwise, when the Honourable Frederick Lamb was my constant visitor, and talked to me of nothing else? However, in justice to myself, I must declare that the idea of the possibility of deceiving Lord Craven, while I was under his roof, never once entered into my head. Frederick was then very handsome; and certainly tried, with all his soul and with all his strength, to convince me that constancy to Lord Craven was the greatest nonsense in the world. I firmly believe that Frederick Lamb sincerely loved me, and deeply regretted that he had no fortune to invite me to share with him.

Lord Melbourne, his father, was a good man. Not one of your stiff-laced moralizing fathers, who preach chastity and forbearance to their children. Quite the contrary; he congratulated his son on the lucky circumstance of his friend Craven having such a fine girl with him. 'No such thing,' answered Frederick Lamb; 'I am unsuccessful there. Harriette will have nothing to do with me.' – 'Nonsense!' rejoined Melbourne, in great surprise; 'I never heard anything half so ridiculous in all my life. The girl must be mad! She looks mad: I thought so the other day, when I met her galloping about, with her feathers blowing and her thick dark hair about her ears.'*

Harriette's memoirs, in which natural history is modified by a naughty restraint, show that while the demi-monde flourished during the Regency, the 'grosser' details could no longer be

---

* All quotations are from the most recent edition: *Harriette Wilson's Memoirs*, with a Preface by James Laver, Peter Davies, London, 1929.

published. As Maurice Quinlan points out in his important *Victorian Prelude*,★ in 1795 a parson would use the word 'whore' without turning his own or anyone else's hair grey; by 1825 the word had undoubtedly become taboo.† Thus, Quinlan writes, Harriette's 'circumlocutions . . . would have done credit to a lady of quality'; despite its mischievous frankness about the intimacies of high life, it contains no 'grossness' whatever. In place of directness, however, we discover many such delights as this:

Fred Beauclerc [a clergyman] is a sly, shy, odd man, not very communicative, unless one talks about cricket. I remember when the Marquess of Wellesley did me the honour to call on me and tell me what a great man he was, and how much he had been talked of in the world, – how often carried on men's shoulders without nags, with other reminiscences of equal interest, Fred Beauclerc . . . [in jealousy] cut me for Moll Raffles [another tart]. . . .

Many public men figured in Harriette's book, which gave the lie to any respectability to which they might have liked to lay claim, and considerably – and delightfully – undermined their dignity. No wonder there was opposition to the publication. Let us follow, as an example, Harriette's own account of her relationship with the Duke of Wellington. Everyone knows that he said 'publish and be damned!', but not so many are in a position to know the whole story, or to enjoy Harriette's telling of it, for the *Memoirs* have not been reprinted for forty years. Here is how Harriette introduced the Duke, in her third chapter:

I was getting into debt, as well as my sister Amy, when it so came to pass, as I have since heard say, that the – immortal!!! No; that's common; a very outlandish distinction, fitter for a lady in a balloon. The terrific!!! that will do better. I have seen his grace in his cotton night-

---

★ Columbia University Press, 1941.

† Has the wheel come full circle? The Bishop of Southwark, writing of the populist Enoch Powell in the London *Evening Standard* in 1969, referred to the notorious rabble-rousing speech on immigration in terms which included the phrase 'before Enoch let his fart'. Christians may note with some dismay that the relationship of the beliefs of both late eighteenth-century parsons and some modern churchmen to Orthodox Christian teaching (Jesus as the literal Son of God, dying for us, etc.) are exceedingly tenuous: like tradesmen, bishops have to bear customers' tastes in mind if they want to stay in business.

cap. Well, then, the terrific Duke of Wellington!! the wonder of the world!! Having six feet from the tail to the head, and – but there is a certain technicality in the expressions of the gentleman at Exeter 'Change, when he has occasion to show off a wild beast, which it would be vanity in me to presume to imitate; so leaving out his dimensions, etc. etc. it was even the Duke of Wellington, whose laurels, like those of the giant in the *Vicar of Wakefield*, had been hardly earned by the sweat of his little dwarfs' brows, and the loss of their little legs, arms, and eyes; who, feeling himself amorously given. – It was in summer. – One sultry evening, ordered his coachman to set him down at the White Horse Cellar, in Piccadilly, whence he sallied forth, on foot, to No. 2 or 3, in Berkeley Street, and rapped hastily at the door, which was immediately opened by the tawdry, well-rouged housekeeper of Mrs Porter, who, with a significant nod of recognition, led him into her mistress's boudoir, and then hurried away, simpering, to acquaint the good Mrs Porter with the arrival of one of her oldest customers. . . .

The Duke had heard of Harriette, and asked Mrs Porter to procure her for him. Eventually she allowed him to call:

'What shall I say to his grace?' Mrs Porter inquired, growing impatient.

'Well then,' said I, 'since it must be so, tell His Grace that I will receive him to-morrow at three; but mind, only as a common acquaintance!'

Away winged Wellington's Mercury, as an old woman wings it at sixty; and most punctual to my appointment, at three on the following day, Wellington made his appearance. He bowed first, then said, –

'How do you do?' then thanked me for having given him permission to call on me; and then wanted to take hold of my hand.

'Really,' said I, withdrawing my hand, 'for such a renowned hero you have very little to say for yourself.'

'Beautiful creature!' uttered Wellington, 'where is Lorne [whose mistress Harriette currently was]?'

'Good gracious,' said I, out of all patience at his stupidity, – 'what come you here for, Duke?'

'Beautiful eyes, yours!' reiterated Wellington.

'Aye man! they are greater conquerers than ever Wellington shall be; but, to be serious, I understood you came here to try to make yourself agreeable?'

'What, child! do you think that I have nothing better to do than to make speeches to please ladies?' said Wellington.

'*Après avoir dépeuplé la terre, vous devez faire tout pour la repeupler,*' I replied.

'You should see me where I shine,' Wellington observed, laughing.

'Where's that, in God's name?'

'In a field of battle,' answered the hero.

'*Battez-vous, donc, et qu'un autre me fasse la cour!*' said I.

But love scenes, or even love quarrels, seldom tend to amuse the reader, so to be brief, what was a mere man. . . . ! ! ! !

Wellington became a frequent caller, though 'a most unentertaining one, Heaven knows', who in the evenings 'looked very like a rat-catcher'. He never gave reasons 'for any thing unconnected with fighting', she said, 'at least since the convention of Cintra'. When once he told her that he had been thinking of her after he got into bed, she replied (she claimed), 'How very polite to the Duchess'.

When, six years later – during which Wellington had visited Harriette on other occasions – he threatened Stockdale (her publisher) with prosecution if he should publish, she wrote at the end of the memoirs:

There is surely something harsh and unmanly in threatening a woman with any kind of law or prosecution, unless she were to do something much worse than telling the truth: and there is a double want of gallantry in threatening a fair lady, whose favours have been earnestly courted! *N'est-ce pas?*

The man who lays his hand on a woman, save in the way of kindness, is a monster, whom it were gross flattery to call coward.

Now what would this excellent author say to Mr Jack Ketch's hand being laid on one [Wellington had told Stockdale that Harriette ought to be hanged – 'beautiful, adored and adorable me, on whom he has so often hung!' she commented], and that not quite in the way of kindness either? Yet, if all the lords and law-givers are like Wellington, in the habit of threatening poor devils of authors . . . with prosecution, hanging, and destruction, as often as they are about to publish any facts which do not altogether redound to their honour and glory, while they modestly swallow all the *outré* applause which may be bestowed

on their luck or their talents for killing men and winning battles. . . .
There's no spirit nowadays.

Not quite fair, perhaps: Harriette – who had fled to Paris in
order to avoid further prosecution, but who was characteristically
able to use the diplomatic bag for correspondence with her
mother-country – was being deliberately mischievous, and seeking
to enrich herself. But she had used her sexual charms to lift herself
out of misery and poverty, and had consequently subjected herself to the lust of several distinguished men; bearing this in mind,
her *Memoirs* are more naughty than malicious. She was a whore
with spirit, and one of those who has upheld – indeed, demonstrated – the dignity of a too despised profession, of which, for all
her reticence on the subject, she must have been a most skilful
practitioner. Her importance lies in her capacity, light-heartedly
and essentially without malice, to see that official male dignity is
very absurd when contrasted with furtive male lust.

Chapter Eight

1

My Secret Life, which runs very approximately to about 900,000 words, is unique in the literature of prostitution. Being the exclusively sexual autobiography of one man – who had in his own estimation some 1,200 women – it naturally amounts to more than a book about prostitutes and their single prodigious client, 'Walter', as he called himself; but the vast majority of Walter's women were in fact prostitutes of one class or another.

My Secret Life has been seriously discussed only in three places: by G. Legman in his introduction to the huge American edition,* by Steven Marcus in *The Other Victorians* and by the Kronhausens in their necessarily limited (and slightly expurgated) selection from and commentary upon *My Secret Life*.† The book is a mine of information about how prostitution actually operated in Victorian England. It also reflects the attitude of a 'gentleman' to the existence of prostitutes. Regardless of the qualities of Walter or of his autobiography, it is a work that ought to have been come to terms with – and has not.

I do not intend to try to turn Walter into a prototype for all men or even for all clients of prostitutes. But he was 'large', he

* Grove Press, New York, 2 volumes, 1965.   † Polybooks, London, 1967.

did 'contain multitudes'; a description of him is bound to reveal
something of every man's sexuality. The overdue consideration
of Walter has, at any rate in its preliminary stages, nothing to do
with whether we think we ought to like him. *My Secret Life* is,
the American critic Robert Phelps has written, 'the other side
of the Victorian novel, what Meredith and Dickens and George
Eliot and Thomas Hardy were obliged to leave out'.

During the eighties of the last century the author, a gentleman
of means, summoned an Amsterdam printer of erotica to London
to discuss the publication of a limited edition of six copies of his
sexual autobiography. It appeared, undated, in eleven volumes
between about 1888 and 1894. There were supposed to be
only six copies, selling at 1,100 guineas each; but it has been
reasonably conjectured that at least one or two more were clan-
destinely run off by the printer. Only six sets, however, are as
yet known.

My Secret Life is written, for the most part, in a bald but, as
the book progresses, increasingly readable style. Such unfamiliar
and not unintelligent detail about sex is so unusual as to be – to a
person free from the usual inhibitions – readable in itself; but
the book is not readable for this reason alone. When it does
pall, it is because of the sheer accumulated weight of subject-
matter – of penis, balls, cunt, fucking, sperm – not the author's
straightforward style. No one need take any notice of the author's
statement at the beginning of Volume I that the book is not really
by him at all, but is the edited autobiography of a dead friend.
Clearly, however, his claim that the work as printed consists of an
edited version of a sexual diary that he has been writing on and
off (mostly on) for the past forty years is correct. Chronologically
it is confused, and it contains many editorial interpolations, in
square brackets, some of which were written at the time of the
experience recorded and others at the time of preparation for
publication. Some passages reveal as many as five layers of composition. However, though names of people and places, dates
and perhaps countries are false, the whole rings true in the sense
that it is certainly a sincerely attempted description of experience:
it is not fantasy, however much fantasy has unconsciously

entered into recollection. Its general authenticity is agreed upon, I think, by all its critics.

G. Legman suggests that Walter was Henry Spencer Ashbee, author of one of the most useful and meticulous bibliographies of erotica ever made. This is admittedly a guess, based on a tradition; but it has much merit. Marcus, however, although he feels that Walter was not Ashbee, writes:

The author of *My Secret Life* was genuinely, though not entirely, concerned to maintain his identity in secret. To this end he suppresses dates, changes names, alters places, and resorts to other devices; but he does this so haphazardly and with such lack of consistency and thoroughness that it is no problem at all to discover whatever is necessary for dating or placing the incidents he describes. (We can assume the self-evident fact that, if he really wanted to keep everything secret, he would not have printed this work or, for that matter, even written the manuscript.)

Elsewhere Marcus writes that the author's 'efforts at obscurity and obfuscation [are] . . . incomplete and perfunctory; he lives by sexual time'. This is making an unjustified assumption, which typifies, I think, Marcus's consistently intelligent and interesting, but often too over-superior approach. How do we know how clever Walter actually was in the matter of disguising himself? Certainly we have not yet proved who he was – nor are we likely to. That he was (sociologically) a gentleman of culture, with fluctuating but usually substantial means, we know; to establish that was in any case absolutely necessary for even an exclusively sexual autobiography. And we know that the whole book was printed by 1894. But we cannot possibly know whether or not he once, or twice, condensed (say) twenty years' experience into five or ten; or whether when he says that he was about twenty-one at the time the railway line between Paris and Rouen was opened (1843), or that he had a French woman in the year of the Great Exhibition, he was deliberately leaving a false trail. (Ashbee was nine in 1843.) Marcus simply does not question these statements. The Kronhausens, too, accept Walter's remarks about himself in the same naïve spirit. Neither seem to have taken into account the fact that discovery – as the author of a 'filthy' book notorious within a year or two of its publication – would have been quite disastrous. The author could not tell how long he might live.

Marcus regards Walter's sexual drives as 'demonic', and treats him as a model pornographic personality: '*My Secret Life* is the record of a life in which the pornographic, sexual fantasy was acted out'. His essentially hostile analysis of Walter's writings is based upon the classically Freudian conviction that while sexuality must be understood, it must be sublimated, directed into other – non-sexual – channels, if civilized culture is to be preserved.

The attitude of the Kronhausens, on the other hand, is that 'sexuality is . . . a positive, benign life force, capable of enhancing individual happiness . . . and of casting a "civilizing" effect on human relations in general', and they therefore see Walter as a forward-seeing hero, a somewhat bizarre view.

Marcus's Freudian analysis of the book is made manifestly inadequate by his (and our) total ignorance of its author. We just do not know what kind of man Walter was in his 'non-sexual' life, or what kind of effect his 'demonic' sexual drives had upon his non-sexual relationships. We should give a great deal to know – and in some detail; but I doubt if we ever shall. *My Secret Life* is a record of Walter's sexual experience. Any incidental detail from his non-sexual experience that is given in it is just as likely to be untrue – a blind – as to be true. We simply cannot know what kind of a man he was. Marcus's view that Walter's unrestrained sexuality was essentially anti-social and anti-cultural therefore remains unproven. Supposing he was Gladstone, the later Wordsworth, Dickens, the Prince of Wales, or the inventor of the electric light bulb . . . ? Who knows?

A further question: has anyone the right to preserve Marcus's superior aloofness from such material as Walter offers us? This is not to say that, when it comes to some of the experiences Walter had, we would not all like to feel superior. But does anyone know enough – even the Director of Public Prosecutions and his advisors, who in England in February 1969 sent a poor little pornographer to prison for two years for printing some of it – to remain happily aloof?*

* See Alan Watkins, 'A Slight Case of Obscenity', *New Statesman*, 14 February 1969.

2

My Secret Life, as stated by the author at its outset, is not the autobiography of a whole man; rather it is the biography of what he variously describes as his 'prick', 'pego', 'red-tipped erection', 'stiff-stander', 'tooleywag', 'persuader', 'stiff stem', 'red prick tube', 'gristly tube', 'pipe', 'prober', 'sperm spouter', 'sugar-stick', 'water pipe', 'doodle', 'rammer', 'fucking machine', 'swollen gristle', 'male piercer', 'cock', 'male cunt stretcher', 'rod', 'cunt-rammer', 'noble stem', 'spindle', 'roly poly pendant', 'red tipped white stemmed sperm spouter', 'cunt-stopper' – and, rather incongruously, 'penis' (he does not use the Frank Harris term, 'manroot'). Inevitably this biography involves continuous mention of the 'cunts', 'cunt-lips', 'cunt-fringes', 'bellies', 'slippery orifices', 'bumholes', and so on and so on, with which it came into contact. Walter's language is entirely non-euphemistic; he shared the private predilection of many men for using just the terms that 'decent' society forbids. At his millions of orgasms – or 'crises', as he frequently liked to call them – he was fond of shouting 'Cunt! Prick! Fuck! Oho!' or some such similar exclamatory phrase. He experimented in the course of his life with more or less every sexual 'deviation', and generally got some sort of satisfaction out of every one of his experiments; but some practices – mainly those connected with homosexuality and the anus – he indulged in caused him, as he admits, more guilt than others, in spite of his frequently reiterated 'philosophy' that anything done sexually between two people, if it gives them pleasure, is ultimately justified. This philosophy was in fact one enormous rationalization, for it is no exaggeration to say that at least one third of *My Secret Life* is taken up with accounts of how Walter persuaded, bribed or forced women to do his will. It never seems to have occurred to him that some of them may actually have been reluctant to perform sexual acts with him.

His special pleasures varied at different periods of his life, but he was consistently fascinated by, in roughly this order: (a) his own and other men's semen, (b) his own and other men's penises, (c) all vaginas (which throughout his life he examined with great care), (d) women pissing, into pots or on him. Like most men, he was fruitlessly and pointlessly obsessed with the size of his penis in erection; but later in his life he became at least satisfied that his was above average. As any other human being would be in the course of nearly a million words, he was inconsistent: many of his experiences he describes as 'the best' of his life. But one may fairly infer that his greatest 'deviant' pleasure was gained from voyeurism, especially when he was accompanied in this by a female confidante whom he could fondle and subsequently have sexual relations with when what he had seen prompted him to it. His capacity for a number of orgasms within a relatively short period of time was not fantastic (it realistically declined as he got older), but suggests that he suffered (if this is the right term) from a mild form of satyriasis. As a boy he suffered from phimosis, and his penis was always very sensitive. Not unnaturally, in view of the amount of use to which he put it, it tended to give him pain throughout his life. His method of seducing women who were not 'gay' was invariably to show them, at what he considered to be the psychological moment, his 'stiff stander', 'carmine with lust'. Since nearly all his girls were from the lowest and therefore poorest classes, doubtless he mistook their reluctant acquiescence (he is both salacious about and contemptuous of the initial reluctance) for something else; hence one of his epithets for his penis, the 'persuader'. However, we do not encounter anywhere else in literature such single-minded persistence. Walter's selfishness is indeed one of the more repulsive aspects of his account of his sexual self, for when he was in what he called his 'rutting fury' he was quite unable to consider any consequences – pregnancy is the most relevant one – for anyone (except, it may be noted, for himself). However, he invariably assumed that when stupid or merely ignorant resistance to his will had finally been overcome – by brutality, trickery or bribery – then it turned out to be 'a pleasure for her!', as he frequently exclaimed.

He was vain but not inordinately vain: of perhaps two or three of the women he met in his sexual life he could actually say that they did not 'like' him sexually. He could not, however, understand any woman, gay or otherwise, not wanting his 'machine' when he showed it to her. But it seems likely, even making allowances for his persistence and his single-mindedness, that he did possess some kind of 'sexual magnetism' – a capacity to fascinate, physically, more women than most men can hope (if I do not offend Mrs Whitehouse) to fascinate. He spent most of his spare time (we cannot put it any higher than that) going after women, usually but not necessarily prostitutes, and he managed to persuade most of them to accede to his demands.

Take *My Secret Life* as not only a unique adventure in sexual autobiography (Frank Harris's boastful and contrived *My Life and Loves* does not compare to it) but also as a cultivated reaction to an environment that was as deliberate as time and nearly a million words could allow, and we may consider Walter in a different light. He may not have known what it was all about; but at least he left us a detailed record about which we may make conjectures. The achievement may incorporate horrible confessions – such as the rape of children; but when others guilty of the same crimes can bring themselves to confess, let us give them similar recognition, even if we do not praise their actions. We should equally admire a volume of political memoirs that recorded real 'facts', of introspection as well as of diplomacy, if it were offered to us. The life of an average modern politician is certainly as squalid and criminal as Walter's life was. Walter did indeed, as Marcus says, 'act out' what he calls 'the pornographic, sexual fantasy'. We do not, of course, admire (say) Hitler, Stalin or certain infamous modern politicians for 'acting out' even more extensive fantasies. But then none of these persons has left or could afford to leave more than perfunctory records.

3

My Secret Life needs to be submitted to several kinds of analysis, notably what would not fashionably be called a 'structuralist' one, in which the way it is built up – the way the language itself functions – is studied independently of the subject-matter. Walter's immense number of experiences need to be classified; every non-sexual descriptive element in *My Secret Life* (true or false) needs to be isolated and carefully examined. But all this work will take a number of years; no intelligent person would suppose that it should not be done. Meanwhile those who have read it are obliged to concentrate upon certain limited aspects of it; my emphasis, naturally, is upon Walter as client – what evidence is there in his text to help us to determine what drove him to seek the services of so many hundreds of prostitutes?

Some of Walter's early experiences were shared with a cousin, Fred, although the first woman he seduced was a servant employed by his mother. His first prostitute put him off: he feared disease, and 'I . . . looked at her cunt, but my prick refused to stand; her being gay upset me'. But Fred, more experienced, then came into the room with another girl:

One was piddling, Fred pulled her up from the pot, shoved her against the side of the bed, bawling out, 'You get the other,' and pulled out his prick stiff and ready. An electric thrill seemed to go through me at this sight, I pulled the other into the same position by the side of Fred's; then the girls objected, but Fred hoisted up his girl and plunged his prick into her. Mine got on to the bed, leaving me to pull up her clothes. The same fear came over me, and I hesitated; Fred looked and laughed, I pulled up her clothes, saw her cunt; fear vanished, the next moment I was into her, and Fred and I, side by side, were fucking.

All four were fucking away like a mill, then we paused and looked at our pricks, as they alternately were hidden and came into sight from the cunts. Fred put out his hand to my prick, I felt his, but I was coming; my girl said, 'Don't hurry.' It was too late, I spent, laid my head upon her bosom, and opening my eyes, saw Fred in the short shoves. . . .

This account exhibits certain characteristics common to a very large proportion of the whole book. First, there is the detail about a girl 'piddling'. All Walter's girls piddled, inordinately, and he makes no bones about the fact that he loved it. But the thousands of gallons of urine expended in the course of the book by tarts suggest a faulty recollection. Secondly, there is certainly a 'blurred' effect in the reportage, as Marcus charges and as the Kronhausens deny. The writing concentrates upon what interests the author, and omits any real or interested observation of the women involved (the Kronhausens claim that Walter was interested in making women happy; but, as the texture of his writing shows, he is really only interested in making them do what interests him). Thus, Walter pulls up the girl's clothes and 'saw her cunt': this is something he invariably liked to do or try to do before going ahead. Thirdly, the account is coarse – in the sense that there is a marked lack of emotional sensitivity, tenderness of feeling or delicacy. In this sense, Walter is a bad natural historian: he is trying to excite himself, not to observe. Fourthly, and most important, what interests the writer is undoubtedly Fred's and his own prick. He gets his confidence, with an 'electric thrill', only when Fred gets his prick out 'stiff and ready'. Further, the two men are said to have looked at and felt each other's pricks: although they are being 'heterosexual' (or, to be precise, we should say that the writer is representing himself as being heterosexual – for he may have imagined the things he makes Fred do in his narrative), they are clearly represented as being as interested in each other's penises as they are in the girls. This tells us something about Walter both as a compulsive sex-seeker and, perhaps, about why men frequently tend to visit brothels in 'packs' when isolated from their own environment (in the army, on shore in the navy, and so on).

According to his own account, Walter realized quite early on that he enjoyed thinking about, and contact with, other men's sperm.

A few years later Walter joined Fred, 'Lord A***' and three whores for an orgy in a house in London. All three men had all the women; in the morning Walter went to bed with one of the girls, Mabel (in order to sleep), and did not awake until late in the day.

Although I did not like Mabel's behaviour and did not care about her having had the other men . . . yet it annoyed me; but it had the effect of giving me a strong letch for her for some time. I used to think as I fucked her, of my prick rubbing where Fred's and Lord A***s' had rubbed, it delighted me to say, 'Should you know it was my prick if you had just awakened?' – 'Did his hurt you, when he pushed like this?' – Shove, shove, – 'Tell me how Fred goes just before he spends?' We used to fetch each other by talking over that night; but she did not recollect very clearly, and declared she was sure I had not had her, although I certainly had her once that night, and when the spunk of Lord A***'s and Fred's was in her. It used to horrify me when I thought of that, such was my masculine inconsistency then.

Fred, who was a soldier, 'went abroad, and was killed in battle'. 'I loved him' is Walter's simple and significant comment.

Walter was never sure whether sex was 'clean' or not, was in fact obsessed with this problem although he suppressed its existence. Once a whore washed in water he had washed in; 'That's not clean,' he told her. Yet sperm is 'the divine life giver', and

I may say here that on several occasions . . . I have frigged myself over a clean sheet of foolscap paper; it was mostly done for curiosity, to see what my sperm was like. . . .

Sometimes the idea of another man's sperm revolted him – but it nearly always excited him; he was never indifferent to it. Of an occasion when he was viewing a couple's sexual activity through a hole in the wall, he wrote 'His spunk lay thick on the black [pubic] hair [of the woman] tho I could barely see it' – this means simply that he saw what he wanted to see, the 'tho' revealing the degree of his accuracy in such details.

4

It is only according to the Kronhausens' own selection – if in this
– from *My Secret Life* that Walter 'outshines, not only in sexual
performance but also in understanding and sexual knowledge,
all the other great lovers. . . '. It is true that Walter's sexual
knowledge was advanced for his times; but in view of his vast
experience his knowledge of women's sexual response was rather
poor. He needed (rather than wanted) to give pleasure, and so
practically every one of the women he describes himself as going
with 'spent'. The Kronhausens explain it thus:

. . . Walter's women came, for the most part, from the lowest socio-
economic levels of Victorian society. And we know from current
sociological research, that, as a group, women of the lower classes
tend to be less inhibited and sexually more responsive. . . .

Alas, this will not do. The sexual response Walter imagined he
obtained from his women is not credible. It proves him to have
been a bad natural historian in yet another important area of
observation. I agree with the Kronhausens that Marcus makes
too much of the fact that Walter – like all his contemporaries –
believed that women experience an emission at orgasm: there is
every justification for thinking this if one does not happen to
know that it is false. But I agree with Marcus that Walter 'projects a male response' on to his women.

The Kronhausens say that there is no evidence in *My Secret
Life* 'to refute the contention that if Walter did not make this
world a better place . . . he certainly did not make it any worse . . .'.
But Walter did make the world worse for some of the people he
met: the girl he raped, the child of ten whom he took by assault,
the young man whom he prostituted to his sodomitic desires by
the temptation of money, the many girls he impregnated, the
women whose tranquillity he shattered. . . . They had not wanted
Walter. This has nothing to do with sex. You might find a man

The eye of the artist: an etching by Félicien Rops (1833–98) (*British Museum*)

Fame and fortune: the apotheosis of Venetia Stanley, from an engraving after
the portrait by Van Dyck (*British Museum*)

who walked into other peoples' houses and who managed to persuade – by means including lying, bribery, inducement of curiosity, flattery – very many of the inhabitants to allow him to stay for a while. This would not be freedom: true sexual freedom, like any freedom, involves freedom for other people. The Kronhausens' presentation of Walter as a sexually free man is grotesque; and in any case, Walter himself was clearly a slave – more even than most of us are – to his compulsions.

However, Marcus is equally irresponsible in stating that 'a work like *My Secret Life* leads one to understand how the deflection of one's sexuality, how even frigidity itself, could have an important social function or purpose'. This, which is based on the pessimistic premise that 'nature' (instinct) is inexorably opposed to 'culture', evades the issue. Marcus, a vigorous though humorous neo-puritan, insists that 'sexuality' consists of nothing more than bestial, insensitive pleasure-seeking; one feels that he is delighted to have the opportunity to use Walter to illustrate the point – that real sexuality cannot, in other words, be anything but compulsive, indecent, selfish, bestial.

Commenting (rightly) on the 'circularity of form' of one of Walter's statements about how he wants 'to fuck, to be frigged, be sucked, all at once' Marcus writes:

We may assume that all such desires for totality are manifestations of a corresponding insatiability, that such fantasies are connected with one's earliest experiences in life and are at once an effort to reconstitute that early state and to overcome the anguish and frustration that our inevitable frustration from that state brings about. In adult life the author strives to recapture the ecstasy of the infant at the breast and the polymorphous pleasures of childhood. In the middle of the nineteenth century, the author of *My Secret Life* undertook to act out in his own life the project which, only a few years ago, Mr Norman O. Brown suggested was the one hope of salvation for our entire civilization.

This is grossly misleading. Though shocked by Norman O. Brown, Marcus may as well get the thesis of his book, *Life Against Death*,* right. It is true that Brown wants to 'abolish

* Wesleyan University Press, 1959.

repression'. But Walter, with his genital obsessions, is a monument to sexual repression – not to sexual freedom. Brown writes:

In Freudian terms, children are polymorphously perverse. But if infantile sexuality, judged by the standard of normal adult sexuality, is perverse, by the same token normal adult sexuality, judged by the standard of infantile sexuality, is an unnatural restriction of the erotic potentialities of the human body. . . . we accept the subordination of sexual activity to the purpose of reproduction as a natural state of affairs. . . . In man infantile sexuality is repressed and never outgrown. . . . The result is that genital organization is a tyranny in man because his peculiar infancy has left him with a lifelong allegiance (i.e. fixation) to the pattern of infantile sexuality.

Walter's account of his sexual life with whores is important because it is certainly a testament to the tyranny of genital organization in himself. If anyone's polymorphous perversities were directed into genital channels then it was this man. . . . His total failure to achieve satisfaction with, to extract meaning from his contacts with, his hundreds of prostitutes is symbolic of the dissatisfaction felt by most of the clients of brothels and street prostitutes: the urge to polymorphous perversity – the urge to indulge in non-genital affectionate physical play – is frustrated by the notion of genital duty, by the conviction that genital 'relief' is being sought. Walter teaches us that many men (like himself) do not go to prostitutes for 'sex' at all. . . . They are looking for something else, but they do not know what they are looking for. If only it had occurred to Walter that he really wanted to *play*, and not to *fuck*. . . . He was looking for something that does not exist. He had separated play, tenderness, delicacy, love, respect, consideration – from lust. Walter could not play because he did not understand that he wanted to do so; and because he could not play, his sexual adventures were an endless quest. Brown quotes Schiller: 'Man only plays when in the full meaning of the word he is a man, and he is only completely a man when he plays.' For such a man (or even for half such a man) love-making is not the self-frustrating activity it was for Walter.

In Sartrian terms, a man partakes of the qualities of – 'is' – what he *prefers*, and Walter preferred sperm. He frequently arranged,

consciously or unconsciously, to fuck in other men's sperm – or
failing that, in his own. Sometimes the woman must wash,
sometimes she must not; but the interest is in the sperm. Marcus is
right to refer to this as evidence of a homosexual component in
his make-up (though to call him a true homosexual would be
a comic contradiction in terms), and to point out that he was
continually re-enacting an Oedipal fantasy. But Marcus is wrong
in his inescapable implication that, sexually, we are all like Walter
– that we can only escape from our 'worst selves', as he might
well say, by sublimation. Nor is this pessimism an inevitable
corollary of Freud's own thinking. This is only to say that
certain people carry our their sexual projects in markedly non-
sexual channels. . . . Their 'sublimation' may not always be
preferable to Walter's non-sublimation. Thus, while Walter rapes
children,* others manufacture armaments, sign death-warrants, sit
in judgement, or agitate for 'racial purity'. Child-rape is not,
however, 'better'; it is not, except presumably to the Kronhausens, 'good'. But it seems *worse* to us only because society
conspires to make 'sex' the scapegoat for its other sins. Thus,
while it is 'manly', 'obedient', 'dutiful' to murder men in battle, it is
reprehensible to rape children, even though British soldiers will
cheerfully queue up, when away from unwoggish Mother England, to have ten-year-old wog girls (as I have myself seen).

For Walter, the infantile delight in withholding and manipu-
lating excrement, with all that this implies, became channelled
into an obsession with sperm. For him, sperm was not only 'the
divine life-giver'; it was also filthy, a viscous excrement (it was
Donne who called it 'excremental jelly') into which he felt
compelled to immerse himself both emotionally and tactilely.
Although Walter manifested Oedipal, homosexual and other familiar enough 'Freudian' elements in his sexual activities – and most
particularly in his characteristically distorted recollections of
them – his project was essentially a narcissistic one. Just as some
judges or politicians use public power to pursue their narcissistic
projects, so Walter used his penis and its sperm-producing capa-
cities to pursue his. All his genital activity is a denial of love,

* To be fair, Walter has only one small girl in the course of the book.

which is of course what he humanly wants. Thus every genital
act he performs is unsatisfying: the present orgasm only breeds
a desire for the next, and so on and so on for ever and ever.

Walter's project was a grandiose and ridiculous one, but those
of many clients of whores, and, indeed, husbands – if they could
write them down as he did his – might parallel it in their smaller
way. Unable to come to terms with the notion of his own death,
he set himself the impossible task of eroticizing death by becoming
God.

Early in his career he had a girl in a churchyard; there is a sudden revelation as he recollects his emotions at the moment when
his desire for perpetual, death-denying orgasm was denied:

'Shove on,' said she, 'I was just coming,' – and she was wriggling and
heaving, – 'Go on.' I could always go on pushing after a spend in those
days [i.e. to get on to the next orgasm as soon as possible] . . . so I
pushed until I thought of doing her a second time; but her pleasure
came on, her cunt contracted, and with the usual wriggle and sigh
she was over, and there were we lying in copulation, with the dead
all around us; another living creature might that moment have been
begotten, in its turn to eat, drink, fuck, die, be buried and rot. . . .

Even when he is patently not lying 'in copulation', but has
unequivocally finished it, he has to deny the fact – for the notion
of it is his only hope of self-perpetuation against the threat of
death, which was of course uncomfortably immediate on this
particular occasion. Commenting on Walter's fascination with
vaginas, which he examined throughout his life on the pretext
of comparing them, Marcus writes:

Either he is looking for something (or someone) that he once saw
or thought he saw, or he is looking for something that is not there. . . .
That something which is not there is of course a penis. . . .

This is right as far as it goes; but I think we can add that Walter
was looking for nothing less than his own penis, and that one of
the many reasons for his 'rutting furies', his drive to 'fuck, fuck
and fuck' (as he himself often puts it), was that he always hoped
that his magical sperm (remember that he could see it when he
could not see it, and that he believed it compensated other people

for any misfortunes he might have caused them) might produce a penis (which, of course, it in a sense could and may have done). Walter did not mention any legitimate children; if he was child-less then this would have given further impetus to his procreative drive.

That the main component of Walter's project was to defeat death is proved by his conclusion to the seventh volume of *My Secret Life*:

It [his narrative] is exuberant, because written for my secret pleas-ure. . . . as I wrote it . . . I almost had my sexual treats over again. . . . newness prevents satiety in sexual frolics. . . . It [the narrative] must remain – written by myself and for myself, none probably will ever see it but myself – therefore why cheat myself? – let it remain.

I wish I had begun this revision earlier, perhaps now I shall never complete it – or complete it only in time to destroy it, before I myself am destroyed. . . .

Of course, Walter sought 'newness' both in order to seek satiety, and to 'prevent' it; and he knew that he would transmit his record to posterity because, as he aged and his sexual powers ran out, that was all he could do.

The anxiety Walter manifested in looking for his own penis in all those cunts (which he then proceeded frenetically to assault, in punishment for its harrowing absence) was originally an exten-sion of one that Freud postulated as common to all civilized men: fear of loss of that instrument with which and only with which one may become reunited with one's mother. In effect Walter, who was sadistic and not at all masochistic, punished his mother in the person of all the women he assaulted: punished her for not having a penis and therefore not being his father-God-Self, at the same time as he vainly tried symbolically to re-unite himself with her. There is undoubtedly an element of this in much brothel- and prostitute-visiting.

All, for Walter, became subordinated to his attempt to be-come a kind of sperm-Midas: if all that he touched could turn into his own sperm, then he could escape death by immersing himself in his own matter (sperm having taken on, for him, the qualities of all excrement).

Walter said that he was a comparatively rich man, and we may at least be sure that this was so. And for him the familiar equation between money and excrement (the essence of this being that 'reserves' of money must always be, by definition, useless in 'civilized' communities) takes on a less familiar look: for Walter, sperm, the paradoxical viscous matter which is both excremental and yet Walter-propagating, actually *is* money. His favourite term for ejaculation is, naturally, 'to spend': always those women with whom he copulates, little penis-endowed Walters in the moment of his recollected spasm, 'spent' too. Thus, of 'H★★★', a lesbian prostitute:

I told her one evening how I had turned N★★le L★★l★e's cunt into a purse, and she wondered if her own would hold as much. I had doubts, for it did not feel to me as large inside as the other . . . but I had H★★★ naked one day and tried. The silver brought was carefully washed [this is Walter engineering things so that he can, curiously, wash his own sperm], and the argental cunt stuffing began. . . . I prolonged the work, not putting in five and ten shillings at a time as I did with the other, when my lustful curiosity was to ascertain a fact, but a shilling or two at a time only. . . . When about forty shillings had disappeared up her belly rift, I put my prick up her, and felt with its sensitive tip the difference between a shilling . . . and the . . . end of her cuntal avenue. . . . Then over the basin she squatted to void the argentiferous stream. It was beautiful. . . . The silver tumbling out of her gaping hirsute cleft. . . . The silver was washed and stored away. 'When you pay any one, tell them that the silver's been up your cunt.' – 'You beast, I will . . .'. Eighty-six or -seven shillings did her cunt hold.

Thus Walter literally fucked not only in his own sperm but also in his own money (he could not, however, understandably, 'spend', and wished he had been able to, 'for it would have been something to remember'). Shortly afterwards he pitched franc pieces at the cunts of a dozen whores in a Paris brothel, while they scrambled for them. . . . It is not without significance that one of Walter's favourite epithets for sperm is 'gruelly': gruel was, of course, what the poor popularly subsisted upon – for the Victorians it was a sadistic symbol disguised as a symbol of charity. Other epithets he used are 'pearly' (= expensive = money), 'thick', 'hot', 'boiling' – but seldom 'sticky'. This may have been because the sticky quality of sperm was what Walter was trying to appropriate to himself, and he could not bring himself to affirm this.

Sartre, writing about sliminess (or viscosity) – a vital concept in his philosophy – says:

> In the slimy substance which dissolves into itself [honey flowing from a spoon back into the jar] there is a visible resistance, like the refusal of an individual who does not want to be annihilated in the whole of being. . . . The slimy is compressible. It gives us the first impression that it is a being which can be possessed. . . . but . . . the softness of this substance . . . gives me the impression that I am perpetually destroying it. . . . The slimy is docile . . . it possesses me. . . .

For Sartre the viscous is the symbol of 'nausea': it is the hideously sticky medium in which 'liquid' human freedom exists, and which threatens to absorb and destroy it in brutishness. At the same time – in Sartrian philosophy – we spend a great deal of our time in plugging up holes because holes mean emptiness:

> the ideal of the hole is then an excavation which can be carefully moulded about my flesh. . . . The obscenity of the feminine sex is that of everything which 'gapes open'. It is an appeal to being as all holes are. . . . sex is a hole.

Few English-speaking people accept Sartre's ideas as being valuable; but I suggest that they clarify *My Secret Life*, which in turn clarifies an important element in male experience with whores. In Sartre's thought the free man creates himself, he chooses to suffer in order to attain liberty. And the bad faith which prevents men from attaining liberty is symbolized – indeed, is – the viscous, the indeterminate state between the fluidity of water and the fixed rigidity of stone.

Walter may not be seen as an 'existentialist hero' precisely because his project was a secret one – he chose to keep it secret. Furthermore, he was no naturalist – though he represented himself as being one. He tried, literally, to immerse himself in viscosity, to perpetuate his non-freedom and simultaneously to pretend that this was free: thus, the dichotomy between his private 'secret' life and his respectable public life (whatever this consisted of) is absolutely typical of male lives of its and our time, but more intense.

If I have one fear about publicity it is that of having done a few things by curiosity and impulse . . . which even professed libertines may cry fie on. . . . from that cause perhaps no mortal eye but mine will see this history.

This is not the language of a man who is free in Sartre's sense; it is indeed the language of a man of 'bad faith', *un salaud*, a filthy stinker.

But Walter did show a certain awareness of a universal human problem when he decided to investigate the meaning of his sexuality. He always found it meaningless because he isolated it – doubtless his impulse to make the investigation in writing originated from a hope that a narrative might confer meaning on what had hitherto been frustratingly meaningless (not that he could ever admit that to himself). Eliot's lines from 'The Dry Salvages' come to mind:

> We had the experience but missed the meaning,
> And approach to the meaning restores the experience
> In a different form, beyond any meaning
> We can assign to happiness.

Walter cannot properly be a hero to anybody. But nor can many people who do worse than he ever did – but with the sanction of society – and never even make the attempt to face themselves or to enquire into their compulsions.

Chapter Nine

1

THE Victorian physician William Acton's *Prostitution* (1857) is the other side of the coin from *My Secret Life*. Acton (*c.* 1814–1875), a married man, the author of a famous passage about women's essentially non-sexual nature and a believer in the horrors of masturbation, wrote what Peter Fryer has called, in his introduction to the reprint of the edition of 1870 'as humane, as clear-sighted . . . as logical [a book], as contemporary morality would permit'.* I myself doubt if Acton really believed in women's sexual passivity, although he told himself that he did. He wrote: 'I should say that the majority of women (happily for them) are not very troubled with sexual feeling of any kind'. But this was what his generation wanted to hear. They expected their 'medical men' to reassure them. What Acton meant was that, officially, wives *ought* not to exhibit sexual desire. If they did, then that was strictly private good luck – not to be talked about: it would be like having a prostitute for a wife. . . . Acton's idea is very like Marcus's, except that Marcus manages (or so it seems to me) to accommodate himself to the horrors of feminine

* Quotations from Acton's *Prostitution* are from Peter Fryer's edition, MacGibbon & Kee, London, 1968.

sexuality: in Acton's implied view men have 'lust' as a terrible burden to carry, while decent, marriageable women are 'chaste', submissive (the latent sadism contained in this concept is obvious) – only prostitutes are 'abandoned'. When I suggest that Acton did not really believe in women's sexual passivity, I mean only that he separated sexual enjoyment from Victorian marriage; that in the privacy of his club (or wherever) he probably indulged in stories of 'loose ladies', but deliberately never made the connection between them and 'wives'. The Victorians frequently knew much more than they would or could admit.

But Acton could be an objective natural historian. He realized that whores did not necessarily come to a bad end, that prostitution was often a transient profession, and much else besides. His account of the prostitution of his time is honest, even if he fails to face up to its implications. Fryer is perhaps too ready to excuse his ridiculosities on the grounds that he was a humanitarian; but he did show courage and humanity. No one can read his book without admitting that, in general, it is sensibly forthright. The following passage is by no means contemptible.

The intercourse, therefore, of man or woman ought to appeal to their threefold organization of body, mind, and spirit. If the first predominates over and excludes the others, sexual desire degenerates into lust; when all are present, it is elevated into love, which appeals to each of the component parts of man's nature. The men who seek gratification for, and the women who bestow it on, one part of their being only are in an unnatural state. And here we may distinguish the indulgence of unlawful love from commerce with prostitutes, the one is the ill-regulated but complete gratification of the entire human being, the other affords gratification to one part only of his nature.

One other distinction also we must carefully notice, and that is that in the one case the enjoyment is mutual, and that in the other the enjoyment is one-sided, and granted not as the expression and reward of love, but as a matter of commerce. But if it be derogatory to their being, and unnatural to bestow gratification on one part of their nature only, what shall we say of the condition of those unfortunate women to whom sexual indulgence affords no pleasure, and who pass their lives in, and gain their living by, affording enjoyments which they do not share, and feigning a passion which has ceased to move them? The woman who abandons herself for gain, instead of in obedience to the promptings of desire – who,

> while her Lover pants upon her breast,
> Can mark the figures on an Indian chest; –

is in an unnatural state, and so is the man who uses her, and obtains for a mere money consideration that enjoyment of the person which should be yielded only as the result and crowning expression of mutual passion. We may further observe that commerce with a prostitute is an ephemeral transaction, which (though it may be followed by serious consequences) yet entails no obligations. Illicit attachments are more lasting, though usually transitory, and entail limited obligations. Both conditions are substitutes for, or imitations of the relationship resulting from love, and known as the married state, which, arising from mutual desire, and granting the highest privileges, imposes corresponding obligations, and is usually as lasting as life itself, and proves at once the mainspring and chief safeguard of society.

The only serious faults here are that Acton's concepts are too rigid and that he is assuming that no woman would really prefer to be a prostitute if she had the chance to work very hard in a factory for a fair wage.

The fact is that some women like being prostitutes at least as much as they like working in factories or being secretaries; they may not always feel like making love, but then nor do typists always feel like typing – and the money is usually better (or seems better at the time). It is risky, in our present state of knowledge, to criticize them: they give, to many people, a certain amount of temporary tactile pleasure (and the more you pay, the less temporary your pleasure, the greater the illusion of a genuine 'affair': by paying enough you can pretend you have conquered the 'will' of the whore, just as Montaigne's Italians did).*

Acton, however, was probably as nearly realistic in public as his age would allow him to be. Tribute should be – and has been – paid to him. His aims were basically humane – which is why I have suggested that he knew more than he let on, and that he may have preached morality and female non-sexuality with his tongue

* See p. 71.

partly in his cheek. In his preface to the second edition of *Prostitution* he was able to say that his first edition had contributed to 'the happiest results [the Contagious Diseases Act 1866], both as regards the health of our army and navy, and the sanitary and moral improvement wrought in . . . unhappy women . . .'. We must remember that if he had not added the occasional 'moral' admonition his book could not have been published at all; besides, 'unhappy women was no more than a Malcolm Muggeridge, say, much less coolly, might bellow forth now.

Acton consistently fought for what (in the same preface) he called 'the RECOGNITION of prostitution by the state'. In one sense at least Butler's law, enshrined in the British Street Offences Act that 'swept prostitution under the carpet', was a step backwards from this. In any case, though this law of 1959 kept the girls off the streets for a few years, it has now failed of its effect: they are coming back, and the police are leaving them alone.

Acton also saw that many women who became prostitutes – to their own eventual material disadvantage – might not have done so had social conditions been better. He advocated a law 'making the seducer substantially responsible for the support of his bastard offspring' and demanded better provisions against overcrowding. It is almost always clear that for Acton the real evils were material – the ravages of syphilis, the consequences of poverty and neglect – rather than 'moral'.

His opening chapter, *Prostitution Defined*, is the first sensible and scientific attempt ever made to establish a working definition of prostitution. That its hard realism was not badly received goes some way towards suggesting that Victorian hypocrisy has too often been exaggerated; true, writers spoke of Acton as not 'being afraid to touch pitch' – but his book was never attacked. Those who actually had to work with the practical problems posed by prostitution were all too aware of its good sense. One cannot point to any opposition to it. Yet Acton was quite certain that 'to attempt to put down prostitution by law is to attempt the impossible'. His description of the various kinds of brothels was clinical and accurate, and although he pays lip-service to morality, there are no signs in his style that his subject-matter either excited or disturbed him; naturalism always takes precedence over politeness.

Acton writes of the tarts in brothels:

They are usually during the day, unless called upon by their fol-lowers, or employed in dressing, to be found, dishevelled, dirty, slipshod and dressing-gowned, in [the common] kitchen, where the mistress keeps her *table-d'hôte*. Stupid from beer, or fractious from gin, they swear and chatter brainless stuff all day, about men and millinery, their own schemes and adventures, and the faults of others of the sister-hood. As a heap of rubbish will ferment, so surely will a number of unvirtuous women thus collected deteriorate, whatever their ante-cedents or good qualities previously to their being herded under the semi-tyranny of this kind of lodging-house. In such a household, all decency, modesty, propriety, and conscience must, to preserve har-mony and republican equality, be planed down, and the woman hammered out, not by the practice of her profession or the company of men, but by association with her own sex and class, to the dead level of harlotry.

There is a cool, naturalistic precision about this; we must make allowances for the comparison of the brothel-women with 'a heap of rubbish' fermenting, at the same time recalling that con-ditions in the houses Acton was describing were probably not calculated to appeal to the aesthetic sensibilities. But note that his pin-pointing of the element that 'hammered out' the women 'to the dead level of harlotry' was courageously accurate: it was not 'sin' ('the practice of her profession') but 'association with her own sex and class'. This is admirably realistic, as is his account of 'the mock refinement' with which well-to-do men could pro-cure prostitutes, with whom they consorted in 'superior haunts'. Acton knew his stuff and he was not embarrassed by it. There was not a trace in him of the notion that those prostitutes who needed medical treatment ought to be 'punished' for their 'sin', even if he does call them 'miserable women' – and after all, many of them were, in the literal sense of the word, miserable.

Acton had 'little faith in the efficacy of lock asylums and peni-tentiaries' as instruments in the prevention of prostitution, but believed 'the only plan' was 'gradually to educate them back to

a sense of decency'. Prostitutes, he thought, should be able to
'ply their trade in a manner as little degrading as possible': this
is still a view worth publicizing. Acton represents conventional
Victorianism at its best; there are still plenty in our midst less
enlightened than he was.

2

Zola's *Nana* is probably the most celebrated of all novels about
whores. It is, as Zola's best critic, F. W. J. Hemmings, says, 'a
coldly austere work' – although the personal courage with which
Zola maintained his naturalistic principles strikes one as being
ultimately far from austere. But for all his desperate honesty – and
this almost continuously overrides his innate puritanism and
bourgeois horror of vice – Zola could not quite manage to turn
Nana into a human being. The best he could do was to introduce
piercingly accurate psychological touches, a kind of series of
brilliant sketches towards a human being; but his real targets
were the rich and corrupt, and Nana herself serves as the 'Golden
Fly' who entices them into her lustful web, the former slum girl
now revenging herself on the class that was responsible for her
misery.

Henriques, in the third volume of his history of prostitution,
attacks *Nana* as being 'designed as a moral tale', and contrasts it
with the real-life success-story of Céleste Mogador, a whore who
eventually married an aristocrat. This subtracts unfairly from
Zola's achievement. *Nana* satirizes the effete and corrupt society
of the French Second Empire, and at the same time provides a
vivid, if humanly incomplete, portrait of a psychopathic whore
who possessed a lust-provoking body. We are not to say that
because whorishness does not of itself imply criminality or a
psychopathic personality therefore no whores are psychopaths.

We may admit that Nana's character played into Zola's puritanical hands; but, once given this particular psychopathic whore, he never played false with her. Zola was a writer of uncompromising honesty: once he had conceived a character, he would go through thick and thin to present him or her in a truthful – a naturalistic – light. To describe a work with the superb realistic detail of *Nana* as merely 'a moral tale' is doltish, for it underrates Zola and his seriousness to an absurd degree. This is a novel that repeatedly transcends its moral and satirical structure. Nor can we judge it as a polemic against sex, even though it provides evidence of how frightened the author himself was of sex. Throughout his life Zola advised continence as a means of 'stirring up' creative energy, so that he must have felt continuously threatened by his own creation as he went on with the book. But he maintained his integrity. We never feel that he is justifying himself, or that he is distorting reality in the interests of his personal predicament.

Beyond informing the reader that Nana has emerged from the slums and that her father was a drunkard, Zola does not tell us exactly why she became a whore. He does not begin to try to answer the question that William Blake posed, in a general way, in a remarkable letter. Blake was talking about theft. (I should make it clear that I am in no way implying that there is an equation between larceny and prostitution.) The point is that some men and women take to certain activities, such as theft or prostitution, and some do not. Poverty is not a sufficient explanation:

But Want of Money & the Distress of A Thief can never be alledged as the Cause of his Thieving, for many honest people endure greater hardships with Fortitude. We must therefore seek the Cause elsewhere than in want of Money, for that is the Miser's passion, not the Thief's.

But Zola's subject was the society of the Second Empire rather than the origins of prostitution.

When *Nana* begins Nana is already a highly successful prostitute, sought after, or at least hotly discussed, by every corrupt aristocrat and government official. She is at the height of her success, appearing as Venus in a deplorable comedy. She is almost loathsomely inadequate as an actress, but when she appears naked

A shiver of delight ran round the house. . . . With quiet audacity, she appeared in her nakedness, certain of the sovran power of her flesh. . . . And when Nana lifted her arms, the golden hairs in her armpits were observable in the glare of the footlights. There was no applause. Nobody laughed any more. The men strained forward with serious faces, sharp features, mouths irritated and parched. . . . Nana was smiling still, but her smile was now bitter, as of a devourer of men.

The American critic Henri Peyre has said that 'not a single scene' in *Nana* is 'ever risqué' or suggestive; but this, and many other scenes, are certainly powerful in their evocation of breathless lust. Hemmings calls them scenes of 'licentiousness'. Seldom has a woman's sexual attractiveness been as vividly conveyed in print; no doubt Zola's own terror of and fascination with raw sexuality had something to do with the power he achieved. Peyre also says that 'Zola . . . rejected the romantic notion of woman as a demon. . . . He himself lived a very bourgeois existence . . . rejoicing in the placid security of his home.' This is misleading. Zola himself did not altogether reject the 'romantic notion of woman as a demon'. As Hemmings rightly points out, 'all unconsciously [Nana] is an avenging angel sent forth by the oppressed and neglected dwellers of slumland'; and as Zola himself makes Fauchery, the journalist, write in an article on Nana,

With her, the infection that was allowed to stew among the lower classes seeped upwards to contaminate the aristocracy. She became a force of nature, a ferment of destruction, without willing it herself, defiling and disrupting Paris between her snow-white thighs . . . a fly . . . taking wing from the dunghill . . . and poisoned men simply by settling on them.

Clearly, then, Peyre is wrong in categorically denying that Zola took what he calls this 'romantic' view of women. He is also misleading when he writes of Zola's 'very bourgeois existence': some eight years after the publication of *Nana* he took a mistress twenty-eight years younger than himself – an affair he kept from his wife for four years, until an anonymous letter arrived – by whom he had two bastards.

Nana, then, exists more as herself, a particular prostitute, than as a prototype of a Paris prostitute of her time. But her psychopathic character – her inability to calculate, or to take advantage of her good fortune – is certainly typical of many 'gutter' prostitutes of modern times. There are many authentic details in the novel, showing that Zola saw Nana as an autonymous character as well as a 'golden fly'. He was unable, however, to concentrate upon her his full naturalistic powers. Thus, when she temporarily disappears – under the influence of Satin, another whore – into the obscurity of the gutter, the exact psychological mechanisms of this move are left undescribed. Nana's crazy and self-damaging impulsiveness is vivid enough; but the mercy Zola might have shown in explicating it is not in evidence, and because it isn't, an emotion of 'disgusting creature!' is generated. That this is not an inevitable weakness of naturalistic fiction is demonstrated by Zola himself in some of his other novels (*La Bête Humaine*, for example) and by Dreiser in *Sister Carrie*.★ Yet Zola never falsifies; he goes as far as he can; he provides, as I have suggested, a series of magnificently precise sketches for a full-sized human portrait.

On the day after her theatrical triumph as Venus, Nana is broke:

Among all those men who had cheered her, to think that there wasn't one to bring her fifteen louis! And then one couldn't accept money in that way! Dear Heaven! how unfortunate she was!

Later, still broke, she gives away money to charity, men having called to see her using this excuse:

She wasn't vexed. It struck her as a joke that men should have got money out of her. All the same they were swine, for she hadn't a sou left. . . .

When the clients come in their dozens to her house, 'sheltering behind her bolted door', she 'began laughing at them, declaring that she could hear them pant'. Reading a novel about a prostitute, she protests that it is untrue, lewd, false. . . . She indulges in a lesbian affair with Satin, simply because Satin wants it. She seems to be represented as the type of prostitute whose driving power, such as it is, is revenge on the father, on men in general and on

★ See pp. 193–4.

society; a type we encounter – almost exclusively – in *Women of the Streets*, by Rosalind Wilkinson,* which is 'a sociological study of the common prostitute' and deals with London tarts at the bottom end of the social scale.

And yet *Nana* is essentially, as Hemmings has well said, a 'denunciation of the erotic peril'. Zola killed his heroine off with smallpox:

Nana was left alone, with upturned face in the light cast by the candle. She was fruit of the charnel-house, a heap of matter and blood, a shovelful of corrupted flesh thrown down on the pillow. The pustules had evaded the whole of the face, so that each touched its neighbour. Fading and sunken, they had assumed the greyish hue of mud, and on that formless pulp, where the features had ceased to be traceable, they already resembled some decaying damp from the grave. One eye, the left eye, had completely foundered among bubbling purulence, and the other, which remained half open, looked like a deep black ruinous hole. The nose was still suppurating. Quite a reddish crust was peeling from one of the cheeks, and invading the mouth, which it distorted in a horrible grin. And over this loathsome and grotesque mask of death, the hair, the beautiful hair, still blazed like sunlight and flowed downwards in rippling gold. Venus was rotting. . . .

A terrible beauty is dead! But although Zola may be said to have engineered the psychopathic character of Nana, and her death by smallpox, he remained admirably objective – naturalist as he was – about details. He did not have it in him, perhaps, to be sympathetic to prostitutes – the subject was intellectually too uncomfortable for him. But, at least uneasy about the matter, he put himself at a certain distance from the view of Nana as a golden fly bred in a dunghill 'disrupting Paris between her snow-white thighs' by representing it as the newspaper article of a journalist (Fauchery) who is by no means one of the 'saved' characters in the book – he himself is presented as a corrupt component of a society rotted by sexual and other indulgences. Indeed, if anyone in the book comes near to being a 'saved' character (this useful term was invented by Northrop Frye) then it is Muffat, the religiously devout Count who becomes Nana's abject slave, and,

* Secker & Warburg, London, 1955. See pp. 186–91.

in a scene borrowed from Otway's *Venice Preserv'd*, allows her to ride him like a horse. (But he is 'saved' only in the sense that he is represented as being a fundamentally decent man corrupted by lust against his will; the corruption of most of the others is simply presented; his is presented as tragic.) The scenes in which Nana humiliates him, making him play at being a horse or a dog, and making him spit on his Chamberlain's uniform, are savagely powerful even if they are supposed to function as terrible warnings about the depths to which lust can drag men down.

'Gee up! Gee up! You're a horse. Hoi! gee up! Won't you hurry up, you dirty screw!'

At other times he was a dog. She would throw her scented handkerchief to the far end of the room, and he had to run and pick it up with his teeth, dragging himself on hands and knees.

'Fetch it, Caesar! Look here, I'll give you what for if you don't look sharp! Well done, Caesar! Good dog! Nice old fellow! Now behave pretty!'

And he loved his abasement, and delighted in being a brute beast. He longed to sink still farther and would cry, 'Hit me harder. On, on! I'm wild! Hit away!'. . .

Then, when once the Chamberlain was undressed and his coat lay spread on the ground, she shrieked, 'Jump!' and he jumped; she shrieked, 'Spit!' and he spat. . . .

It is significant that Zola is uneasy about this character, too: he never comes to life, but operates as a mere symbol. This was doubtless because in depicting his masochistic humiliation Zola felt himself direly threatened. Naturalism could operate for him as a self-defensive mechanism as well as a means of revealing reality: by 'measuring' what he felt to threaten him, he could distance himself from it.

Nana herself, however, is alive and vital, though not fully characterized: Zola was not capable of the sin of dehumanizing or sentimentalizing even what he most feared.

3

Zola's *Nana* should be contrasted with a famous novel that appeared thirty-two years before it: *La Dame aux Camélias* (1848) by Alexandre Dumas the younger. Dumas invented the term *demi-monde* (after the title of one of his plays), to describe the world of women who were neither professional prostitutes nor yet faithful wives – the world, indeed, of 'fallen women'; later it came to be applied more exclusively to socially successful professional tarts. He was an anti-romantic moralist, whose writings had no literary merit but a correspondingly wide influence: *La Dame aux Camélias* was turned into a play in 1852, and in the following year Verdi used it as the basis for *La Traviata*, with a libretto by Piave. Although one of Verdi's most popular operas, it is by no means one of his best: its virtues can best be defined as those occasions when his music and dramatic genius transcend the sickly and nauseous story.

For, like the audience he wrote to gratify, the illegitimate Dumas *fils* was a snob, a hypocrite and a fantasist, and *La Dame aux Camélias* is pure sentimental fantasy, designed to appeal solely to an anti-naturalistic mentality. Camille is a representative of a male fantasy-figure, 'the tart with the heart', that was created by nineteenth-century public morality. When tarts were, by and large, taken for granted, there had been less need to endow them with hearts of gold. But the triumph of public morality caused what was in fact indulged in as much as ever to become 'forbidden', so that forbidden fruit guiltily needed to be endowed with impossibly sentimental qualities of self-sacrifice and nobility. This was one of the main reasons for the nineteenth-century French sentimentalization of the whole concept of prostitution: these women who took your money were not *really* taking your money and threatening the stability of the marriage union: they were tragic, noble, good hearted. . . .

The story of *La Dame aux Camélias* is too well-known to need retelling here. The main ingredients are Camille's nobility in rejecting her lover at his father's behest, and her subsequent death of consumption brought on by a broken heart – i.e. the prototype of a purely physical sexual liaison is transformed into a full-blooded romantic love-affair that cannot be respectably consummated because of the heroine's 'tragic' social position. The hidden ingredient is Camille's lush (tubercular) sexiness, and all the bed-work that is never mentioned. Marie Duplessis, a real high-class tart upon whom Dumas modelled Camille, had recently died of tuberculosis – but the facts of her life bore no real relation to the plot of *La Dame aux Camélias*.

In his invention of the *demi-monde* Dumas did what most moralists do. His *demi-monde* began where wives were faithless and ended where tarts took straight cash-payments. Thus he created a 'tragic' fantasy-category of women (he made no attempt to moralize about the position of males): lush, sexy pieces unhappily robbed of the chance of respectability, and therefore all the more excitingly 'abandoned' in bed.

The chief fantasy element in Dumas's novel is the 'pure passion' the socially accursed Camille conceives for her lover. This is seen as redeeming her character. However, her actual marriage to her lover is simultaneously seen as totally impossible. In reality, amorous passion is a complex phenomenon, and the element of 'purity' that Dumas (and so many others) introduce into it is wholly artificial. But it is useful fantasy-food. For while the institution of marriage remains sacrosanct, some really hot sex-work can be expected from the dream-girl. The element of 'purity' also casts her in the role of wife: thousands of Dumas's male readers wanked themselves dry by superimposing the novel image of sexy Camille on the reality of their familiar and therefore sexually dull, but nevertheless respectable wives.

Nana, by an author who had perhaps just as serious personal sexual problems as Dumas *fils* – but who was a consistently honest naturalist – may be seen as a deliberate reaction to the sickly sentimentality which *La Dame aux Camélias* epitomized. For even if Nana's mechanisms are not fully explained, she remains a real tart where Camille embodies the shabby fantasy of a million self-deluding sugar daddies.

4

Zola's contemporaries Guy de Maupassant and Jean-Marie-Mathias-Philippe-Auguste, Comte de Villiers de l'Îsle-Adam, were more relaxed and more sophisticated about the subject of sex than Zola. Maupassant as a man, in any case, resembled Walter rather more than he resembled Zola (whose disciple he felt himself in many ways to be): there is Frank Harris's famous story, which is probably true, about how Maupassant told him 'I suppose I am a little out of the common sexually, for I can make my instrument stand whenever I please. . . . Look at my trousers . . .', and how he claimed to be able to go on having orgasms for a prodigiously long time. And we know, of course, that he died of syphilis. It was, perhaps, Maupassant's more casual sexuality that made 'Boule de Suif' – too well-known for me to need to outline it here – such a moving story. As F. W. J. Hemmings writes, '[Maupassant's] prostitutes are never anything but prostitutes, never, like Nana, mystical embodiments of the corruption of slumland spilling over and infecting the cultivated classes' (while this is true, I think it is stated in a manner somewhat unfair to Zola's superb integrity). In 'Boule de Suif' it is the prostitute who is warm and human, and who has honour and patriotism – the others lack it. At the end, in the carriage,

> Nobody looked at her, nobody thought of her. She felt herself drowning in the flood of contempt shown towards her by these honest scoundrels who had first sacrificed her and then cast her off like some unclean and useless thing.

She begins, in one of the most touching scenes in French literature, to cry. 'Madame Loiseau gave a silent chuckle of triumph and murmured, "She is crying over her shame".'

Few stories or novels contain such a damning indictment of the society that both condones and condemns prostitution, regarding it as 'shameful' and 'criminal' only in order to satisfy its own basest instincts. No one can fail to recognize the essential reality, the utterly unmanufactured quality, of Boule de Suif herself; but generations have read this story, have paid lip-service to its art – and have continued to regard prostitutes just as the people in Maupassant's story regarded Boule de Suif.

Villiers de l'Îsle-Adam was a more savage and tortured critic of society than Maupassant. In 'The Bienfilâtre Sisters', one of the *Contes Cruels* (1883), Villiers mocked the absurd relativity of moral concepts. But the two tarts came out of it little better than their hypocritical environment. Olympe and Henriette have 'lent a hand' to their poor family by being 'sisters of pleasure' 'from early childhood'. ' "God blesses our efforts," they would sometimes say.'

When they were asked if their labours, which were sometimes excessive, were not detrimental to their health, they used to reply evasively, with that gentle, embarrassed expression which is born of modesty, and with downcast eyes: 'Every way of life has its special graces . . . .'.

Regular in their ways, they shut up shop on Sunday. And being sensible creatures, they paid no attention to the flattery of young men-about-town, who are good for nothing but enticing girls away from the narrow path of duty and work. . . . Their motto was 'Speed, Safety, Discretion'; and on their visiting-cards they added: 'Specialities'.

Alas, Olympe goes 'astray'. She 'yielded to the temptations to which she was more exposed than other people. . . . She fell in love'. The irony of this needs no explication.

Henriette pretends not to recognize her, begs her 'to keep up appearances'. 'Perhaps she hoped by these words to produce a return to virtue.' Maxime (the boy-friend) asks her father for Olympe's hand – ' "Swine!" Bienfilâtre . . . exclaimed . . . disgusted by this "cynicism" '.

Olympe becomes ill, 'literally dying of shame'. She cannot bring herself to return to her profession. A priest arrives to confess her: ' "I have had a lover!" murmured Olympe, thus admitting the stain on her honour'.

Then Maxime enters, 'triumphantly chinking' money which his

parents have sent him for his examination fees. 'Failing at first to
notice this important extenuating circumstance', Olympe stretches
her hands out 'in horror', which the priest interprets as 'a final
farewell to the object of a guilty, immodest pleasure'.

In reality it was simply the young man's *crime* which she was rejecting – and this crime consisted of not being 'serious'.

But just as the august pardon was descending upon her, a heavenly
smile lit up her features; the priest supposed that she felt she was saved.
. . . Olympe had in fact just caught a glimpse of the pieces of sacred
metal shining between Maxime's transfigured fingers. . . . A miracle
had happened! . . . her lips parted and she exhaled her last breath,
like the perfume of a lily, murmuring these words of hope:

'He's shelled out!'

Probably this is ultimately anti-woman, although it does not
attempt to distort reality, but instead accepts, with a savagely
ironic intelligence, the facts of lust, which Villiers seems to have
seen as a fatal, a 'diabolical' masculine burden. But 'The Bienfilâtre
Sisters' is more than merely frigid and clever: it is as much an
indictment of bourgeois hypocrisy about prostitution (and
French bourgeois hypocrisy is particularly repulsive) as it is an
ironic comment upon the nature of women. Reality is not falsified.

George Gissing, who developed into an excellent and still
underrated novelist, could not bring himself to accept the fact of
prostitution with any kind of naturalistic aplomb. His second
published novel, *The Unclassed* (1884) – there was an unpublished
one before it – deals with the problem courageously but falsely.

Gissing himself had ruined his highly promising scholastic
career by getting caught pilfering sums of money from his
fellow-pupils at Owens College, Manchester. He did this to
help a Manchester prostitute with whom he imagined himself
in love. He went off to the United States, where he nearly starved.
Unfortunately for him, the prostitute was waiting when he returned. She became a drunkard, and he left her (but paid her
over half his miserable earnings); when she died he picked up a
servant-girl in a park, married her, and repeated his previous
sufferings.

So Gissing knew as much about prostitution as Maupassant –

perhaps more. But *The Unclassed* is an abject failure. Osmund
Waymark, an idealized portrait of Gissing himself – but with the
sour bitterness disingenuously left out – meets Ida Starr, a beautiful young prostitute. In an unconvincing passage (it takes place
on Hastings beach) Ida tells Waymark how she became a prostitute; but this is no more than the old tale of becoming a man's
mistress when unfairly dismissed from a menial position, and then
being forced on to the streets owing to the villainy of another
man who wanted her. . . . Ida's motives in becoming a prostitute
are not examined; the question is evaded. True, Gissing is at
some pains to draw attention to her essential 'nobility'; but this
nobility is quite unreal, and becomes much more so when Ida
takes to welfare work. . . .

Actually, Ida Starr, the prostitute of *The Unclassed*, is not a
portrait of Gissing's wife at all: she is the unreal woman whom
he invented when he was a young man and projected onto a
real prostitute. What the humourless Gissing wanted was the
smug satisfaction of rescuing a 'fallen woman', of being seen to
be a tolerant idealist – he also wanted the special sexual satisfaction
of having a 'fallen woman'. Thus while Ida is a quite impossible
character, Gissing gave himself erections (we may fairly guess)
describing her physical appearance. His real wife he portrayed
as Harriet, the drunken wife of Waymark's friend Julian Casti,
the villainess of the book. Although Gissing was eventually to
portray his rather unfortunate self with real genius and objectivity
as Godwin Peake in *Born in Exile* (1892), in the early novel he
could not come to terms with the psychopathic nature of the
woman he had married. And so he cruelly pillories Harriet, making her into an unconvincingly melodramatic villainess, while
Ida is turned into a saint. It is no coincidence that Harriet accuses
Ida of stealing jewellery which she has planted, and gets her sent to
prison: this is Gissing's way of revenging himself on his real wife
for not living up to his idealized and sentimentalized vision of her.
Julian Casti was Gissing's portrait of his nagged and horribly
harried self at the time he lived with his wife, although he tried
to imagine himself in the part of the too admirably cold, dis-
passionate novelist Waymark, who is priggishly shown as slowly

but surely learning that misfortune is not mere 'material' for writers. Poor Casti (being the sort of miserable Gissing that the author wanted to get rid of) is killed off by consumption; Waymark in due course gets Ida (and the delights of an experienced bedfellow); Harriet, a wreck, ends in an invalid home – maintained by the noble Ida.

Gissing's failure of humour and objectivity in *The Unclassed* is well illustrated by part of one of Waymark's pompous perorations (to Casti):

'In the prostitute you have the incarnation at once of the greatest good and the greatest evil, the highest and the lowest, that which is most pure associated with that which is most foul, – using all these words in the conventional sense. Love is the supreme in human life; and love brought to market, the temple of ecstatic worship degraded to a house of entertainment for the merest bodily need, the ideals of a young girl's heart little by little corroded and envenomed and blotted out by the reeking mists of debauched imagination, the fair bodily form corrupting with the degradation of the soul and metamorphosed to a horror. . . .'

This has no merit. It commits the ancient error of regarding the body and the mind as separate entities; and behind it lies Gissing's self-unacknowledged sexual fascination with prostitutes – his desire to ennoble himself while taking sexual advantage of the 'reeking mists of debauched imagination'. As a more mature writer he would have approached this theme – for him, admittedly, a difficult one – more honestly; unfortunately he died young, and before he was able to do so.

5

Two very different pieces of nineteenth-century writing form a contrast to Zola and Gissing – and, indeed, to Maupassant and Villiers, none of whom were seriously interested in why whores become whores. One is Tolstoy's novel *Resurrection* (1900), and the other is a letter, written to *The Times* on 24 February 1858 by an intelligent prostitute who signed herself simply 'Another Unfortunate'. (See Appendix, p. 199. This formed part of a correspondence on the subject in *The Times*.)

Resurrection, as most readers must know, is about a rich and bored young man, Prince Nekhlyadov, who is asked to serve on a jury in a poisoning case. Maslova, a prostitute (with the two others who have committed the crime), is charged with poisoning one of her clients, a rich merchant. Nekhlyadov realizes with horror that the girl on trial is a servant whom he had seduced on his aunt's estate many years ago.

Because of legal incompetence on the part of the judge, Maslova is sent to Siberia; Nekhlyadov, whose life (of constructively trying to undo the harm he has done to Maslova) now has meaning, follows her. In Siberia he does much good, in spite of the cruel indifference of officialdom, which Tolstoy portrays to excellent effect; and he eventually obtains Maslova's release. He asks her to marry him. She is in love with him, but chooses for his sake to go to live with another man who wants her: she feels that she, as an ex-prostitute, would ruin him.

In *Resurrection* we get, instead of the familiar Christian lament for the sins of the flesh, a serious account of how a certain type of prostitute feels and is. Social attitudes, and in particular the loathsome cruelty of institutionalized Christianity in late nineteenth-century Russia, are mercilessly exposed. (Tolstoy was excommunicated by his Church.) Tolstoy never adapts his portrait of Maslova, who clearly presented him with a problem, to suit philosophical or moral or theological presuppositions. His sketch of her life is laconic, non-moralistic, and exact. Having described her childhood (a bastard, neglected by her mother, she came to live in the house of Nekhlyadov's aunts by luck; she was brought up as 'half servant, half young lady'), Tolstoy goes on to tell how Maslova (called Katusha) fell in love with the rich young nephew at the age of sixteen. Then:

Two years later this same nephew stayed four days with his aunts before proceeding to join his regiment, and the night before he left he seduced Katusha, and, after giving her a one hundred ruble note, went away. Five months later she knew for certain that she was pregnant. After that, everything seemed repugnant to her, her only thought being how to escape from the shame awaiting her; and she not only began to serve the ladies in a half-hearted and negligent way, but once, without knowing how it happened, she was very rude to them, though she repented afterwards, and asked them to let her leave. They let her go, very dissatisfied with her. Then she got a housemaid's place in a police-officer's house, but stayed there only three months, for the police-officer, a man of fifty, began to molest her. . . . It was useless to look for another situation, for the time of her confinement was drawing near, so she went to the house of a village midwife and illicit retailer of spirits. The confinement was easy; but the midwife, who had a case of fever in the village, infected Katusha, and her baby boy had to be sent to the foundlings' hospital, where, according to the old woman who took him there, he died at once. . . .

Then she went to live with her aunt in town. Her uncle, a bookbinder, had once been comfortably off, but he had lost all his customers and taken to drink, and spent all he could lay hands on at the public-house. The aunt kept a small laundry and managed to support herself, her children and her wretched husband. She offered Katusha a place as assistant laundress; but, seeing what a life of misery and hardship her aunt's assistants led, Katusha hesitated, and applied to a registry office. A place was found for her with a lady who lived with her two sons, pupils at a public day school. A week after Katusha had entered the house, the elder, a big fellow with moustaches, threw up his studies and gave her no peace, continually following her about. His mother laid all the blame on Katusha, and gave her notice.

It so happened that after many fruitless attempts to find a situation Katusha again went to the registry office, and there met a woman with bracelets on her bare, plump arms and rings on most of her fingers. Hearing that Katusha was badly in want of a place, the woman gave her her address and invited her to come to her house. Katusha went. . . . In the evening a tall man, with long grey hair and white beard, entered the room and sat down at once near Katusha, smiling and gazing at her with glistening eyes. He began joking with her. The hostess called him away into the next room, and Katusha heard her say, 'A fresh one from the country.' Then the hostess called Katusha away and told her that the man was an author, and that he had a great deal of money, and that if he liked her he would not grudge her anything. He did like her, and gave her twenty-five rubles, promising to see her often. The twenty-five rubles soon went; some she paid to her aunt for board and lodging, the rest was spent on a hat, ribbons, and suchlike. A few days later the author sent for her and she went. He gave her another twenty-five rubles and offered her a separate lodging.

Next door to the lodging rented for her by the author there lived a jolly young shopman, with whom Katusha soon fell in love. She told the author, and moved to a small lodging of her own. The shopman, who had promised to marry her, went off to Nizhny on business without mentioning it to her, having evidently thrown her up, and Katusha remained alone. She meant to continue living in the lodging by herself, but was informed by the police that in that case she would have to get a yellow (prostitute's) passport and be subjected to medical examinations. She returned to her aunt. Seeing her fine dress, her hat, and mantle, her aunt no longer offered her laundry work. According to her ideas, her niece had risen above that. The question as to whether she was to become a laundress or not did not occur to Katusha either. She looked with pity at the thin, hard-worked laundresses, some already in consumption, who stood washing or ironing with their thin arms in the fearfully hot front room, which was always full of soapy steam and very draughty; and she thought with horror that she might have shared the same fate. It was just at this time, when Katusha was in very narrow straits, no 'protector' appearing upon the scene, that a procuress found her out. . . .

The procuress brought all sorts of dainties, to which she treated the aunt, and also wine, and while Katusha drank she offered to place her in one of the largest establishments in the city, explaining all the advantages and benefits of the situation. Katusha had the choice before her of either going into service to be humiliated, probably annoyed by the attentions of the men and having occasional secret sexual connection; or accepting an easy, secure position sanctioned by law, and open, well-paid regular sexual connection – and she chose the latter. Besides, it seemed to her as though she could, in this way, revenge herself on her seducer, and the shopman, and all those who had injured her. One of the things that tempted her and influenced her decision, was the procuress telling her she might order her own dresses: velvet, silk, satin, low-necked ball-dresses – anything she liked. A mental picture of herself in bright yellow silk trimmed with black velvet, with low neck and short sleeves, conquered her, and she handed over her passport. That same evening the procuress took an *izvozchik* and drove her to the notorious house kept by Caroline Albertovna Kitaeva.

From that day a life of chronic sin against human and divine laws commenced for Katusha Maslova, a life which is led by hundreds of thousands of women, and which is not merely tolerated but sanctioned by the Government, anxious for the welfare of its subjects; a life which for nine women out of ten ends in painful disease, premature decrepitude, and death.

Heavy sleep until late in the afternoon followed the orgies of the night. Between three and four o'clock came the weary getting-up from a dirty bed, soda water, coffee, listless pacing up and down the room in bedgowns and dressing-jackets, lazy gazing out of the windows from behind the drawn curtains, indolent disputes with one another; then washing, perfuming and anointing the body and hair, trying on dresses, disputes about them with the mistress of the house, surveying one's self in looking-glasses, painting the face, the eyebrows; rich, sweet food; then dressing in gaudy silks exposing much of the body, and coming down into the ornamented and brilliantly illuminated drawing-room; then the arrival of visitors, music, dancing, sexual connection with old and young and middle-aged, with lads and decrepit old men, bachelors, married men, merchants, clerks, Armenians, Jews, Tartars; rich and poor, sick and healthy, tipsy and sober, rough and tender, military men and civilians, students and mere schoolboys – of all classes, ages, and characters. And shouts and jokes, and brawls and music and tobacco and wine, and wine and tobacco, from evening until daylight, no relief till morning, and then heavy sleep; the same every day and all the week. Then at the end of the week came the visit to the police station, as instituted by the Government, where doctors – men in the service of the Government – sometimes seriously and strictly, sometimes with playful levity, examined these women, completely destroying the modesty given as a protection not only to human beings but also to animals, and gave them written permissions to continue in the sins they and their accomplices had been committing all the week. Then followed another week of the same kind: always the same every night, summer and winter, work days and holidays.

This account does speak of 'chronic sin against human and divine laws'; but its biographical detail is basically naturalistic. Tolstoy's attitude is his own, but he does not project this on to the facts. And he makes it clear in the rest of the novel – and, of course, in his other writings – that he does not regard 'illicit' sex as the only, or indeed the most important kind of 'sin'; his guess about the eventual destiny of the Russian prostitutes of his time (that nine out of ten died in misery) is certainly correct. Maslova, unlike Nana, is not a psychopath; but she is not happy in her profession – she feels ashamed and unreal, and takes refuge in a defeatist slovenliness and drink. We gather that she does not enjoy her work. Tolstoy also points out that she was in one sense forced into becoming a common prostitute by the law: she could not live alone unless she would accept a yellow ticket.

The main theme of *Resurrection* – which is probably Tolstoy's weakest novel, though only by the high standards he himself set – is the hypocrisy of society. Tolstoy is at his best when he is most angry, in describing the hideous minutiae of officials' reactions to statements of truth or justice. Maslova happens to be a prostitute because this makes an easy way for Nekhlyadov to be responsible for her plight; but she need not have been. The novel is not, in other words, about prostitution. The genuinely highminded Tolstoy could not quite come to terms with this, and so gave Maslova her famous enigmatic squint, which substitutes for the element in her character (which Tolstoy cannot define) that enabled her to become a prostitute.

The extremely literate London prostitute who wrote at length to *The Times* in 1858 (it is tempting to think of Walter as having been one of her clients) began by announcing that she was 'a stranger to all the fine sentiments' that 'lingered in the bosom' of a previous correspondent. This letter corrects several false impressions; but, chiefly, that prostitutes cannot have self-respect and that the Victorians were incapable of plain speaking. It is a dignified piece of writing of great social importance – equalled in this century only by 'Sheila Cousins's' autobiography *To Beg I Am Ashamed*. Clearly it is not a put-up job, a concoction by a sophisticated group. It is informed by a justified anger, and caused the leader-writer of *The Times* of the following day to comment: 'They [prostitutes] have their virtues, like others. . . .' Further

comment seems superfluous and impertinent. The letter is quoted
in full in the Appendix on page 199.

6

The French novelist Charles-Louis Philippe, who died of menin-
gitis at the age of thirty-five in 1909, has not had his due in the
English-speaking countries. Among his six novels is a classic
account of a young prostitute: *Bubu de Montparnasse* (1901).
Philippe was the son of poor parents and he had to struggle
against ill-health as well as poverty in order to realize his gifts.
Born at Cérilly in the Bourbonnais countryside, some 150 miles
south of Paris, he did well at the local lycée. After an initial failure
to establish himself as a writer, he went to Paris, lived in a hotel,
took a job as a clerk, and studied to become a naturalistic writer
steeped in the working classes. Convalescence from an illness
gave him the opportunity to begin his first novel, *La Mère et
L'Enfant*.

Soon after he returned to Paris and his dull clerking job he
met on the Boulevard de Sébastopol a young prostitute, Maria,
the Berthe of *Bubu de Montparnasse*. He formed exactly the
attachment to her that Pierre Hardy forms for Berthe in *Bubu*.

The story of *Bubu*, which is a simple and poignant one, is true.
Berthe is sent into whoredom by a brutal pimp, Maurice, whose
nickname is Bubu. She gets syphilis and goes to hospital. While
Bubu is in prison for a theft she takes up with Pierre and makes an
attempt to leave her profession, returning to her original job as a
flower-seller. But one night while Pierre and she are in bed, Bubu,
released from prison and accompanied by a gang of toughs,
returns to claim her: he needs her to provide him with cash:

She went into a world where individual benevolence has no power,
because there is love and money, and because those who wreak evil

are implacable and because prostitutes carry the brand of it from the start like passive animals that are led to the common pasture.

The downstairs door banged. Pierre already understood.

'Oh, I know that you will weep! My God, but I have no luck! You haven't courage enough to deserve happiness. Weep and die! Even though you were alone, you should have gone down in your shirt and your bare feet and cried out: "Help!" You should have gone down into the street and clutched hold of the passers-by, and cried: "Come quickly. They're murdering a woman up there!"'

The real-life Berthe, Maria, eventually emancipated herself from her pimp, although not before Philippe had found himself another girl (not, this time, a prostitute). Philippe and his friends got together enough money to send her away to Marseilles and a new life as a florist; but it seems that she failed to find work, and relapsed into the profession she wanted to abandon.

Philippe described Maria as 'the most exquisite little creature in the world, very kind, very intelligent, very sweet and very much corrupted'. Berthe is all of these things except intelligent: this she is not, and one suspects that Philippe described Maria as such because he found in her strange, crushed passivity – and gratitude for his unfamiliar kindness – a reflection of his own at that time unconscious shrewdness.

Philippe has been rightly described as essentially a naturalist, but with a streak of poetry running through his work; the poetry is pure lyricism, youthfulness, love of life, of pleasure and of the sun. His natural immaturity comes across, in *Bubu*, in the form of this freshness and lyricism. But for all that, it is natural history on as high a level as *Nana*; it only lacks Zola's huge social scope. Berthe's 'corruptness' is not specifically of a sexual nature; essentially, it is the process of an illiterate innocent's passive learning of the real grammar of life, of which loveless, affectionless, brutalized sex is but one element. Philippe was the least intellectual, the most 'natural', of the French naturalists. He saw and described things he enjoyed – determinism in his fiction is markedly unphilosophical – but these never interfered with his portrayal of things and people as they are. The brutalities of the world he mourned, but he set nothing against them in the form of a 'philosophy'; that his own passion for truth functions as something more than a criticism of them is incidental to his own unusually pure naturalistic intentions. He was a 'sincere socialist'; but only casually so: he had no use for politics or politicians. The sad beauty of *Bubu* lies not only in its account of how youthful hopes become blighted but also in its unobtrusive celebration of truth.

Although Bubu, the pimp who destroys Berthe's innocence, is brutal and horrifying, the portrait of him is by no means a distorted one. He is presented as a victim of circumstances, though not as poignant a one as Berthe herself. His 'wisdom' is ironically presented as purely practical; thus

She [Berthe] needed a great deal of approval. She was weak and needed someone to lean upon; she was gentle, and she needed kind words said to her. . . . But he [Bubu] knew that in business one must always seem exacting. Women wouldn't do another stroke of work if you listened to their chatter.

This 'skill' in handling his girl does not, however, prevent Bubu from committing a clumsy burglary and getting sent to prison for it. All, in fact, that Bubu 'knew' was (as Philippe says) that 'it was necessary to have money and a woman'.

When Pierre first encounters Berthe he falls in love with her – or with the idea of her. But she, although 'gentle and still new to the trade', cannot regard 'this big passionate boy' as anything more than 'one more man to undergo': 'prostitutes curtail their clients' love because it is harmful'. As she enters his hotel with him she ponders,

This young man would make use of her at least twice. The others would want their money's worth. Men abuse and destroy our bodies to let us have bread. And these ideas swarmed in her head like a world of black insects that buzz and sting and do harm to little children.

They reached Pierre's door. On the threshold, he took her in his arms and said: 'I love you so much, my little Berthe!'

Then he fumbled in her blouse.

Hope, joy and romantic love are seen as destroyed not only by circumstance and by the brutal realities of prostitution but also

by Pierre's own lust. Where this particular, and helpless, prostitute needed only kindness, Pierre has to accompany it with lust:
to use her in the way he mourns that she allows herself to be
used. For this, in Berthe's case, is literally using her up: using up
her individuality. She has been a lovely girl – and Philippe has
well hinted at the qualities of her loveliness – but a few months
of enforced prostitution has eaten into it. Thus, when she goes to
hospital with syphilis she writes this letter to Pierre:

Pierre,
    I got your letter which made me sick but I expected it the nerve to
put it all on me but you think you can get away with it but you're
wrong there I always knew you gave me that dreadful disease. But
you're right I never said nothing because you helped me but now you
think I have enough like this but I suffer I'm so sad I could die and
you're happy at what you've done and to how many other young
girls to who you give a few francs for their trouble of giving themselves to you you make them rotten. Perhaps these young girls have
killed themselves like me if I hadn't thought about my family but I
thought my father had suffered enough with my mother dying without
hearing about my death also. Then I didn't think I'd meet my executioner one day boulevard Sébastopol July 15. The tears I've cried
since that day but it's too late and I must resign myself and I say this
because I'm sure you gave it to me and made the misery of my whole
life. And I'm going to have more days of terrible suffering and others
also will suffer and I pity them those people who have to suffer because of you for me the people who know you gave me this disease
hate you more than me but I listen to no one's advice that's why I
suffer in silence. You must know I'm not a dirty girl because if I wanted
I also could make lots of men rotten but I prefer to take care of myself
and when I'm cured I'll see what to do but never I'll forgive you.
You don't deserve it a man who did me so much bad which I didn't
deserve either and I didn't think one day I'd go on the rack for you
know right now I'm suffering something awful in the throat at this
moment. I know very well you don't care but this relieves me and
you must know more than me what one feels with the head in this
state and then the lint I picked up one day on the floor you don't
wash your feet with it and then the ointment which is on the night
table below the basin you give yourself frictions with it it's good for
the pox and not for nothing else also. . . . But the sickness exacts it

or you'll have worse accident than you have and the woman who goes
with you will get it at once but what is a nuisance is when you're
excited an accident comes and you give it to others then you ditch
her and it's another's turn and you are jealous because others have not
got it bad like you. But Pierre I beg you take care of yourself like me
and that way you won't give nothing otherwise you might get worse
and injure yourself this is bit of advice. As for your doctor that is
invention because you are through with me and that's all.

I hope you won't be too angry with me but you see I am not wicked
I only want one thing just to never meet you for you are not a friend
like you are you say less than nothing or the pavement I walk every
day but you will keep my souvenir in your memory like I keep yours
but like a man not worthy to have a girl like me for I am the best girl
one can find in Paris and it's always like that. At last I dain to answer
your letter and tell you I think of you in spite the hate I have for you:

Mademoiselle BERTHE

the girl and poor miserable creature who has only hate for the man
that made her rotten.

This letter, which must surely be close to an actual one Maria
wrote to Philippe, is natural history at its purest; it illustrates
better than any description the exact state of Berthe's mind.

Yet *Bubu* is not an indictment of prostitution as such; it contains none of the empty moralizing that characterizes Gissing's
The Unclassed, which is not natural history but a disguised personal case-history. *Bubu* is a particular story, and it would be
impossible to generalize from it. Thus, Blanche, Berthe's sister,
although sordid, is happier in her prostitution than Berthe. And
Berthe herself is a particular case: we cannot use her to assert that
all pimps corrupt all the girls who work for them. The life of
some factory-girls was as sad, and sweated labour was sometimes
as corrupting as sweated sex. . . . When at the end of the book
Bubu claims Berthe as his rightful property, it is not the sexual
life in which she will be engulfed that is dismaying, but the
pimp's unaware brutality and the girl's lack of freedom of
choice.

An American novella that in certain respects resembles *Bubu* was published nine years before it: Stephen Crane's *Maggie: A Girl of the Streets* (1892). Crane, whose genius was not recognized until the appearance of *The Red Badge of Courage* in 1895, certainly could never have heard of Philippe; but it seems possible – even likely – that Philippe at least knew of *Maggie*, for this was acknowledged as a masterpiece of naturalism by the time he began to write *Bubu*.

Crane was a man who to some extent uncannily anticipated his own future in his fiction. He wrote *The Red Badge of Courage*, a classic study of war, when he had never been near a battlefield; soon afterwards he became a war-correspondent and saw plenty of battles (in the Spanish-American war). His first book, *Maggie*, dealt with a prostitute; in 1898, in London, he married a good-looking blonde woman older than himself called Cora Taylor, whom he had met in Jacksonville, Florida, where she kept a brothel. Whether she had herself been a prostitute is not clear; but, though obviously his social inferior – he came of an old family – she was a devoted wife.

No publisher would touch *Maggie* in 1892, and so Crane had to borrow $700 from his brother and pay for its publication himself. The printers were afraid to display their name on the covers, and even Crane, who had to earn his living as a journalist, could not use his own name – it was published as by Johnston Smith. Although the story that most of the copies were used to light Crane's fire is probably untrue, it is certain that the book was a commercial failure; but it gained Crane the friendship of the novelist and early naturalist Hamlin Garland, and helped him on his way to his success three years later.

Crane wrote *Maggie* out of his experiences on the Bowery and under the direct influence of Zola. Of *Nana* he observed:

. . . the girl in Zola is a real street walker. I mean, she does not fool around making excuses for her career. You must pardon me if I cannot agree that every painted woman on the streets of New York was brought there by some evil man. Nana, in the story, is honest.

Maggie, however, is distinctly American, and it already displays the kind of temperamental pessimism – really a gloominess about human nature rather than any kind of philosophically tinged determinism – that characterized his mature writing, and especially his poems. *Maggie* is truly naturalistic in that it treats people as dominated by instincts; and although Crane's sympathies are with Maggie, there is no explicit moralizing and no attempt to offer a 'solution'.

Maggie Johnson's background is the Bowery, where 'gruesome doorways gave up loads of babies to the street and gutter'. Maggie's family is continually fighting; as the novel starts, in her childhood, her brother Jimmie is fighting in the street, his father catches him and beats him, Jimmie beats Maggie, and then his mother beats him again. . . . The baby, Tommy, gets knocked down in the scuffle. The mother is a drunkard: 'You better let up on the bot', ol' woman, or you'll git done', her husband tells her. Jimmie eats 'with feverish rapidity', while Maggie swallows her fried potatoes 'like a small pursued tigress'. When there is a noise from the Johnsons' apartment, a neighbour asks 'Is yer fader beatin' yer mudder, or yer mudder beatin' ye fader?'

Jimmie grows up, 'his sneer . . . chronic'; without any respect for any thing or body, 'he menaced mankind at the intersections of streets'. 'Nevertheless, he had, on a certain star-lit evening, said wonderingly and quite reverently, "Deh moon looks like hell, don't it?" '

Maggie grows up pretty. She goes to work in a sweatshop turning out collars and cuffs. A friend of Jimmie's, Pete, takes to her: 'Say, Mag, I'm stuck on yer shape. It's outa sight'. Her mother, now widowed and famous throughout the district as a drunk and a fighter, taunts her and tells her that she has gone to the devil. Pete seduces her, and Mrs Johnson shrieks: 'May she be cursed for ever! . . . May she eat nothing but stones and deh dirt in deh street. May she sleep in deh gutter an' never see deh sun shine again. . . . Ah, who would t'ink such a bad girl could grow up in our fambly. . . .' Jimmie, himself pursued by two women whom he has impregnated, recoils in virtuous horror at his sinful sister when she returns after being finally rejected by Pete; she is turned away. His new girl-friend, an experienced hustler, says of Maggie: 'Did you note the expression of her eyes?

There was something in them between pumpkin pie and virtue.'
She goes on the streets, and dies. The novel ends as her mother
says, 'I'll fergive her!'

The details of Maggie's prostitution are passed over in silence;
there is no description of her feelings. Crane's main purpose,
beyond describing life as it was in the Bowery, seems to have been
to emphasize the religious hypocrisy of the working-class society
from which Maggie came, and the manner in which men went
uncondemned for 'sins' that made women into outcasts. It was
impossible for him, in the early 1890s in New York, to be more
specific about Maggie herself, so that her personality and her
reactions tend to become lost in the pitiless picture he draws of
her environment. *Bubu* is much more specific; but, so far as he is
able to go, Crane is a natural historian of absolute integrity.

Chapter Ten

1

THIS century has not seen more enlightened – although it has seen more – novels on the subject of prostitution than the last. But there have been some serious and objective studies. Henriques's three-volume work I have often mentioned in the course of this book. It is distinguished by some dry sympathy for prostitutes and by an unmoralistic tone, though not by any marked talent for literary criticism.

Rosamund Wilkinson's *Women of the Streets*, mentioned in the last chapter, deals with streetwalkers, mostly psychopaths or near-psychopaths, of the pre-Butler (Street Offences Act) era. Mrs Wilkinson's purposes, apart from attempting to give statistical data about 'the population of prostitutes who came to the notice of the police in London', were to investigate the early history of prostitutes, 'to discover how and why they became prostitutes', to find out about the incidence of venereal disease among them, and to inquire generally into the social, economic, legal and criminal factors. The objectivity preserved by Mrs Wilkinson is admirable, and no fault can be found with her manner of interviewing or the way she writes it up. But, while *Women of the Streets* is an important survey, it should be noted

that it deals only with prostitutes who have come to the notice
of the police: that is, with the lower end of the scale. For successful and really expensive prostitutes, while they are successful and
really expensive, which may be for the whole of their professional
careers, do not come to the notice of the police. The majority
may not even think of themselves as prostitutes, although by
definition this is what they are. The women on whom Mrs
Wilkinson so exhaustively reported were, without exception,
'hustlers', who got their trade by soliciting on the streets; they
were members of a socially ostracized sorority, and they understood, accepted and even liked their positions in this respect.

Mrs Wilkinson established that very few of her prostitutes were
criminals, habitual drinkers or dealers in drugs, and that (she
wrote before the Act put prostitutes off London's streets, upon
which they are now – ten years later – beginning to come back
in force, and so far without much molestation) the police and
the girls had 'come to . . . a working, though pointless, compromise'. The police were on the whole tolerant, if casual in
their sense of justice; the prostitute-client relationship they
regarded as 'natural' as contrasted with male homosexulaity.
Probation had had no discernible effect in deterring girls from
returning to prostitution. Police activity did not stop women
soliciting, but 'to some extent' modified their behaviour. One
prostitute who gave it up did so on her own: 'the influence of the
law in forming her decision . . . was slight'. 'Bribery of police by
prostitutes,' Mrs Wilkinson asserted, 'either in cash or in kind, is
uncommon.' This, despite widespread opinions to the contrary,
seems to be correct for the pre-Butler period: there is little hard
evidence to disprove it. Street prostitution seemed to Mrs
Wilkinson 'to be far from the "easy life" it is reputed to be' (but
now that many of the former street-girls solicit from their own
rooms, as 'models', it may be less hard on the feet). The attractive girls did very much better than the plain or dull ones, as one
would expect. On the whole all prostitutes were 'earning far
more than [they] could in any job open to [them]'.

Her prostitutes in general, Mrs Wilkinson found, were 'completely without physical or emotional feeling for the man'. The

men more often wanted – pathetically – to buy some form of personal relationship; but on the other hand many men succeeded physically only with prostitutes because they could despise and dominate them.

I should interpolate here that I know of whores (of the 'model' type) who, I am convinced, take pleasure in their work. One told me that she 'had her kicks' about once a day, with whomever of her customers pleased her. Although dowdy and by no means attractive, her assertion that she enjoyed her life more than marriage (which she had 'tried') was convincing. She lived in the flat in which she worked, and particularly enjoyed 'lolling around on Sunday afternoons when I'm not working and don't have to put make-up on'. She was uncomplicated and perfectly frank: a thoroughly nice woman. It is just possible that the opportunities created by the Street Offences Act have (fortuitously, one need hardly add) helped a certain kind of woman, who wants to be a tart but does not want to associate with other tarts or be a part of their ostracized world. When I asked one 'model' in Shepherd Market what she knew about the street-girls there – they are now again numerous, although they make their forays sporadically and can utterly vanish in an instant – she said indignantly, 'How can I know anything about them if I'm working up here?' There seems little doubt that street-life suits some girls and not others. For the former, it is mainly the thrill of *la chasse*, the securing of custom, that acts as a cohesive force. A point of honour amongst them (as Mrs Wilkinson points out) is that they should not be seen to be getting pleasure – only getting money.

It is significant that Mrs Wilkinson found a distinct difference in attitude when she encountered a French woman, Annette, who had come to Soho at the beginning of the last war. She was more objective (showing up the flaws in the blasé approach of some of the Mayfair women), and reported that for 'a long time I was really happy in the life'. 'You do not know what the man wants, but he tells you and then you know and you do it'. But at thirty-five Annette began 'not to like it': 'I feel bad and am ashamed. . . . I do not feel comfortable now when I stand in the streets'. This change could be attributable to two factors: advancing age and the consequently increasing difficulty of getting custom, and infection by British social attitudes.

Any view of whores based only on the British variety would, as Mrs Wilkinson's experience with Annette suggests, certainly be an incomplete one. The puritanism that seems to be innate in the British character certainly plays its part in the formation of British whores' character, attitude and behaviour. It is no male myth that French, Italian and German prostitutes are 'better' than their British counterparts. Quite simply, they generally give their clients a better time. This, I suggest, is because they have a much more straightforward attitude to the act they are asked to perform. If they, too, often simulate desire or passion, they do so sincerely and not in a bored, petulant or incompetent manner. They establish a more personal relationship with their clients, and entirely lack the proverbial British whore's attitude of 'Feel better, dearie?' They are not afraid of the idea of sexual pleasure.

With the exception of Annette, all of Mrs Wilkinson's prostitutes might be said to have been typically 'British' in this respect: the sex they (and their clients) made was, one may reasonably infer, remarkably joyless. But this is, as I have suggested, something inherent in the British, or Anglo-Saxon, character, and as it is observable in all spheres of British life it does not tell us anything about prostitution as an isolated phenomenon.

One apparently distressing piece of excellent natural history is quoted by Mrs Wilkinson from police records (the name of Peter Davies is fictitious):

11.1. p.m. Mrs Davies successfully accosted a man and went with him to a tree.

11.3 p.m. Mr Davies arrived from the direction of Marble Arch and he stood on the grass watching Mrs Davies and the man by the tree.

11.12 p.m. The man left Mrs Davies, and she returned to Broad Walk where she unsuccessfully accosted a number of men.

11.31 p.m. Mr Davies went and joined Mrs Davies and stood talking to her for a short time. He grabbed her handbag, put his hand inside and then swung the handbag, hitting her on the side of the head, saying something to her in a loud voice and she started to cry. He caught hold of her hair and dragged her on the grass striking her about the body and face with his left hand. Mrs Davies was crying and screaming. I heard her say to him, 'Don't be silly, Pete. I can't help it, there has been no men about.' He then walked away from her and she followed and I heard her shout, 'It's all right for you sitting in the pub in the warm. I keep you and I bought you a new coat and then you're not satisfied.' He then took the coat off, walked towards her and threw the coat over her head and shouted, 'Take the bloody thing.' They then walked towards Marble Arch, Mrs Davies was carrying the coat and they were arguing.

11.50 p.m. Mr and Mrs Davies arrived on the Meeting Ground, where he took the coat from her and put it on. They then left the Park.

This might well be taken as an argument for the savage punishment of pimps. But in fact (as Mrs Wilkinson tells us in her admirably laconic and objective manner) the prostitute in question was self-consciously tough (and fairly unattractive), adored the man, badly wanted his child, and stated that she would 'murder anyone' who tried to part them. The man was young, 'pleasant looking', had been discharged from the Forces with a good character (this means, in practice, without a viciously criminal character), and yet had chosen to go to live 'with this rough, physically unattractive prostitute', who was described on her approved school reports as 'sly and underhand'. The picture conjured up by the police report, then – which is a generally accepted one – of the pimp as a savage taskmaster beating up his unwilling slave, is not borne out at all. Indeed, since the girl in question obviously accepted her pimp's physical violence as a matter of course, it could even be argued that she had corrupted him. . . . If two people agree to choose to live in this way, outside the bounds of society, then society has no right to interfere, and makes a fool of itself by doing so. This is a very different story from the equally non-fictitious one told by Charles-Louis Philippe in *Bubu of Montparnasse*. We may justifiably regard the relationship observed by Mrs Wilkinson as coarse and brutal; but something personal – and possibly, in its moments, tender – was nevertheless involved.

Wayland Young's chapter on prostitutes in *Eros Denied* may

conveniently be mentioned here: it leans very heavily on Mrs Wilkinson's book and on the originally Freudian concept of 'vaginal' orgasm being 'more mature' than 'clitoral' orgasm: Young represents all tarts as 'clitoral', and concludes that they are universally superficial, frigid and with lesbian tendencies.

The controversy about clitoral and vaginal orgasm has loomed large in recent years. Some women, while experiencing orgasm in both the clitoral and vaginal (and other) areas, regard the latter as more pleasurable (i.e. longer, more intense, more satisfying). Other women experience orgasm only in the clitoral area. No woman I have heard of who experiences both types of orgasm 'prefers' the clitoral. This, however, does not disprove the recent assertion that the physiological origin of all orgasm is in the clitoris, which is much more richly endowed with nerve-endings than the walls of the vagina. Nor is there any reason to suppose that because some women can experience vaginal orgasms they are therefore more 'mature'. Research into these matters is, for obvious reasons, extremely difficult; the significance of laboratory experiments, in which women are observed while love-making and while masturbating (with a special, plastic, adjustable dildo), and in which they therefore perform differently from how they perform in private, may not perhaps have been as helpful as some have supposed. So far as prostitutes are concerned, there is no serious evidence that, when they do have a 'kick', it isn't as 'good' as anyone else's. Their predisposition to frigidity is largely mythical, I think – although it is encouraged by the obvious fact that as their work is sex then nine times or more out of ten they don't get any kick at all. . . . Young is right to represent the world of the ordinary tart and her client as a sad and sordid one; the trouble is that many other areas of life are equally sad – if not as obviously sordid. The kind of lower middle-class marriage recorded so truthfully by Cliff Ashby in his novel *The Old Old Story** is just as sordid. 'Frigidity' in women is an appalling sin in the eyes of most males, and it is predictable that the average view of whores should be that they are 'frigid'. However, if there is any special factor that

* Hodder & Stoughton, London, 1969.

predisposes certain women to become tarts, I doubt if 'frigidity' is an element in it; it is just that men would like to think that it is.

As for the alleged lesbianism of tarts: they are no more or less lesbian than any other group. But being sexually uninhibited they perform more experiments.

Again, Young writes that 'The only way out of the game is feet first'. Is that true of today? The historical evidence does not warrant it. Certainly those prostitutes who are also psychopathic remain on the game, and may end up in a helpless state; but then this is the almost invariable fate of psychopaths, people who (amongst other things) are incapable of taking into account the consequences of their actions. There are plenty of prostitutes who are stable, and who may even know how to tease earnest social workers and interviewers. By far the most sensible and comprehensive of all the modern books on the subject is Harry Benjamin's and R. E. L. Masters's *Prostitution and Morality*, to which I have already referred. This is admirably objective, unpatronizing and humane. The authors' final conclusion, a justifiable one (thinking in terms of, say, one's own daughter), is that they would not recommend the profession 'to anyone who has a real alternative', and they urge those who are prostitutes to get out of the life if they can. But this is because of society's attitude – and because of the serious problem of ageing. They are realists, who spend their lives working with prostitutes; they urge that prostitutes:

. . . should be freed of any feelings of guilt or inadequacy, and should be able to conduct their chosen work with safety and under decent conditions.

They (alas rightly) remain sceptical about the reception their suggestions will meet with.

The best book ever written by a prostitute was 'Sheila Cousins's' *To Beg I Am Ashamed*.* Its first paragraph is splendid:

Because I was born a lady and still look one, 'How on earth do you come to be doing this?' is the first question most men ask me when they

---

* Published in the 1930s in Great Britain, and reprinted, Richard Press, London, 1954; published in the U.S.A. under the title *Prostitute*, New York, 1962.

pick me up on the streets. I came to be a prostitute for many reasons, but in the end because I deliberately chose to be.

'What? Impossible!' would be the reaction of most psycho-analysts and of many social workers. And yet Sheila Cousins's lucid account of her life shows it to be true in her own case. Those who read her book without prejudice will be unable to avoid the conclusion that she is a dignified and hard-working woman, who has chosen her way of life deliberately and who has not a trace of self-pity. Like any other profession, prostitution has its occupa-tional hazards and its particular worries. Sheila sometimes felt 'the contempt of the world' weighing heavily upon her; those who read her book honestly will take a little weight off her shoul-ders. She is probably not working now (by my calculation she must be nearing sixty); I hope she made out.

2

Only a few novels from this century deserve mention. Such in their time celebrated novels as Hermann Sudermann's *Das hohe Lied* (translated as *Song of Songs*, London, 1913), and Patrick MacGill's *The Rat Pit* (London, 1915) are quite properly for-gotten. For both these authors, prostitution is a terrible moral misfortune in itself; their only concession to good sense is that it is men who create the market.

Theodore Dreiser's *Sister Carrie* (1901), his first novel, is in an altogether different category; but Carrie, based partly on his own sister, is not a street prostitute. Before becoming a successful actress, she lives with two men, and causes the ruin of one – which is the real theme of the novel. But there is no moralizing: Dreiser was freer than Zola from inhibitions: he had a full appetite for women and exercised it without guilt. His scruples, as he made clear in *The Genius*, were all to do with the effect his own pro-miscuity would have on the women in his life.

His great achievement in *Sister Carrie* is the manner in which he conveys Carrie's curious indifference – half passivity, half repressed aggression – to the emotions of the men who desire her. Dreiser gives a startlingly vivid and truthful portrait of a certain type of successful 'promiscuous' woman, who manages to advance herself (by selling her body) without really knowing what she is doing. This sexual numbness, surprisingly not accompanied by an overt 'frigidity' – that is to say, by an indifferent attitude, a passivity, in actually making love – must characterize many prostitutes, especially those in the higher echelons.

If the American David Graham Phillips, who worked upright for fear of appendicitis and was shot by a madman (who then shot himself), had possessed any talent as a novelist, then his posthumous *Susan Lenox: Her Fall and Rise* (1919) would have been a remarkable book. As it is, it is a truthful documentary about the 'fall' of a bastard into prostitution and her 'rise' as a world-famous actress. Its psychology is good; but Phillips had no intuition, and although he never sentimentalized his heroine he failed to get inside her mind. The psychology is therefore in sociological rather than in individual terms. The novel, gallantly faithful to Susan's feminine viewpoint, creaks along, and is hard to read – if it were not for this, it would be worthy of reprinting. The Greta Garbo film of the same title is not recognizably based on Phillips's novel.

Colin MacInnes in *Mr Love and Mr Justice* (London, 1960), the story of a pimp, his whore and a bent policeman, gives one of the most intelligent and comic treatments of the subject. Essentially, its purpose is to show that criminal and policeman are two sides of the same coin, and that both are human. At the beginning the policeman, Edward, tells his girl that ponces should be destroyed because 'they're making money out of love'. At the end, because both Frankie the ponce and he the policeman are human – rather than those abstractions, the 'criminal' and the 'policeman' – he understands him. He needs to, because both are side by side, physically damaged, in hospital. This is a charming latter-day morality by a writer with the precious gifts of feeling and good temper.

3

The profoundest literary insights into prostitution always assume, if they do not state, that prostitutes exist because in modern cultured societies women have been split by men, and have consequently split themselves, into 'wife' and 'whore'. This is nowhere more apparent than in pornography (which is, of course, anything but profound). Gillian Freeman has dealt with this in *The Undergrowth of Literature*,* and I do not wish to trespass unnecessarily on her domain. But current pornography is pertinent to my subject in as much as it never deals with prostitutes (except to provide usually false lists of addresses and telephone numbers of 'models'). It is written for men by men. (The women who pose for the photographs incorporated in its crudely cyclostyled sheets are in a sense prostitutes – but they never look as if they are much interested in what they are doing.) And no participant in any of the thousands of these productions is ever represented as getting his satisfaction from a prostitute.

Yet the creations of the pornographers are ideal – imaginery – prostitutes: they do what the prostitutes themselves cannot do for their clients: they submit, they satisfy. My example is *Corpun* 5,† described as a 'spanking' production: it consists of 'My Sadistic Husband' and 'Greta's Cousin Paul', 'Two stories of pain and pleasure through pain'.

'My Sadistic Husband' is the story of Rebecca, and is told 'by' Rebecca. Thus the male writer creates the illusion, for the male reader, that this woman is the sexual ideal: 'she' really experiences the sexual emotions 'she' states. Her clergyman father had beaten her severely with a ruler until on one occasion she 'blacked out'. She felt a 'flush of shame as I felt his [her father's] eyes on my naked bottom'. After the fainting fit her father stopped beating her – this, as we shall see, is what it is really all about.

Then she marries John Halliday. On the wedding night he

* Nelson, London, 1967 † London, no date.

tells her 'we are going to make a woman of you'. But she felt only
'excruciating pain', and could not respond. The next day he comes
home to find overcooked food (his name has now changed to
Henry, an example of how little identity matters in these books):

'So I've married a woman who cannot even get me a decent meal. . . .
No good in bed. . . . Take off your frock, will you, and your other
clothes.'

The outcome is predictable: Rebecca gets to like 'punishment',
and even invites it. She 'learns' 'to enjoy' the birch and to 'eagerly'
anticipate being whipped on her 'pussy', which sends 'waves of
pleasure' through her and gives her her 'first true orgasm'. She
learns to give John-Henry the 'last moments of his pleasure' in
her mouth, and he tells her to swallow 'every drop of his spunk',
after which he works himself up again by 'slashing' at 'the lower
part of my cunt until he was ready to come'.
        Then the sudden conclusion:

The terrible thing is that my husband died a few weeks ago and I
am the loneliest, most miserable woman in the world. . . . will I ever
find a man to whom I can give myself in slavish submission. . . . Meanwhile something has happened that might develop in the direction
I wish. I am staying with old father again and the other day I happened
to wear some white knee-length socks. My father noticed them and
I saw a strange look come into his face. . . . it will not be long before
he puts me once again over his knee to luft [sic] my skirt, pull down
my knickers and slap me!

In the other story Cousin Paul catches Greta (a school-girl)
masturbating her dog while she masturbates herself. He gives her
the usual sadistic punishments, in particular 'slashing' her 'cunt
lips'. Eventually they marry,

And after two years of marriage the same routing [sic] continues
unaltered every night of their lives, and in the real sense of the word
their marriage yet remains to be consummated.

There is a kind of terrible despair about these loveless fantasies.
Both are incestuous and easily explicable in Oedipal terms; both
are infantile; perhaps both are ultimately homosexual. But the

point is that the two 'females' in them are what sadistic males want prostitutes to be; they explain what kind of infantile fantasies they desire prostitutes to help them re-create. The masochistic male reads 'male bondage' stories, which are equally infantile.

They are terrible in their lovelessness, and yet strangely harmless. By illustrating the kind of services clients expect from prostitutes, they reveal something of the psychological difficulties of the profession. But those who specially seek to suppress this kind of literature, who will not allow it into the open, stifle the infantile wails of their own repressed sexuality. For were the imaginary prostitutes, the whipped and the whippers, allowed to be in the open, discussed by us all as examples of our universal sexual confusion and sickness, then we might be able to advance to some kind of freedom.

4

It is not likely that one day in the future we shall pass signposts reading 'WANT TO GET POXED? DON'T HAVE AN AMATEUR. STATE WHORES ARE CLEANER, CHEAPER AND BETTER ON THE JOB AND THEY ARE TRAINED TO ENJOY YOU.' Or 'GET FUCKED, FRIGGED, GAMA-HUCHED OR MOCK-WHIPPED BY HENDON ESMERALDA: THE STATE WHORE.'

Society would not tolerate such satire upon its hypocrisies. But out attitude to whores is a disgrace; with the Street Offences Act we confirmed it. It is now time to put the profession on a proper footing. One could write a book about inland-revenue men or armament-manufacturers as if they were universally reprehensible; but no one has had to plead for their human status. By nationalizing prostitution, providing attractive pensions for whores, and giving them expert training, we should considerably improve the national temper as well as the national economy.

A brothel in the House of Commons would improve the quality of debate by releasing sexual tensions in the proper place. The pathologically shy, the crippled, the hopelessly perverse, would all be catered for. The prostitute, paid a decent salary, would have a place of honour in the community as a highly skilled worker. The often diseased amateur would be put out of business (since those who like to 'pick up' their women would be catered for by the Secret Pleasure Corps, highly paid girls posing as amateurs). Those who were shocked and wished to preach could work off *their* sexual needs by paying to thunder to Sunday audiences of whores. The Ministry of Sex would see to it that all organization was unobtrusive; thus squalor, for the men and women who require it, would appear to exist; poverty and despair would be instantly enactable anywhere; pain would be real only to those who needed real pain and not a fantasy of it.

This one learns from the enlightened writers. For while we insist on separating sexual pleasure from love, there will have to be 'fallen women'.

Appendix

LETTER FROM A LONDON PROSTITUTE

(Reprinted from *The Times*, 24 February 1858.)

My parents did not give me any education; they did not instil into my mind virtuous precepts nor set me a good example. All my experiences in early life were gleaned among associates who knew nothing of the laws of God but by dim tradition and faint report, and whose chiefest triumphs of wisdom consisted in picking their way through the paths of destitution in which they were cast by cunning evasion or in open defiance of the laws of man.

I do not think of my parents (long in their graves) with any such compunctions as your correspondent describes. They gave me in their lifetime, according to their means and knowledge, and as they had probably received from their parents, shelter and protection, mixed with curses and caresses. I received all as a matter of course, and, knowing nothing better, was content in that kind of contentedness which springs from insensibility; I returned their affection in like kind as they gave it to me. As long as they lived, I looked up to them as my parents. I assisted them in their poverty, and made them comfortable. They looked on me and I on them with pride, for I was proud to be able to minister to their wants; and as for shame, although they knew perfectly well the means by which I obtained money, I do assure

you, Sir, that by them, as by myself, my success was regarded as
the reward of a proper ambition, and was a source of real pleasure
and gratification.

Let me tell you something of my parents. My father's most
profitable occupation was brickmaking. When not employed at
this, he did anything he could get to do. My mother worked with
him in the brickfield, and so did I and a progeny of brothers and
sisters; for somehow or other, although my parents occupied a
very unimportant space in the world, it pleased God to make
them fruitful. We all slept in the same room. There were few
privacies, few family secrets in our house.

Father and mother both loved drink. In the household expenses,
had accounts been kept, gin or beer would have been the heaviest
items. We, the children, were indulged occasionally with a drop,
but my honoured parents reserved to themselves the exclusive
privilege of getting drunk, 'and they were the same as their
parents had been'. I give you a chapter of the history of common
life which may be stereotyped as the history of generation upon
generation.

We knew not anything of religion. Sometimes when a neighbour died we went to the burial, and thus got within a few steps
of the church. If a grand funeral chanced to fall in our way we
went to see that, too – the fine black horses and nodding plumes –
as we went to see the soldiers when we could for a lark. No parson
ever came near us. The place where we lived was too dirty for
nicely-shod gentlemen. 'The Publicans and Sinners' of our cir-
cumscribed, but thickly populated locality had no 'friend' among
them.

Our neighbourhood furnished many subjects to the treadmill,
the hulks, and the colonies, and some to the gallows. We lived
with the fear of those things, and not with the fear of God before
our eyes.

I was a very pretty child, and had a sweet voice; of course I
used to sing. Most London boys and girls of the lower classes sing.
'My face is my fortune, kind sir, she said', was the ditty on which
I bestowed most pains, and my father and mother would wink
knowingly as I sang it. The latter would also tell me how pretty

she was when young, and how she sang, and what a fool she had been, and how well she might have done had she been wise.

Frequently we had quite a stir in our colony. Some young lady who had quitted the paternal restraints, or perhaps, had started off, none knew whither or how, to seek her fortune, would reappear among us with a profusion of ribands, fine clothes, and lots of cash. Visiting the neighbours, treating indiscriminately, was the order of the day on such occasions, without any more definite information of the means by which the dazzling transformation had been effected than could be conveyed by knowing winks and the words 'luck' and 'friends'. Then she would disappear and leave us in our dirt, penury, and obscurity. You cannot conceive, Sir, how our ambition was stirred by these visitations.

Now commences an important era in my life. I was a fine, robust, healthy girl, 13 years of age. I had larked with the boys of my own age. I had huddled with them, boys and girls together, all night long in our common haunts. I had seen much and heard abundantly of the mysteries of the sexes. To me such things had been matters of common sight and common talk. For some time I had coquetted on the verge of a strong curiosity, and a natural desire, and without a particle of affection, scarce a partiality, I lost – what? not my virtue, for I never had any. That which is commonly, but untruly called virtue, I gave away. You reverend Mr Philanthropist – what call you virtue? Is it not the principle, the essence, which keeps watch and ward over the conduct, the substance, the materiality? No such principle ever kept watch and ward over me, and I repeat that I never lost that which I never had – my virtue.

According to my own ideas at the time I only extended my rightful enjoyments. Opportunity was not long wanting to put my newly-acquired knowledge to profitable use. In the commencement of my fifteenth year one of our be-ribanded visitors took me off, and introduced me to the great world, and thus commenced my career as what you better classes call a prostitute. I cannot say that I felt any other shame than the bashfulness of a noviciate introduced to strange society. Remarkable for good looks, and no less so for good temper, I gained money, dressed

gaily, and soon agreeably astonished my parents and old neighbours by making a descent upon them.

Passing over the vicissitudes of my course, alternating between
reckless gaiety and extreme destitution, I improved myself greatly;
and at the age of 18 was living partly under the protection of one
who thought he discovered that I had talent, and some good
qualities as well as beauty, who treated me more kindly and con-
siderately than I had ever before been treated, and thus drew
from me something like a feeling of regard, but not sufficiently
strong to lift me to that sense of my position which the so-called
virtuous and respectable members of society seem to entertain.
Under the protection of this gentleman, and encouraged by him,
I commenced the work of my education; that portion of education which is comprised in some knowledge of my own language
and the ordinary accomplishments of my sex; – moral science,
as I believe it is called, has always been an enigma to me, and is
so to this day. I suppose it is because I am one of those who, as
Rousseau says, are 'born to be prostitutes'.

Common honesty I believe in rigidly. I have always paid my
debts, and, though I say it, I have always been charitable to my
fellow creatures, I have not neglected my duty to my family. I
supported my parents while they lived, and buried them decently
when they died. I paid a celebrated lawyer heavily for defending
unsuccessfully my eldest brother, who had the folly to be caught
in the commission of a robbery. I forgave him the offence against
the law in the theft, and the offence against discretion in being
caught. This cost me some effort, for I always abhorred stealing.
I apprenticed my younger brother to a good trade, and helped
him into a little business. Drink frustrated my efforts in his behalf.
Through the influence of a very influential gentleman, a very
particular *friend* of mine, he is now a well-conducted member of
the police. My sisters, whose early life was in all respects the
counterpart of my own, I brought out and started in the world.
The elder of the two is kept by a nobleman, the next by an officer
in the army; the third has not yet come to years of discretion,
and is 'having her fling' before she settles down.

Now, what if I am a prostitute, what business has society to abuse me? Have I received any favours at the hands of society? If I am a hideous cancer in society, are not the causes of the disease to be sought in the rottenness of the carcass? Am I not its legitimate child; no bastard, Sir? Why does my unnatural parent repudiate me, and what has society ever done for me, that I should do any-thing for it, and what have I ever done against society that it should drive me into a corner and crush me to the earth? I have neither stolen (at least since I was a child), nor murdered, nor defrauded. I earn my money and pay my way, and try to do good with it, according to my ideas of good. I do not get drunk, nor fight, nor create uproar in the streets or out of them. I do not use bad language. I do not offend the public eye by open indecencies. I go to the Opera, I go to Almack's, I go to the theatres, I go to quiet, well-conducted casinos, I go to all the places of public amusement, behaving myself with as much propriety as society can expect. I pay business visits to my tradespeople, the most fashionable of the West-end. My milliners, my silk-mercers, my bootmakers, know, all of them, who I am and how I live, and they solicit my patronage as earnestly and cringingly as if I were Madam, the Lady of the right rev. patron of the Society for the Suppression of Vice. They find my money as good and my pay better (for we are robbed on every hand) than that of Madam, my Lady; and, if all the circumstances and conditions of our lives had been reversed, would Madam, my Lady, have done better or been better than I?

I speak of others as well as for myself, for the very great maj-ority, nearly all the real undisguised prostitutes in London, spring from my class, and are made by and under pretty much such con-ditions of life as I have narrated, and particularly by untutored and unrestrained intercourse of the sexes in early life. We come from the dregs of society, as our so-called betters term it. What business has society to have dregs – such dregs as we? You railers of the Society for the Suppression of Vice, you the pious, the moral, the respectable, as you call yourselves, who stand on your smooth and pleasant side of the great gulf you have dug and keep yourselves and the dregs, why don't you bridge it over, or fill it up, and by some humane and generous process absorb us

into your leavened mass, until we become interpenetrated with
goodness like yourselves? What have we to be ashamed of, we
who do not know what shame is – the shame you mean?

I conduct myself prudently, and defy you and your policemen
too. Why stand you there mouthing with sleek face about morality? What is morality? Will you make us responsible for what we
never knew? Teach us what is right and tutor us in what is good
before you punish us for doing wrong. We who are the real
prostitutes of the true natural growth of society, and no im-
postors, will not be judged by 'One more unfortunate', not
measured by any standard of her setting up. She is a mere chance
intruder in our ranks, and has no business there. She does understand what shame means and knows all about it, at least so it
seems, and if she has a particle left, let her accept 'Amicus's' kind
offer as soon as possible.

Like 'One more unfortunate' there are other intruders among
us – a few, very few, 'victims of seduction'. But seduction is not
the root of the evil – scarcely a fibre of the root. A rigorous law
should be passed and rigorously carried out to punish seduction,
but it will not perceptibly thin the ranks of prostitution. Seduction
is the common story of numbers of well brought up, who never
were seduced, and who are voluntary and inexcusable profligates.
Vanity and idleness send us a large body of recruits. Servant girls,
who wish to ape their mistress' finery, and whose wages won't
permit them to do so honestly – these set up seduction as their
excuse. Married women, who have no respect for their husbands,
and are not content with their lawful earnings, these are the worst
among us, and it is a pity they cannot be picked out and punished.
They have no principle of any kind and are a disgrace to us. If I
were a married woman I would be true to my husband. I speak
for my class, the regular standing army of the force.

Gentlemen of philanthropic societies and members of the
Society for the Suppression of Vice may build reformatories and
open houses of refuge and Magdalen asylums, and 'Amicus' may
save occasionally a 'fallen sister' who can prevail on herself to be
saved; but we who never were sisters – who never had any relationship, part, interest, or communion with the large family of

this world's virtues, moralities, and proprieties – we, who are not fallen, but were always down – who never had any virtue to lose – we who are the natural growth of things, and are constantly ripening for the harvest – who, interspersed in our little, but swarming colonies throughout the kingdom at large, hold the source of supply and keep it fruitful – what do they propose to do with us? Cannot society devise some plan to reach us?

'One more unfortunate' proposes a 'skimming' progress. But what of the great bubbling cauldron? Remove from the streets a score or two of 'foreign women', and 'double as many English', and you diminish the competition of those that remain; the quiet clever, cunning cajolers described by 'One more unfortunate'. You hide a prurient pimple of the 'great sin' with a patch of that plaster known as the 'observance of propriety', and nothing more. You 'miss' the evil, but it is existent still. After all it is something to save the eye from offence, so remove them; and not only a score or two, but something like two hundred foreign women, whose open and disgusting indecencies and practices have contributed more than anything else to bring on our heads the present storm of indignation. It is rare that English women, even prostitutes, give cause of gross public offence. Cannot they be packed off to their own countries with their base, filthy and filthy-living men, whom they maintain, and clothe, and feed, to superintend their fortunes, and who are a still greater disgrace to London than these women are?

Hurling big figures at us, it is said that there are 80,000 of us in London alone – which is a monstrous falsehood – and of those 80,000, poor hardworking sewing girls, sewing women, are numbered in by thousands, and called indiscriminately prostitutes; writing, preaching, speechifying, that they have lost their virtue too.

It is a cruel calumny to call them in mass prostitutes; and, as for their virtue, they lose it as one loses his watch who is robbed by the highway thief. Their virtue is the watch, and society is the thief. These poor women toiling on starvation wages, while penury, misery, and famine clutch them by the throat and say, 'Render up your body or die'.

Admire this magnificent shop in this fashionable street; its front, fittings, and decorations cost no less than a thousand pounds. The respectable master of the establishment keeps his carriage and lives in his country-house. He has daughters too; his patronesses are fine ladies, the choicest impersonations of society. Do they think, as they admire the taste and elegance of that tradesman's show, of the poor creatures who wrought it, and what they were paid for it? Do they reflect on the weary toiling fingers, on the eyes dim with watching, on the bowels yearning with hunger, on the bended frames, on the broken constitutions, on poor human nature driven to its coldest corner and reduced to its narrowest means in the production of these luxuries and adornments? This is an old story! Would it not be truer and more charitable to call these poor souls 'victims'? – some gentler, some more humane name than prostitute – to soften by some Christian expression if you cannot better the un-Christian system, the opprobrium of a fate to which society has driven them by the direst straits? What business has society to point its finger in scorn, to raise its voice in reprobation of them? Are they not its children, born of the cold indifference, of its callous selfishness, of its cruel pride?

Sir, I have trespassed on your patience beyond limit, and yet much remains to be said. . . . The difficulty of dealing with the evil is not so great as society considers it. Setting aside 'the sin', we are not so bad as we are thought to be. The difficulty is for society to set itself, with the necessary earnestness, self-humiliation, and self-denial, to the work. To deprive us of proper and harmless amusements, to subject us in mass to the pressure of force – of force wielded, for the most part, by ignorant, and often by brutal men – is only to add the cruelty of active persecution to the cruelty of passive indifference which made us as we are. I remain, your humble servant, Another Unfortunate.

INDEX

Acton, William, Victorian doctor and writer on prostitution, 155–60
Alcibiades, 18
Alciphron, post-Christian Greek writer, 19, 20, 21, 22, 22–3, 24, 26
Allen, Walter, 112
Aristotle, 17
Ashbee, Henry Spencer, Victorian collector of erotica and possible author of *My Secret Life*, 138
Ashby, Cliff, 20th-cent. English novelist and poet, 191
Athenaeus, 2nd-cent. Egyptian-Greek anthologist, 19
Augustine, St, 57
Auletrides, classical Greek prostitutes, 18, 26

Bartholomew Fair, see Jonson, Ben
Bassermann, Lujo (pseud. H. O. L. Schreiber), 20th-cent. German popular writer on prostitution, 19, 20
Belle de Jour, film by Buñuel, 43
Benjamin, Harry, and Masters, R. E. L., 20th-cent. joint-writers on prostitution, 7, 59, 192
'Bienfilatre Sisters, The', see Villiers de l'Îsle d'Adam, Comte de
Black, Sir Cyril, 69, 103
Blake, William, 16
Blundell, Sir Robert, 20th-cent. celibate, magistrate, 103
Bonger, W. A., 20th-cent. Dutch criminologist, xi

Born in Exile, see Gissing, George
Boswell, James, 115–29
'Boule de Suif', see Maupassant, Guy de
Brandon, the Rev. S. G. F., 46
Brantôme, Pierre de Bordeilles, Seigneur de, 16th-cent. French scandalous writer and unordained Abbé, 72
Brinton, Crane, 20th-cent. social historian, 27
Brown, Norman O., 20th-cent. psychoanalyst of history, 147–8
Bubu de Montparnasse, see Philippe, Charles-Louis
Buggery, 17
Byzantium, 6th cent., 57–61

Catullus, Gaius Valerius, 31–5
Charles II, King of England, 100, 101
Christ, Jesus, self-styled Jewish Messiah, 45, 46, 47, 48–52
Clarissa, see Richardson, Samuel
Cleland, John, 18th-cent. writer, 102–115
Coleridge, Samuel Taylor, 115
Confessions of Felix Krull, Confidence Man, see Mann, Thomas
Contes Cruels, see Villiers de l'Îsle d'Adam, Comte de
Corinthians I, 47–9
Corpun 5, 20th-cent. cyclostyled pornography, 195–7
'Cousins, Sheila', pseud. of 20th-cent prostitute, 177, 192–3
Crane, Stephen, 182–5